Women in the Works of Lou Andreas-Salomé

Studies in German Literature, Linguistics, and Culture

Women in the Works of
Lou Andreas-Salomé

Negotiating Identity

Muriel Cormican

 CAMDEN HOUSE
Rochester, New York

First published 2009
by Camden House

Camden House is an imprint of Boydell & Brewer Inc.
668 Mt. Hope Avenue, Rochester, NY 14620, USA
www.camden-house.com
and of Boydell & Brewer Limited
PO Box 9, Woodbridge, Suffolk IP12 3DF, UK
www.boydellandbrewer.com

ISBN-13: 978-1-57113-414-1
ISBN-10: 1-57113-414-X

Library of Congress Cataloging-in-Publication Data

Cormican, Muriel, 1969–
  Women in the works of Lou Andreas-Salome: negotiating identity /
Muriel Cormican.
      p. cm. — (Studies in German literature, linguistics, and culture)
  Includes bibliographical references and index.
  ISBN-13: 978-1-57113-414-1 (hardcover: alk. paper)
  ISBN-10: 1-57113-414-X (hardcover: alk. paper)
  1. Andreas-Salomé, Lou, 1861–1937 — Criticism and interpretation.
2. Women in literature. 3. Women — Identity. 4. Identity (Psychology)
in literature. I. Title. II. Series.
  PT2601.N4Z615 2009
  838.'809 — dc22

                                                              2009021016

A catalogue record for this title is available from the British Library.

This publication is printed on acid-free paper.
Printed in the United States of America.

Dedicated to my mother, Bridie

Contents

Acknowledgments

MANY PEOPLE AND INSTITUTIONS have provided support of varying sorts during the writing of this book. William Rasch introduced me to Lou Andreas-Salomé a long time ago and oversaw my first readings of her works. Raleigh Whitinger's intellectual generosity has been incredible. Although I have never met him in person, he commented on my work, shared insights with me, and encouraged me for years. The advice of someone whose work I respect so much enriched the book and my intellectual life in general. I am indebted to my colleagues and friends in the field and at UWG who organized conference sessions and read parts of the manuscript over the years: Cynthia Chalupa, Nikhil Sathe, Mary Beth O'Brien, John Blair, Gary Schmidt, Amy Cuomo, and Mark Weiner, among others. The support of the people at Camden House, in particular Jim Walker, has meant a great deal, as have the immensely helpful responses of the anonymous readers for Camden House. I am grateful and proud to have benefited from the work with all of those mentioned. Any shortcomings that remain are my own.

My home institution, the University of West Georgia, as well as the Carl von Ossietzky Universität in Oldenburg offered contexts in which I could deliver newly emerging readings and receive immediate feedback. UWG supported my conference travel and CvO gave me the opportunity to teach a *Hauptseminar* on the topic of this book in the summer semester of 2007. The students in that course were a delight to work with, and I thank them too. The libraries of both institutions also provided support. I thank their staff, particularly the interlibrary loan staff at UWG. I also thank Channa Cole, our departmental secretary, for last minute, long-distance help with some quotations.

My mother, Bridie Cormican, has always been a model of strength and tolerance for me, and I am thankful to her and to all my family for their steady companionship and support. But it is to John Blair that I owe and extend my deepest gratitude. He has been my reader and partner for so many years and in so many ways, that I cannot imagine having arrived at the point of writing acknowledgements without him, *mo chroidhe dhil.*

Oldenburg, July 6, 2009, MAC

Introduction

BECAUSE OF HER ASSOCIATIONS, correspondence, and collaboration with Nietzsche, Rilke, and Freud, Lou Andreas-Salomé (1861–1937) has always been of interest to German literary scholars. Until the mid- to late 1980s scholarship on her was dominated by biographical studies inspired by a fascination with the great literary and cultural giants she befriended rather than by curiosity about the woman herself and her literary works.[1] In assessing the need for Rudolph Binion's extensive study *Frau Lou: Nietzsche's Wayward Disciple* in the late sixties, for example, Walter Kaufmann pointed to the importance, above all, of her "successive friendships with Nietzsche, Rilke, and Freud."[2] In 1984 Angela Livingstone similarly assumed that her contemporary readership's interest in Andreas-Salomé would center on her subject's "acquaintance with . . . influential persons."[3] Early biographers such as Peters, Binion, and Livingstone typically acknowledge Andreas-Salomé's intellectual deftness, deferring to the high regard in which her well-known modernist contemporaries held her, but write off her literary works as veiled recastings of her own experience, as essayistic, and thus lacking in artistic merit.[4]

Beginning in the 1980s, a series of German biographies written almost exclusively by women sought to redress the one-sided focus of their predecessors and shed new light on elements of Andreas-Salomé's life that had previously been ignored: her own intellectual endeavors, long term and intimate relationships with less famous men (Paul Rée and Friedrich Pineles), her connections to women (Frieda von Bülow and Helene Klingenberg), and her position vis-à-vis the German women's movement.[5] Leonie Müller-Loreck's *Die erzählende Dichtung Lou Andreas-Salomés: Ihr Zusammenhang mit der Literatur um 1900* (Lou Andreas-Salomé's Narrative Works. Their Connection to Literature around 1900, 1976) is the first study to focus on Andreas-Salomé's fictional works in their contemporary literary context, tracing their thematic ties to *Jugendstil* (art nouveau).[6] With the exception of this book and some cogent and path-breaking readings by Gisela Brinker-Gabler and Uta Treder in the mid-eighties, it was not until the early 1990s that literary readings of Andreas-Salomé's fiction began to constitute the norm.[7]

On the heels of these critics, critics in the 1990s began to emphasize the engaging subtlety with which Andreas-Salomé treats prominent themes and problems of the day in her fictional works. Book-length studies by Biddy Martin, Caroline Kreide, Birgit Wernz, and Chantal Gahlinger treat Andreas-Salomé's fiction from varied perspectives.[8] Reevaluating her relationship to German modernity, Martin analyzes her life as much as her texts, and as if it were a text, rejecting the idea that the suppression of biographical details was an adequate response to the cult of biography around Andreas-Salomé (2). A long overdue, thorough, and complex study, *Woman and Modernity* devotes only one chapter to Andreas-Salomé's fiction, namely to the 1898 pair of novellas, *Fenitschka* and *Eine Ausschweifung* (Deviations, 1898).[9] Basing her findings on close analyses of a number of the non-fictional works, Caroline Kreide weighs in on an ongoing debate about Andreas-Salomé's relationship to the German women's movement and feminism in general, convincingly demonstrating that while Andreas-Salomé was not a self-professed or politically engaged feminist, there can be little doubt that her thoughts and ideas paralleled those of a variety of contemporary feminists, radical and otherwise.[10] Except for in the final chapter, in which Kreide analyzes the marriages in *Das Haus: Eine Familiengeschichte vom Ende vorigen Jahrhunderts* (The House: A Family Saga from the Turn of the Last Century, 1921), she too pays limited attention to the fictional works. Although Birgit Wernz offers numerous interesting insights into Andreas-Salomé's fiction in *Sub-Versionen: Weiblichkeitsentwürfe in den Erzähltexten Lou Andreas-Salomés,* reading a selection of works through the lens of deconstruction and French Feminist theory, her clear and detailed explications of the theories tend to relegate the analysis of the literary texts to second place. Chantal Gahlinger's *Der Weg zur weiblichen Autonomie: Zur Psychologie der Selbstwerdung im literarischen Werk von Lou Andreas-Salomé* addresses questions similar to my own (path to individuation; female psychological development) but from a decidedly psychological perspective and with more emphasis on the possibility of achieving closure. My intention with this study, then, is to build on and complement the pioneering work of these and other critics.[11]

Brigid Haines, Raleigh Whitinger, Gisela Brinker-Gabler, and Julie Doll Allen have variously and cogently interpreted *Fenitschka, Eine Ausschweifung,* and *Menschenkinder* (The Human Family, 1899) in article-length publications. All of these path-breaking studies go a long way toward remedying the earlier negative scholarly reception of Andreas-Salomé's fiction by demonstrating how she contributed substantively, critically, and innovatively to literary developments of the time.[12] These critics have paved the way for the study at hand by challenging the arbitrary notions of artistic merit responsible for the frequent dismissal of Andreas-Salomé's fictional works. They have spearheaded the work that Ruth Ellen Boetcher Joeres deems necessary in the case of women authors not entirely lost to literary history, namely the removal "of past interpretive ideological layers" before one can see what other interpretations or representations of their works are possible.[13] In its close readings of the by-now-relatively-well-known pair of novellas, *Fenitschka* and *Eine*

Ausschweifung, as well as of still further neglected prose works — *Ma: Ein Porträt* (Ma: A Portrait, 1901), *Jutta, Das Haus, Menschenkinder,* and *Ródinka: Russische Erinnerung* (Ródinka: A Remembrance of Russia, 1923) — this book emphasizes the variety and complexity of the critical dialogue that Andreas-Salomé carried on a century ago in her fiction with conventional conceptions of identity, sexuality, and gender and the narrative structures and conventions that represented them.[14]

My analysis of Lou Andreas-Salomé's texts has a twofold agenda. First, I hope to offer an account of a larger body of her literature, deemphasizing biographical and psychoanalytical/psychological perspectives without ignoring the sociopolitical, historical, and cultural contexts in which her works were written. Second, I hope to add to contemporary theoretical discourses on gender, feminism, and identity and to show how Andreas-Salomé's work prefigures discourses of identity politics that have emerged in feminist and queer theory in the late twentieth and early twenty-first centuries. Close readings of the wide range of representations of women and men in her fiction, together with a resolve to let contradictions in and among her texts stand rather than pursue coherent and definitive statements, uncover the many points of convergence between Andreas-Salomé's understanding of gender, identity, sexuality, and narrative, and the understanding of more recent commentators on the same, such as Judith Butler, Luce Irigaray, and Julia Kristeva.[15]

As far back as the late nineteenth and early twentieth centuries, Andreas-Salomé's fiction drew attention to what is now commonly acknowledged as a shortcoming of feminist discourse: its claims to universality. More than simply presenting thematic explorations of women's changing roles in society, her works investigate how narrative shapes thought and influences the conceptualization of woman's experience. In a global sense Andreas-Salomé is as much concerned with a cultural crisis of femininity and masculinity as with the identity crises of her individual women characters, exploring how even subtle shifts in women's and men's understanding of themselves, their sexuality and their identity, might affect cultural norms from something as practical as the division of roles in marriage to something as abstract as narrative formulas and narration.

Andreas-Salomé's position vis-à-vis the women's movement was complex and contradictory. In her lifetime her works met with significant acclaim and were widely read by members of the women's movement, who saw in her a model for woman's social and sexual freedom, even as they heavily criticized some of the views on women she espoused in her essays, views that seemed in stark contrast to her own approach to life.[16] On the one hand, her personal choices — she was intellectually and artistically active, married but involved in other love affairs, not tied to the home — and her fiction about the struggles of women who wanted more than traditional roles implied that she could only be in favor of the changes feminists sought for women. On the other hand, she explicitly criticized feminism and promoted an active appreciation of a naturalized motherhood and submission to a husband's will and desire, sometimes pointing to both as panaceas for women's identity crises. "Der Mensch als Weib" ("The Human Being as Woman," 1899), for example, represents motherhood as a state of uniquely mystical wholeness that eludes all women who cannot or do not reproduce.[17]

In "Reaktion in der Frauenbewegung" ("Reactions within the Women's Movement," 1899), Hedwig Dohm criticized the neo-Romantic essay "Der Mensch als Weib" for what she argued was its betrayal of the feminist cause.[18] Although the essay delineates and argues for the superiority of the feminine principle, that superiority is rooted in a passive, self-effacing, and submissive attitude. Woman, as figure, becomes an all-encompassing natural phenomenon, incapable of producing art because she remains at one with the universe, does not complete a process of individuation, and thus fails — and herein, paradoxically, lies her success — to achieve the kind of differentiation necessary for reflection and artistic distance. Silvia Bovenschen refers to "die imaginierte Weiblichkeit" ("imagined femininity") in 1979 in her book of the same name, suggesting that when women in the real world do not attain this mythical state, they are subjected to rejection and condemnation; this imagined femininity constitutes the focus of Hedwig Dohm's 1899 socially and economically aware criticism of "Der Mensch als Weib."[19]

In her fiction Andreas-Salomé similarly invokes romantic idealizations of women as wives and mothers but then complements and complicates these ideals in two ways. She depicts each woman's psychic life as complex and replete with contradictions and uncertainties, and she fills her texts with a variety of women — submissive, independent, feminist, masculine, sexually liberated — all of whom are granted legitimacy. Although she repeatedly suggests that the "ideal" woman, or at least the most serene woman, is one who finds happiness in an implicitly natural marriage of subordination and in motherhood, she also consistently makes it clear that not all women can or want to conform to such a life. At a time when women were under attack from many sides, not least from themselves — those who chose or advocated more conservative routes in life were criticized by feminists; those who challenged the conservative routes were criticized by antifeminists — Andreas-Salomé validates a myriad of life choices, attempting to draw her readers' attention repeatedly to the discursive construction of a femininity deemed natural. She depicts how the judgment and self-judgment of an individual in accordance with prescriptive and frequently internalized ideologies of "the natural" function in the messy internal churning out of a sense of self, as well as in attempts to articulate that sense of self.[20] In her first-person narrative stories such as *Jutta* and *Eine Ausschweifung*, she demonstrates how the creation of subjectivity is tied to telling, how the act of narrating is not the representation in writing of something that already exists but part of the act of creation itself. These novellas also show how the creation of a narrative about self-doubt, a loss of control, and confusing confrontations between desire and duty provides a forum in which control can be reconstituted. Andreas-Salomé suggests that feminist tendencies can just as easily be inscribed in an organic and natural femininity as are traditionally sanctioned female roles. In the contradiction between her own construction of femininity in her essays and her treatment of her female characters in her fiction, she most clearly reveals not only how femininity is a discursive construct but also how that construct has very real impact on the shaping of both women's and men's identities, sexualities, and lives.

This book underscores how identity emerges in Andreas-Salomé's works as a process of endless negotiation. Moving back and forth between close readings of individual texts and the identification of overarching patterns, it attempts to let the details of her narratives stand without forcing them into a neat and tidy set of authoritative conclusions. Andreas-Salomé points to how new ways of understanding male and female identity come about in a confrontation and intertwining of theoretical thinking, narration, social realities, and acquired and inherited characteristics. If there is a constant in Andreas-Salomé's depiction of women, then this constant is, paradoxically, that there is no constant. Whereas her representation of women's identity negotiations frequently involves what might be seen as uniform conflict between an ingrained desire to submit and an instinctive drive toward self-sufficiency and self-fulfillment, the process of and results of the negotiation are anything but uniform.[21] In *Menschenkinder,* for example, each story presents a different female "type": some are outspoken feminists, some timid wives, some are masculine individualists, but all of them, and the male figures too, find themselves in endless negotiations with themselves and others with regard to their place in the world and their desires and needs. Her characters present us with instances in which internal psychic concepts of sexuality, identity, gender, and self come into contact with external historical, political, and social realities of identity politics. Like Wernz, I read the works published at the turn of the century as counter-narratives to the dominant scientific and psychological narratives of femininity that had appeared in the latter half of the nineteenth century, and indeed continued to appear, by authors as varied as Freud, Weininger, Scheffler, Krafft-Ebing, and Schopenhauer.[22] Her corpus also offers, I argue, a corrective to the narratives of both conservative and radical representatives of the women's movement.

Andreas-Salomé's fiction indicates that she recognized in the German women's movement a fault that Judith Butler has tackled in her book *Gender Trouble,* namely the failure to see that the unified subject whom feminists speak of as "woman" and claim to represent is as much a questionable projection and discursive creation as the "woman" of the patriarchal ideology they seek to undermine.[23] Butler argues that "the construction of the category of woman as a coherent and stable subject" is "an unwitting regulation and reification of gender relations" and that it is perhaps the case that "'representation' will be shown to make sense for Feminism only when the subject of 'woman' is nowhere presumed" (5–6). Butler's criticism of certain aspects and assumptions of feminist discourse offers a useful model for understanding Andreas-Salomé's more implicit critique of the German women's movement. Women have certain recurring characteristics in Andreas-Salomé's works — as do men — but her repertoire of characters is so expansive and diverse that any attempt to settle on a unified concept of woman or female subjectivity or identity fails. Although Andreas-Salomé deals to some degree in stereotypes in her texts, nowhere are they unthinkingly validated. Neither are they rejected and dismissed, however. They are performed, weighed, and examined in a manner that makes her implied questions about gender, identity, and sexuality, as well as the subsequent muddling through such questions, more important than the arrival at definitive answers to them.

The works that form the focus of this study — written, though not all published, in the two decades surrounding 1900 in the midst of a discursive explosion on (and by) women — deal predominantly with women's roles in society, and women's sexual and psychic lives. Andreas-Salomé's exploration of the themes outlined above leads to reflections on the formal aspects of narrative. Additionally, these themes force a consideration of the meaning of concepts such as decadence and modernity for women. Although her investigations of identity and subjectivity tend to be played out almost exclusively in female characters, they are unmistakably of general human interest, underscoring identity as multicentered, overdetermined, performative, and fluid, or, in Jane Flax's words, as "a shifting and always changing intersection of complex, contradictory, and unfinished processes."[24] Andreas-Salomé's characters, whether male or female, Jews or gentiles, middle or working class, feminist or antifeminist, constantly negotiate with both themselves (internalized expectations and roles) and others (social expectations and roles) in their search for a satisfying relationship to the world. In short, in her fictional texts she develops a fundamental and programmatic ambivalence toward cultural norms and their scientific justifications in late nineteenth and early twentieth-century Europe, particularly, though not exclusively, as they pertained to female identity. In its reflection of the general uncertainty that surrounded the woman question at the time, her rhetorical ambivalence is insightful and provocative and presents her readers with a critical point of entry into the multifaceted and pervasive fin-de-siècle discourse on woman.

While one could not accuse Andreas-Salomé of a radical aesthetics, in that she does not conspicuously disrupt the mimetic illusions of the realist and naturalist traditions, the novels, novellas, and short stories analyzed here include a manipulation of literary narrative and form, an unresolved tension between differing viewpoints on contemporary issues, and a lack of narrative closure. Her constant return to a depiction of unresolved tensions constitutes a performative insistence on a more inclusive epistemological system than the public and professional discourse tolerated at the time, namely the inclusion of the layperson's perspective and experience. The refusal of narrative closure highlights her important questioning of the Western Cartesian concept of the subject so central to the development of the then emerging field of psychology and to narrative traditions in general. Undercutting the teleological narrative of identity — a narrative that begins with a sexed body, leads it through prescribed and definite stages of development, and has it emerge in the end into its "natural" gendered self — she impresses on the reader at the end of her narratives that the negotiation of identity that dominated the narrative has by no means been resolved. As Whitinger argues in his studies of the relationship of both *Fenitschka* and *Eine Ausschweifung* to the tradition of the Bildungsroman, Andreas-Salomé questions the standard notion of *Bildung* as the progressive striving toward a viable and rewarding sense of completion and wholeness.

The manipulation of narrative and form in the service of her exploration of female identity provides for an irony and aesthetic self-consciousness that underscores her critical engagement with literary and artistic traditions and the limitations of those traditions. For Andreas-Salomé, narrative is more than the literary organization of a story; it is an everyday tool that helps shape one's life, and that one can consciously use to attempt to do this. Like any tool, it provides a certain amount of freedom in how it is used, but it also has limits and determines to some degree in advance the kinds of shaping that it can achieve. Narrative structures and forms, she suggests, are replete with unquestioned ideological perspectives that force any articulation of identity toward preestablished categories. She grapples with both the difficulties and the possibilities of authoring one's own life within limiting and limited rubrics, and she seems particularly interested in how these questions apply to women. However, she does not see the dilemma she examines as singular to women. The biggest question she asks is how one might be able to adapt the narrative conventions and structures available in such a way as to provide a satisfying fit between the personal and the general, between individual identity and the socially acceptable categories for men and women as described, defined, and prescribed in narrative. She harps on the human being's need for absolutely contradictory things, privileging the coexistence of contradictions as something that provides for insight and truth. In terms of narrative, for example, she foregrounds our contradictory needs to negotiate between the general and the particular, between the linearity imposed on a life by narrative and the episodic and fragmentary nature of an actual life that no narrative can adequately represent and which seems, nonetheless, absolutely incomprehensible without the imposition of some kind of narrative structure. Dealing in aporias, Andreas-Salomé questions the possibility of radical and revolutionary breaks that would allow for the easy and clear determination and articulation of individual and collective identities. There is, she submits, only a patient and persistent chiseling that might slowly give way to new orders.

Each of Lou Andreas-Salomé's fictional works deals with numerous strands of women's identity and examines how those strands interweave. Emphasizing the impossibility of completely prying these strands apart, she considers repeatedly how art, marriage, sexuality, masochism, narrative, decadence, nationality, and their inherent gendered connotations play into the development of a sense of self. Mimicking what I perceive to be the movement in Andreas-Salomé's own work, the movement of this book may appear contradictory in that I attempt to discuss the elements listed above separately from each other, cognizant nonetheless of the fact that any such separation is artificial and unsustainable, and thus I tolerate slippage and overlap. Each chapter focuses on the role of a particular one of these in the negotiation of identity and on Andreas-Salomé's exploration of it in particular works.

Chapter 1 examines one of her theoretical excursions on female identity, analyzing, in particular, woman's relationship to art and artistic production in "Der Mensch als Weib." In this essay she polarizes artistry and femininity, positing the former as a phenomenon that takes over the human being in such a way as to render him practically genderless and the latter as a mythical serenity and union with the cosmos. The contradictions that come to light reveal an understanding of a discursively constructed femininity as an ideal that the engagement with art can only pervert. Comparing then her essayistic pronouncements on figurative woman's (*das Weib*) relationship to art to her narrative investigation of a particular female character's relationship to art in *Eine Ausschweifung,* I argue that Andreas-Salomé experienced theory as a realm of the imagination in which aesthetics played as fundamental a role as it did in poetry or art. Reading "Der Mensch als Weib" and *Eine Ausschweifung* in tandem brings to light Andreas-Salomé's larger and lifelong project of maintaining a clear distinction between theoretical discourses, in which woman functions as a figure, and concrete circumstances, in which women must function as freely as possible as people. Interested in an aesthetically and theoretically pleasing ideal of femininity to which both women and men ("der Mensch") might aspire, she nonetheless warns against allowing such ideals to shape real-life expectations.

Chapter 2 tackles the role of marriage in women's negotiation of identity, specifically in *Das Haus,* written six years later in 1904, though not published until 1921. In contrast to most of the other works addressed in this study, *Das Haus* steers our focus toward women who choose traditional paths in life. Although it conveys criticism of the repressive and authoritative underpinnings of bourgeois marriage and the family, the novel nonetheless reflects Andreas-Salomé's ambivalent position vis-à-vis the feminist project of woman's emancipation. Reluctant to reject either conservative or progressive perspectives on female identity and women's lives, she depicts women and men of varying generations and outlooks who are all forced to navigate through and balance a series of conflicting desires and expectations. In both Anneliese and Anneliese's daughter, Gitta, she reconciles the somewhat contradictory poles of femininity and autonomy, showing that whatever their choices ultimately, women rarely slip easily and without ongoing compromise into social and familial roles. Because this is a novel in which women who choose traditional paths in life are shown to be active, intellectually engaged, and very aware of the limitations and benefits of their choices, it must have been a breath of fresh air in a discursive arena defined by overly simplistic oppositions such as the old and new woman.

While *Das Haus* raises questions of the expression and containment of female sexuality within marriage, *Jutta,* a novella written in 1898 but not published in German until after Lou Andreas-Salomé's death, looks at a young woman's irrepressible sexual attraction to her brother's friend and at the psychological consequences of acting on this attraction. Jutta indulges in premarital sex, and chapter 3 examines the novella, which masquerades as her diary entry about this lapse. This diary entry allows us insight into Jutta's complicity in a moral code according to which she would now be categorized as dishonorable. While she does not explicitly criticize or question the double standard of this code, her attempts to understand how she could have instinctively behaved in a manner that she intellectually rejects hints at the critique she proves unable to articulate. Jutta is not caught in the act, but her formidable superego causes an identity crisis by constantly returning her to a moment in which she gives in to her physical urges. Even if Jutta does not manage to verbalize the problems of the double moral standard, the novella effectively communicates them.

Like marriage, the subject of motherhood has always been intimately linked to the subjects of woman's identity and sexuality. The maternal instinct is not unusual in Andreas-Salomé's female characters, even if it is not always linked to biological motherhood. Anneliese of *Das Haus* feels motherly toward her husband, Branhardt, for example, and Adine of *Eine Ausschweifung* feels motherly toward Benno, her former fiancé, at the end of the novella. In Anneliese and Adine, as well as in the theoretical woman of "Der Mensch als Weib," motherhood represents more than a biological phenomenon, becoming practically synonymous with empathy and representing, in this form, a tie to another human being that proves superior to biological motherhood. But in *Ma: Ein Porträt,* the focus of chapter 4, Andreas-Salomé traces how biological motherhood relates to subjectivity and masochism, presenting the reader as always with a differentiated and knotty notion of motherhood and giving voice to aspects of woman's experience that rarely found literary expression at the time. She points to Ma's twenty years of motherhood as punctuated by moments of self-dissolution and sacrifice but also makes it clear that motherhood need not involve woman's self-abnegation and the dormancy of personal identity and development. Taking on dominant contemporary concepts of masochism, as she does in *Eine Ausschweifung,* she also questions the tendency to essentialize feminine masochism and investigates incidences of pathological and non-pathological masochism in both men and women.

In its analysis of *Menschenkinder,* a collection of ten novellas published in 1899, chapter 5 turns to theories of the Gaze developed in Film Studies and draws parallels between those theories and Andreas-Salomé's understanding of the power of looking. I trace acts of looking and being looked at in these novellas and analyze narrative perspective in order to highlight how the author moves from descriptions of literal looking to the more generalized and theoretical implication that to look is to be in the masculine position, to be looked at in the feminine position. She also introduces possibilities for the subversion of these constellations, however, and examines the relationship between the gaze and power, the gaze and spatial arrangements, and the gaze and self-representation.

Further exploring themes of self-representation, the final chapter considers what may well be Andreas-Salomé's most widely read and critically received fictional work, *Fenitschka,* emphasizing the central role of the regularly sidelined male protagonist, Max. This analysis elucidates the novella's investigation of the relationship of narration to the negotiation and articulation of identity. Max presumes that his professional knowledge and authority grants him superior knowledge of his female counterpart, Fenitschka. He seeks to intervene repeatedly in her life and to offer correctives to her when she, as he sees it, goes astray. Fenitschka, however, demands the right to speak for herself, to navigate a fresh narrative of female identity, and Max, not incorrigibly domineering in his convictions, gradually learns from her over the course of their acquaintance. Through their debates, Andreas-Salomé reveals the inadequate nature of normalizing tendencies in contemporary discourses on woman and exposes them as stories that are simply widely accepted and thus imposed on, and often internalized by, men and women alike. In what can be read then as a riposte to the contemporary medical, psychological, and philosophical discourses on gendered identity, *Fenitschka* presents and criticizes a prevalent rhetoric whereby woman is denied the ability to speak for and understand herself (hysterization).[25]

The conclusion summarizes the arguments presented throughout the book by pairing the concepts of gender and motion.[26] In some of the literary texts already analyzed, as well as in *Ródinka*, literal and physical movement within the texts are shown to correspond to figurative and psychical movement. Subverting typical notions of progress as one-way, forward motion, Andreas-Salomé's body of work, I argue, defines progress as the possibility of back and forths, comings and goings, of numerous coexistent alternatives. New possibilities of self-determination and self-definition do not need to preclude more traditional ones. The restlessness of Andreas-Salomé's female characters points to them as works in progress. Arriving only to quickly depart again, they are in perpetual motion and steering toward no predictable endpoint.

Notes

[1] For an excellent and succinct overview of the biographies available on Lou Andreas-Salomé, see Caroline Kreide, *Lou Andreas-Salomé: Feministin oder Antifeministin? Eine Standortbestimmung zur wilhelminischen Frauenbewegung* (New York: Peter Lang, 1996), 3–16.

[2] Walter Kaufmann, "Foreword" in *Frau Lou: Nietzsche's Wayward Disciple*, by Rudolph Binion (Princeton, NJ: Princeton UP, 1968), v.

[3] Angela Livingstone, *Lou Andreas-Salomé: Her Life and Work* (New York: Moyer Bell, 1984), 10.

[4] H. F. Peters, *My Sister, My Spouse: A Biography of Lou Andreas-Salomé* (London: V. Gollancz, 1963).

[5] Cordula Koepcke, *Lou Andreas-Salomé: Ein eigenwilliger Lebensweg; Ihre Begegnungen mit Nietzsche, Rilke und Freud* (Freiburg im Breisgau: Herder, 1982) and *Lou Andreas-Salomé: Leben, Persönlichkeit, Werk; Eine Biographie* (Frankfurt am Main: Insel, 1986); Linde Salber, *Lou Andreas-Salomé* (Reinbek bei Hamburg: Rowohlt, 1990); Ursula Welsch and Michaela Wiesner, *Lou Andreas-Salomé: Vom "Lebensurgrund" zur Psychoanalyse* (Munich: Verlag Internationale Psychoanalyse, 1988).

[6] Leonie Müller-Loreck, *Die erzählende Dichtung Lou Andreas-Salomés: Ihr Zusammenhang mit der Literatur um 1900* (Stuttgart: Akademischer Verlag Hans-Dieter Heinz, 1976), 8.

[7] See Uta Treder, *Von der Hexe zur Hysterikerin: zur Verfestigungsgeschichte des "Ewig Weiblichen"* (Bonn: Bouvier, 1984) and Gisela Brinker-Gabler, "Feminismus und Moderne: Brennpunkt 1900," in *Kontroversen, alte und neue: Akten des VII. Internationalen Germanisten-Kongresses, 1985* 8 (Tübingen: Niemeyer, 1986), 228–34. See also Gisela Brinker-Gabler, "Perspektiven des Übergangs: Weibliches Bewußtsein und frühe Moderne," in *Deutsche Literatur von Frauen*, ed. Gisela Brinker-Gabler (Munich: C. H. Beck, 1988), 2:169–205.

[8] Chantal Gahlinger, *Der Weg zur weiblichen Autonomie: Zur Psychologie der Selbstwerdung im literarischen Werk von Lou Andreas-Salomé* (Bern: Peter Lang, 2001);

Biddy Martin, *Woman and Modernity: The Lifestyles of Lou Andreas-Salomé* (Ithaca, NY: Cornell UP, 1991); Birgit Wernz, *Sub-Versionen: Weiblichkeitsentwürfe in den Erzähltexten Lou Andreas-Salomés* (Pfaffenweiler, Germany: Centaurus-Verlagsgesellschaft, 1997). After the completion of this manuscript and at the time of going to press, a further book-length study on Lou Andreas-Salomé appeared: Karin Schütz, *Geschlechterentwürfe im literarischen Werk von Lou Andreas-Salomé unter Berücksichtigung ihrer Geschlechtertheorie* (Würzburg, Germany: Königshausen & Neumann, 2008).

[9] Lou Andreas-Salomé, *Fenitschka, Eine Ausschweifung: Zwei Erzählungen,* ed. Ernst Pfeiffer (Frankfurt am Main: Ullstein, 1983). In English, *Fenitschka and Deviations: Two Novellas,* trans. Dorothee Einstein Krahn (Lanham, NY, and London: UP of America, 1990).

[10] Compare van Santum, especially 316–17. Lisa A. Rainwater van Santum, "Hiding Behind Literary Analysis: Heinrich Heine's *Shakespeares Mädchen* and Lou Andreas-Salomé's *Henrik Ibsens Frauengestalten,*" *Monatshefte* 89 (1997): 307–23.

[11] Another important work on Lou Andreas-Salomé's writings is the special issue of *Seminar* edited by Raleigh Whitinger in 2000, which brings together nine voices that move away from "a perspective dictated by masters and master-narratives and toward revealing Andreas-Salomé as a writer of theoretical works and fiction that developed a subtly critical dialogue with the modes of discourse and writing in which she was previously considered to be more of a follower than an instigator or progressive thinker." *Seminar: A Journal of Germanic Studies; Special Issue on Lou Andreas-Salomé,* 36:1 (Feb. 2000): 2.

[12] Julie Doll Allen, "Male and Female Dialogue in Lou Andreas-Salomé's *Fenitschka,*" in *Frauen: Mitsprechen, Mitschreiben: Beiträge zu Literatur- und sprachwissenschaftlichen Frauenforschung,* ed. Marianne Henn and Britta Hufeisen (Stuttgart: Akademischer Verlag Hans-Dieter Heinz, 1997), 479–89; Gisela Brinker-Gabler, "Renaming the Human: Andreas-Salomé's 'Becoming Human,'" *Seminar* 36:1 (Feb. 2000): 22–41; Brigid Haines, "'Ja, so würde ich es auch heute noch sagen': Reading Lou Andreas-Salomé in the 1990s," *Publications of the English Goethe Society* 62 (1992): 77–95, "Lou Andreas-Salomé's *Fenitschka:* A Feminist Reading," *German Life and Letters* 44 (1991): 416–25, and "Masochism and Femininity in Lou Andreas-Salomé's *Eine Ausschweifung,*" *Women in German Yearbook* 8 (1993): 97–115; Raleigh Whitinger, "Lou Andreas-Salomé's *Fenitschka* and the Tradition of the Bildungsroman," *Monatshefte* 91:4 (Winter 1999): 464–81 and "Echoes of Lou Andreas-Salomé in Thomas Mann's *Tonio Kröger: Eine Ausschweifung* and its Relationship to the Bildungsroman Tradition," *The Germanic Review* 75:1 (Winter 2000): 21–36.

[13] Ruth Ellen Boetcher Joeres, *Respectability and Deviance: Nineteenth-Century German Women Writers and the Ambiguity of Representation* (Chicago and London: U of Chicago P, 1998), 9.

[14] Lou Andreas-Salomé, *Ma: Ein Porträt* (1904; repr., Frankfurt am Main: Ullstein, 1996); *Das Haus: Familiengeschichte vom Ende vorigen Jahrhunderts* (1921; repr., Frankfurt am Main: Ullstein, 1987); *Amor, Jutta, Die Tarnkappe: Drei Dichtungen,* ed. Ernst Pfeiffer (Frankfurt am Main: Insel Verlag, 1981);

Menschenkinder: Novellencyklus (Stuttgart: Cotta, 1899); *Ródinka: Russische Erinnerung* (1923; repr., Frankfurt am Main: Ullstein, 1985).

[15] Karla Schultz has refered to Kristeva and Andreas-Salomé as "sisters across the decades" and performs an excellent comparative reading of Kristeva's *Tales of Love* (1983) and Andreas-Salomé's two essays "Gedanken über das Liebesproblem" ("Thoughts on the Problem of Love," 1900) and "Narzißmus als Doppelrichtung" ("Narcissism as Dual Directionality," 1921). See Schultz, "In Defense of Narcissus: Lou Andreas-Salomé and Julia Kristeva," *The German Quarterly* 67:2 (Spring 1994): 185–96.

[16] Until the mid-eighties Andreas-Salomé satisfied neither traditional nor feminist evaluations of what is good and necessary in a work of art, and her works were labeled either trivial as literature or not radical enough as feminism. At least partially for these reasons, her works have been treated, with the recent exceptions that I have listed, as biographical source material. They were, however, welcomed in her own time as literary texts (Salber, *Lou Andreas-Salomé*, 7–8).

[17] Lou Andreas-Salomé, "Der Mensch als Weib," *Neue Deutsche Rundschau* 10 (1899): 225–43, repr. in Lou Andreas-Salomé, *Die Erotik: Vier Aufsätze,* ed. Ernst Pfeiffer (Frankfurt am Main: Ullstein, 1985), 7–44.

[18] Hedwig Dohm, "Reaktion in der Frauenbewegung," *Die Zukunft* (18 Nov. 1899): 279–91.

[19] Silvia Bovenschen, *Die imaginierte Weiblichkeit: Exemplarische Untersuchungen zu kulturgeschichtlichen und literarischen Präsentationsformen des Weiblichen* (Frankfurt am Main: Suhrkamp, 1979).

[20] In "Perspektiven des Übergangs: Weibliches Bewußtsein und frühe Moderne," Brinker-Gabler analyses how what she identifies as the "Weltwende" (world change) of the time was experienced and depicted by a number of female authors. She offers an excellent overview of concerns and themes that cropped up repeatedly in women's texts, including the "Verschiebung des 'Zwiespalts' von Innen/Außen auf den Zwiespalt im Inneren selbst" (170; displacement of the "inner/outer" dichotomy onto an internal dichotomy). Her discussion of Andreas-Salomé in this context spans pages 190–98 and comprises a discussion of the hitherto neglected *Ruth* as well as of *Fenitschka*.

[21] Biddy Martin develops this idea of conflicting drives in *Woman and Modernity:* "Salomé figured feminity and feminine subjectivity as the fluid interaction of conflicting drives — the impulse toward self-assertion or individuation on the one hand and toward erotic submission and dissolution on the other" (4).

[22] See Ann McGlashan's dissertation, *Creating Women: The Female Artist in Fin-de-Siècle Germany and Austria* (PhD diss., Indiana U, 1996) for an overview of the treatment of "woman" in texts by Freud, Weininger, and Scheffler.

[23] Judith Butler, *Gender Trouble: Feminism and the Subversion of Identity* (New York: Routledge, 1990).

[24] Jane Flax, "Multiples: On the Contemporary Politics of Subjectivity," in *Disputed Essays on Psychoanalysis, Subjects Politics and Philosophy* (New York: Routledge, 1993), 108.

[25] Ironically she would later be the victim of such rhetoric herself in the annals of literary history where Nietzsche's, Rilke's, and Freud's comments on her became the measure of the woman.

[26] I want to thank Beth Muellner of The College of Wooster for first drawing my attention to this productive pairing of concepts when she organized a panel for the 2007 German Studies Association entitled "Women in Motion." Her pithy title inspired me submit and present the paper "Motion, Performance and Identity in Lou Andreas-Salomé's Fiction."

1: Woman versus Women: Gender, Art, and Decadence in "Der Mensch als Weib" and *Eine Ausschweifung*

> *Oh, draw, by all means, little girl, but please don't aspire to be an artist*
>
> — Geraldine Brooks

IN "DER MENSCH ALS WEIB," Andreas-Salomé argues that a woman who corresponds to what she defines as "das Weib" cannot be an artist. These two forms of being are mutually exclusive. In the novella *Eine Ausschweifung,* published in the same year, the main character, Adine, struggles significantly because her desire to devote herself to art clashes with a vestigial drive to be a wife and mother. Although the word "decadence" does not appear in either text, each text's representation of the chasm between the submissive, nurturing woman (wife/mother) and the emancipated, artistic woman conjures up elements of discourses on decadence. "Der Mensch als Weib" reiterates common turn-of-the-century definitions of woman. *Eine Ausschweifung,* too, while depicting life possibilities for women that go beyond the traditional roles of wife and mother, tends toward nostalgia for women's traditional roles. These two texts address similar issues but in different manners. Whereas "Der Mensch als Weib" is a theoretical essay about femininity, woman, and humanity, *Eine Ausschweifung* is a novella that examines how theories of femininity play out in the lives of individual women. Reading the two texts in tandem provides an enriched reading experience of both, opens up new and productive avenues of interpretation, suggests Andreas-Salomé's concomitant appreciation for and reservations toward gender theories and theory in general, and sheds new light on the gendering of decadence.[1]

Theory and Femininity

"Der Mensch als Weib: Ein Bild im Umriß" appeared in the *Neue Deutsche Rundschau* in 1899, a year after the publication of the novella *Eine Ausschweifung.* As Caroline Kreide points out, the focus of "Der Mensch als Weib" is the philosophical-theoretical dimension of femininity and the woman question rather than the socio-legal dimension.[2] *Eine Ausschweifung,* on the other hand, examines how spoken and unspoken theories of femininity and gender expectations manifest themselves in the psyche and social interactions of a particular woman. Andreas-Salomé offers us her own theory of gender difference in the second part of "Der Mensch als Weib" (13–20). Femininity becomes a mystical union with the cosmos, and "etwas Selbsteigenes" (something entirely independent) rather than half of a whole in which the masculine represents the other half (15).[3] Nonetheless, she does not deny the inescapability of the binary pair — masculine/feminine — and continues with her own set of binary distinctions. In her narrative, "das Weib" (woman) represents an intact harmony with the world, a primitive state. It (das Weib) is self-sufficient, aristocratic, original, and completely involved in the sex act in which it produces no visible substance. It is organic, unified, less cultivatable, beyond the law, and its understanding is based on feelings. The opposite of this construct is "der Mann" (man) and it, in Lou Andreas-Salomé's rendering, represents a necessary and forceful progression and development. It is restless, an upstart, an accessory to the original, and only partially involved in the sex act in which it produces a visible substance. It is differentiated, inorganic, excessively cultivated, immersed in tradition, and its understanding is historical and logical. Andreas-Salomé repeats many erstwhile distinctions between masculinity and femininity but chooses to celebrate the feminine as superior and as a model for humanity, for the "Mensch" (human being). In this sense, her theory comes very close to ideas of conservative bourgeois feminists of her time and reads as merely another limiting paradigm of femininity.

At times, however, Andreas-Salomé interrupts the unfolding of her argument in order to call for absolute freedom for real women, freedom to do as they wish, including the freedom to write and participate in artistic activities, freedom, therefore, even from whatever constraints her own theory of femininity imply: "man [kann] daher nur Freiheit und immer wieder Freiheit predigen . . . weil man mehr Grund hat, den Sehnsuchtstimmen im Menschen selbst zu trauen, selbst wenn sie sich falsch ausdrücken, als vorgefaßten und zurechtgemachten Theorien" (29–30; thus one can only preach freedom, freedom, and more freedom . . . because we have more reason to trust the yearnings within a human being herself, even when spuriously expressed, than preconceived and tidy theories). Together with the themes developed in *Eine Ausschweifung,* this interruption and a similar one later in the essay point to Andreas-Salomé's understanding of theory as something that does not have a one-to-one correspondence to life but exists as a realm of the idealistic. Rather than see the distance between theory and reality as an undermining aspect of theory, however, she insists on simply forging ahead, on preserving, but remaining cognizant of, the gulf between the theoretical and the real.[4]

Andreas-Salomé does not purport to report on women and femininity in "Der Mensch als Weib" in a so-called scientific-objective fashion, as those practitioners of science whom she quotes do — Karl Claus, Johannes Rankes, Rudolf Virchow. In the first part of the essay she gives short shrift to contemporary scientific discourses on femininity and masculinity. Not questioning the mapping of physical difference onto the psyche per se, she examines Rankes's theory that establishes the sperm as active and the egg as passive and argues that scientists have confused the place in which fertilization takes place with the feminine element in fertilization (11).[5] She proposes that the egg is not inactive and in need of completion through the active and life-giving force of the sperm simply because it remains in the body in which it is produced and concludes:

> Mit gleichem oder weit größerem Schein von Recht hätte statt jener Phrase [vom weiblichen Element als dem passiven Anhängsel des schöpferischen männlichen] die Rede sein können von dem männlichen Bestandteil als dem anschlußbedürftigern, bedürftigern überhaupt, — vom "hingebendern" sozusagen, der von der weiblichen gewährenden Selbstsucht als willkommene Zutat in ihrer Entwicklung aufgebracht wird. (13)

> [With the same, or an even greater, appearance of authority, one could have spoken of the masculine rather than the feminine element as the element most in need of completion, indeed simply as the most needy — one could have spoken of the more surrendering element that is incorporated by the confidently selfish feminine element as a welcome addition to its development.]

Thus she shifts the reader's focus from concepts of truth, of unbiased scientific description, and of a one-to-one correspondence between language and reality to the notion of plural truths or "the untruth of truth,"[6] rhetorical agility, the aesthetics of theory, and language as something that shapes our reality as much as it describes it. She does not claim that she can replace widely accepted theories of gender with the truth but points instead to language as an ideological tool that she can engage at once very similarly to and yet differently from her predecessors on the subject of gender difference.

Drawing attention to two potential models of gender difference, the traditional model of gender difference that she cites and the altered, though still quite traditional, model that she puts forward, she reveals both as constructs and makes visible the gulf that separates whatever physical and biological differences there may exist between men and women from the articulation of corresponding psychic differences. Implicitly then, theoretical and scientific narratives on gender have similar qualities to fictional narratives. Constituting exercises in linguistic dexterity, they are reductive models of a complex reality that depend as much on aesthetics and on a particular prevailing ideology as on truth. Pursuing a project similar to Foucault's genealogical inquiry into sexuality, Andreas-Salomé redistributes and inverts cause-and-effect relationships and questions the authority of those who would claim to objectively map biological difference onto gendered psyches and real lives.[7] Refusing to engage the scientists she quotes on their own terms, she indicates that she does not accept the premises and assumptions of the scientific discourse in which they maneuver. In yet another inversion of the expected, readers find themselves confronted with a text in which the author demonstrates as much interest in revealing the dependence of scientific argumentation on ideology, imagination, and fantasy as she shows in the subject matter announced in the title.

"Der Mensch als Weib" outlines a seductive theory of femininity, elevating "das Weib" to the status of a model for human beings. "Das Weib" is a positive, undifferentiated being who, completely at home in the world, lacks the ego problems that lead to demands for recognition. Because Andreas-Salomé's "Weib" simply is and enjoys being, she is freed from the usual human psychic and egotistical ailments. This clearly one-sided and idealized image of woman ("das Weib") invites a feminist critique, to be sure, but the one-sidedness is counteracted by her depiction of femininity in fictional texts. In them she adds to the complexity of the theoretical ideas she presents in this and other essays, fleshing them out, examining them in a social context, and providing a corrective to them. *Eine Ausschweifung,* for example, serves as a site for the negotiation of expected gender behaviors as represented in the figure of "das Weib" and for the development of individual identities in discrete women. Whereas "das Weib" is transcendent, seductive not only to the readers of Andreas-Salomé's "Der Mensch als Weib" but also to Adine, the main character in *Eine Ausschweifung,* the novella offers a broader treatment of the concept of "das Weib," examining what happens when theory meets lived experience. Adine wrestles with the tension between her great pleasure in and commitment to art and an ingrained drive to prostrate herself in marriage, to make her own activity secondary to that of Benno, her fiancé, and thereby to give up everything that is not immediately connected with taking care of him and their household.[8] Investigating how theories and traditional understandings of femininity clash with new opportunities available to women, *Eine Ausschweifung* points to the establishment of a sense of one's own identity as a woman at the turn of the century in Germany as an undertaking fraught with pitfalls.

A first-person narration, *Eine Ausschweifung* is Adine's letter to her would-be lover, explaining why she is incapable of truly loving him or any other man. Despite an apparently monologic set-up — everything is filtered through the consciousness of the first-person narrator — the text produced is dialogic, accommodating voices that represent viewpoints very different from Adine's. In one of the first articles to do justice to the complexity of this novella, Brigid Haines emphasizes the text's ambivalence toward masochistic behaviors in women.[9] The ambivalence underscored by Haines in relation to masochism bleeds over, I contend, into attitudes toward femininity and the changes made possible by feminism. Alternative perspectives and a polyphony of voices coexist with and complicate Adine's perspective, producing a palpable ambivalence toward the woman question in general. Whereas Andreas-Salomé's argument in "Der Mensch als Weib" shores up traditional understandings of femininity and women's roles in life to a certain degree, and whereas Adine's positions on femininity and the relationship between "Weib" and "Kunst" (art) do the same, *Eine Ausschweifung* as a whole makes it explicit that Andreas-Salomé is not only aware of but also sympathetic toward the psychic and social struggles of individuals, both women and men, and the complexity of the relationship between theory and life, between generalizations and the particular.

Andreas-Salomé's responses to contemporary discourses call for a multidimensional approach that she mirrors in her fiction. She does not intervene in monologic discourses by merely replacing one monologue with another, but rather by using a multiplicity of voices and perspectives and thus producing a polylogue in each work. *Eine Ausschweifung* presents us with a variety of female characters: Adine herself, her mother, her masochistic wet-nurse, her neighbor Gabriele, who longs for freedom from her domestic chores, Gabriele's younger sister, Mutchen, who is consumed by her sensuality, and the physically deformed Daniela, who deifies Benno, Adine's erstwhile fiancé. In her attempt to understand herself and to create a narrative that accounts for her difference from and similarity to "woman," Adine reflects on these women's lives and her conversations with them.

Adine's father encourages her artistic side from childhood on, but when her puberty and his death coincide, she falls for her cousin Benno, influenced by both his and her mother's more conservative notions of femininity. She gives up her art in submission to Benno and her prospective wifely duties. Her new focus makes her physically and mentally ill and Benno, in consultation with her mother, breaks off the engagement and sends Adine away from her home town of Brieg. With time she recovers from her illness and broken heart, takes an atelier in Paris, and returns to art as a full-time occupation. For six years she does not return to Brieg. The privileges of Adine's life, her freedom from her family and home town and her devotion to art, are associated with her class, to be sure, but also with the gains and advances made for women by feminism. Nonetheless, Adine clings to a distinctly antifeminist viewpoint on topics such as love, marriage, careers, and individual agency, romanticizing the submission of her mother to her father and the violence she witnesses her wetnurse's husband inflict on his wife. She romanticizes the lives of women who manage, whether by necessity or choice, to subordinate themselves to men and become self-effacing.

Gabriele, her upstairs neighbor of a lower class, on the other hand, validates aspects of the women's movement by trying to make Adine aware of the advantages she has had. The contrast between the two women qualifies Adine's perspective on femininity and feminism. Gabriele has longed for but been unable to enjoy the sorts of opportunities for self-development that Adine takes for granted. When Adine first gets to know Gabriele, she imagines that Gabriele enjoys doing the household chores at which she appears to be very good. But Gabriele soon reveals ulterior motives. She has agreed to keep house for a time in return for the chance to go to Berlin, where she hopes to enroll in a teacher-training school. Gabriele has no interest in domestic life or in marriage. Ironically, six years later, Adine, who chided Gabriele for her lack of interest in men and marriage and for her determination to escape the narrow and conservative world of Brieg, has escaped instead, has made a career, and has become independent. When Gabriele congratulates Adine for her achievements, Adine denies that any conscious feminist desire determined her current lifestyle, insisting that she was merely presented opportunity on a silver platter. Gabriele's annoyed reaction emphasizes both her envy and scorn: "Du bekommst es eben geschenkt — wir andern müssen es erobern" (95; "Well, you received it as a gift, other people have to work for it," 69).[10] Whereas Gabriele sees no contradiction between her identity as a woman and her desire for an unconventional lifestyle, Adine persistently rejects seeing the direction her life has taken as something she willed.

Twice Adine admits, however, that she admires Gabriele. When she first discovers that Gabriele has long-term goals, she is impressed (78). And later, when she returns to Brieg and finds that Gabriele is still determined to do what she had wanted to do six years earlier, despite increasing odds against her, Adine is again impressed (94–95). Although she argues against Gabriele in dialogues about marriage, love, and men, claiming that these are the foundation of a real woman's life and women are best off when they can accept their masochistic and self-effacing nature, Adine cannot help but respect a woman who rejects these ideas. Her respect for Gabriele and the fact that years later Gabriele's criticisms remain with her gives Gabriele's voice authority within this text. That Gabriele desperately wants and cannot have something that Adine has and repeatedly undermines in discussion points to the distinction between the bourgeois and proletarian women's movements, suggesting that it is easier to pay lip service to traditional notions of femininity and motherhood when one has the means to escape them. In her juxtaposition of Adine and Gabriele, Andreas-Salomé acknowledges the proletarian feminist critique of bourgeois feminism's lack of interest in social conditions and class.[11]

The echoing of Gabriele's voice and criticisms by Adine's mother, Lisette, whom Adine similarly respects and admires, emphasizes another perspective at odds with Adine's. Lisette condemns her daughter's ideal-ization of the Baroness Daniela's physical deformities and of the mental illness of their maidservant, Anna. A former patient of the insane asylum where Benno works, Anna imagines that she is in service to the emperor of China as she goes about her daily duties. Daniela is a nineteen-year old girl with an incurable deformity of the hips and shoulders, whom Benno encourages and supports by regularly meeting her to discuss literature and philosophy. She tells Adine that she is nothing to Benno, that he only meets with her because he is sorry for her, and that she rejoices in her inferiority. Adine idealizes Daniela's self-subordinating relationship to Benno, entitling a sketch she makes of Daniela's face "das Glück" (109; "Happiness," 79). Lisette's reaction to the sketch underscores Adine's blind spot: "Aber das ist ja die kleine Baronesse . . . nur gar so schön wie du ihren Kopf gezeichnet hast, ist sie doch nicht, Kind" (109; "This must be the little baroness. . . . But it is not quite right, my child. Her head is not as beautiful as you have sketched it here," 79). When Adine continues to lionize illness and deformity, wishing for both Daniela's and Anna's afflictions for Christmas, her mother chastises her, again drawing atten-tion to Adine's tendency to glorify disability. Adine casts it as aestheti-cally and psychically pleasing because it takes away certain choices that she finds cumbersome.

Gabriele criticizes Adine for glorifying what Adine sees as the previ-ous generation of women's "natural" subordination to man and accuses her of speaking like her grandmother when she pronounces a man's tyr-anny to be his most enchanting trait. For Gabriele, Adine's concepts of gender and love are old junk with no place in contemporary woman's practical life concerns. Gabriele shows little patience for Adine's privileg-ing of the aesthetic over the quotidian: "Du bist eben eine Künstlerin, Adine. Ich sage ja nicht, daß du mit Gefühlen spielen würdest, aber *ihre Tuglichkeit fürs Leben ist dir doch nicht alles* — wenn sie dich irgendwie künstlerisch anregen" (96; "Well, you are an artist, Adine. I am not say-ing that you play with emotions, but *their purpose in life is not of the great-est importance to you* as long as they stimulate your artistic creativity," 70, emphasis added). Gabriele's and Lisette's interventions serve as qualifica-tions to Adine's narrative as a whole, encouraging the reader to question her perspective of her own development and its relationship to femininity. Like her sketch of Daniela's face, the text Adine writes constitutes a cre-ative attempt to deal with her overwrought emotions and may well have similar shortcomings. Unlike the sketch of Daniela's face, however, the text includes other voices and exists, despite the fact that it has a single author, as a more dialogic form than the sketch.

Lisette's and Gabriele's critiques of Adine's narratological tendencies also provoke reservations in the reader about Adine's representation of the natural and satisfying feminine masochism she projects onto her mother and her wet nurse. While Adine was very much in control in her own home, she saw the women around her leading lives of subservience and devotion to their husbands. The hierarchy within her family was clear: ". . . mein liebes Mütterchen tat alles, was mein Vater wollte, er aber alles was ich wollte" (73; ". . . my dear little mother did everything as my father wanted it, and he in turn did everything that I wanted," 52). Raised to be in control, she nonetheless sees her female role models as deferential and associates this with love, marriage, and motherhood, which she in turns associates with true femininity. In her parents' marriage, which she refers to as "wahrhaft musterhaft" ("exemplary"), her mother is self-effacing (83; 52). Her wet-nurse, as Adine remembers it, rejoices in the physically abusive attention of her husband. Although Adine's upbringing and socialization seem to instill in her a sense of her own self-worth, her own will, and the importance of her artistic endeavors, they also teach her that a woman in love is a woman who is subservient and self-effacing, and who has no occupation other than that of wife and mother. Her childhood consists, it seems, of sets of conflicting messages, and so her masochism and desire to submit come to manifest themselves in her sensual side but are counterbalanced by a self-assertiveness and independence in her artistic side. Adine's attempts to understand herself and her psyche make room for complexity and intricacy, but her use of other women in the narrative construction of her identity ignores the possibility of similar complications for them. Differentiating her masochism from that of her mother and her wet-nurse, she sees only hers as debilitating:

> Durch diese gewaltsame Unterordnung unter ihn vermischte sich in meiner Leidenschaft das Süßeste mit dem Schmerzlichsten, fast mit dem Grauen. Das ist ja gewiss nicht der Fall, wo ein Weib schon an sich viel untergeordneter ist als der Mann. Sonst aber kann es zu einer furchtbaren Würze der Liebe werden, zu einer so ungeheuren Aufpeitschung der Nerven, daß das seelische Gleichgewicht notwendig verlorengehen muß. (79)

> [In this forced submissiveness to him, my most delightful feelings of passion became mixed with the most painful, even with horror. That is certainly not usually the case since women are already subordinate to their men. But it can add such enormous excitement to their love that all inner peace and balance are lost. (57)]

She assumes the absence of inner conflict in her caregivers, reproducing contemporary understandings by Freud and Krafft-Ebing, among others, of masochism as generally natural in women and pathological in men.[12] Given how she distinguishes the masochism of her mother and wet-nurse from her own, Adine implies that she suffers from a symptom of the times, of her generation.[13] Thus she writes nostalgically of a time and place in which the conflicts she experiences did not exist. But she also draws a beautiful portrait of Daniela, erasing Daniela's deformities, struggles, and problems. Both the sketch and the letter point to potential oversights in the interest of reductive but aesthetically pleasing theories and an imagined utopia. Functioning as legitimate alternatives to Adine's ideas and perspectives on women, love, and marriage, Gabriele's and Lisette's voices add depth and complexity to Adine's views of the women's movement and of the previous generation.

In *Eine Ausschweifung*, Andreas-Salomé revisits aspects of the theory of femininity she develops in "Der Mensch als Weib" in more concrete circumstances and illustrates deviations from that theory, highlighting the chasm that separates theories of femininity from manifestations of femininity in the lives of multiple women. Toward the end of the novella Benno mulls over his role in the failure of his relationship to Adine:

> "Ich [erkannte] allmählich, wodurch ich dich verloren hatte: durch den Mangel an Einsicht in das, was kraftvoll und gesund in dir war, und nur deshalb krankhaft erschien, weil man deine Entwicklung unterband, weil man dich nicht in den Stand setzte, es künstlerisch aus dir herauszugeben." (103)

> ["Only gradually I understood why I had lost you, through the lack of insight in what was important for you, the inability to understand what was strong and healthy in you. You appeared to become ill, and I did not realize it was only because you were stifled in your development, because you were prevented from expressing yourself through your art." (75)]

His insight reads as a direct overlap with an argument Andreas-Salomé puts forth in "Der Mensch als Weib," when she calls for absolute freedom from prescription and norms for individual women so that they might develop in accordance with their own internal feminine compass:

> denn nichts vermag ein Weib so tief und wahrhaft zu emanzipieren als die Ahnung, daß man ihr durch irgend eine Enge, in der man sie künstlich hält, den Weg verwehrt, auf dem sie zu voller frommer Hingebung und Andacht dem Leben gegenüber gelangen könnte, — den Punkt finden könnte, von dem aus das Leben und sie selbst ihre geheimnisvoll ineinanderrinnende Harmonie feiern. (39)

> [for nothing enables a woman to so truly and profoundly emancipate herself than the sense that one is using artificial constraints to deny her access to the path on which she could achieve a completely

pious devotion to and zeal for life — the path that could lead her to
that point at which she could celebrate the secret fusing of her own
and life's harmony.]

For Andreas-Salomé, emancipation is not necessarily positive, at least
not for "das Weib," but generates the kinds of psychic upsets, inner conflicts, and identity problems that Adine experiences in *Eine Ausschweifung*.
In an interesting twist, however, she argues that constraining women in
any way is more likely to damage their natural femininity than any apparently unfeminine behavior in which they might indulge. Valorizing a primitive utopia in which woman has no choice but is simply driven by physical
impulses and satisfied with those impulses, Andreas-Salomé intimates that
nothing threatens femininity more than civilization. She at once defines
femininity in very conservative terms and refuses to pin it down completely
or to see it as necessarily damaged or undermined by particular actions or
behaviors. She suggests that femininity does not need to be safeguarded or
regulated in an increasingly civilized world but is hardwired in woman. In
a fascinating circularity, she establishes femininity as that which individual
women do. That is, femininity simply is. Discourses and rules or laws that
attempt to limit women, to prescribe behavior, run the risk of damaging
femininity because they confine, narrow, and pervert what always already is.
Femininity, she suggests, polices itself.

Adine's defense of her theories of self-effacing femininity similarly
recalls aspects of "Der Mensch als Weib." She tells Gabriele that her theory
might be old junk but is nonetheless beautiful: "Aber er [alter Plunder]
kann den praktischen Gerätschaften so unendlich überlegen sein durch
seine Schönheit" (96; "But it can be vastly superior to some of the practical objects because it is beautiful," 69–70). Given that Adine's concept
of ideal femininity corresponds to the concept of "Weib" in "Der Mensch
als Weib," *Eine Ausschweifung*'s plural voices represent, if not a corrective,
then certainly a complement, to the arguments put forth in "Der Mensch
als Weib." Reading these texts side by side amplifies the emergent concept
of theory in the essay, that theory, if treated as a kind of poetic fiction, can
be beautiful in its nostalgic creation of lost utopias but ought not be used
to regulate femininity and the lives of individual women.

In their introduction to *Feminism, Bakhtin, and the Dialogic*, Dale
M. Bauer and Susan Jaret McKinstry state that the object of their project
of feminist dialogics is not

> to produce a feminist monologic voice, a dominant voice that is a
> reversal of the patriarchal voice . . . but to create a feminist dialogics
> that recognizes power and discourse as indivisible, monologism as
> a model of ideological dominance, and narrative as inherently mul-
> tivocal, as a form of cultural resistance that celebrates the dialogic

voice that speaks with many tongues, which incorporates multiple voices of the cultural web. (4)[14]

Eine Ausschweifung is multivocal in the way these authors suggest. Even the form of the novella — a letter to a friend — suggests exchange, dialogue, and the potential for response. The manner in which the text breaks off abruptly further emphasizes the lack of resolution of Adine's specific problem and of the issues that this problem inevitably touches upon. By creating a text with a variety of perspectives and a variety of positions on important contemporary issues, Andreas-Salomé creates a rhetorical ambivalence that undermines the idea of definitive knowledge, including the notion of definitive self-knowledge — the reader cannot know Adine because she cannot even know herself. This rhetorical ambivalence underscores the importance of questions and dialogue rather than conclusions and resolutions.

While I have emphasized the role Gabriele's and Lisette's voices play as correctives to Adine's antifeminist notions, it is important to recognize that Andreas-Salomé also underscores problematic aspects of a feminist agenda, particularly one that sought equality with men in the world of work and careers. Adine is surprised, for example, when six years after their initial relationship she returns home and discovers that Benno is dissatisfied with his lot. She has always assumed that Benno was defined by his work and that he enjoyed and even lived for that work. At dinner one evening, he refers to work as "Sklavendienst. Sklaverei von früh bis spat" ("slave labor. Slavery from morning to night"), complaining that his dedication to his profession has resulted in one-sidedness and in a lack of personal development in all areas other than the professional (97; 70). Expressing surprise at the fact that he is not completely fulfilled by his job, Adine reminds him that women are currently very eager to emulate professional men. By drawing attention to Benno's inner conflict and his disgruntlement, Andreas-Salomé underscores blind spots in contemporary feminism too. She argues extensively against woman's emulation of the male lifestyle in "Der Mensch als Weib," and here too she appears to warn against making man's life into a model of fulfillment.

In her theoretical works Andreas-Salomé similarly emphasizes the importance of questioning resolutions, even her own.[15] Throughout her writings she wavers, changes direction, and remains flexible in both her style and her themes.[16] If she seems more traditional in her theoretical and essayistic writing than in her fiction, the nature of the writing can explain this. In order to be taken seriously when writing theoretical tracts, the author must articulate a coherent line of reasoning from an authoritative position. Narrative, on the other hand, offers the author the opportunity to present a wide range of characters. The polyphony of voices, the ambiguities, and the ambivalence that pervade *Eine Ausschweifung* leave the reader with questions, aspects of a debate, perspectives, but no solutions, and thereby better represent Andreas-Salomé's own position on many of the issues of her time. The changes in Adine, Gabriele, Benno, and even Lisette, point to identity as an ongoing endeavor, as something that rarely if ever culminates in the kind of satisfying and comfortable relationship of the self to the world that the theory of "das Weib" represents. Rather, the novella drives home how identity is forever in flux, involving daily negotiations, rewritings, setbacks, successes, and failures; and the differences inherent in her various female figures are a reminder, whether intentional or not, of her own call for freedom for women in "Der Mensch als Weib."

The Limits of the Figurative

In "Reaktion in der Frauenbewegung" Hedwig Dohm accuses Andreas-Salomé's "Der Mensch als Weib" of antifeminism, recognizing that its elevation of "Weib" to the level of superior human being occurs at the cost of denying her equal participation in intellectual and public life.[17] She also recognizes that Andreas-Salomé's description of women and women's lives bore little or no resemblance to the limited domestic life as wives and mothers that many women then lived, not to mention to the lives of women over the age of forty who were no longer — if indeed they ever had been — the beautiful shade-giving trees that Andreas-Salomé imagined her "Weib" to be. Rose-Maria Gropp and Caroline Kreide dismiss Dohm's critique, claiming that she fails to recognize the symbolic value of "das Weib."[18] However, their resistance to the idea that "Weib" has a referent in the real world, namely real women, is questionable. Andreas-Salomé's own text even appears to acknowledge the problem that Dohm identifies. Her second interruption of the unfolding of her essay constitutes a conflation of the desire for emancipation with "truly" feminine desire and seeks to preempt the use of her theories to regulate women's behavior: "Sehr vieles, was an einer Frau emanzipationslustig aussieht, ist nichts weiter als das, und löst die scheinbaren Proteste und Verneinungen in einem tieferen Sinn doch wieder in Bejahungen auf" (Much of what seems like an emancipation fervor in women is really nothing more than that, and the apparent protests and denials soon dissolve again into more meaningful affirmations, 39). Having implicitly and explicitly criticized feminism and the goal of emancipation for much of the essay, she backpedals, arguing that many so-called emancipated women are simply struggling against constraints that get in the way of self-development. This interruption, along with the one discussed earlier, indicates her awareness that, try as she might, she cannot divest "Weib" of its reference to real women.

To see Andreas-Salomé's "Weib" in "Der Mensch als Weib" as solely figurative not only ignores the ambiguity of the term "Weib" in "Der Mensch als Weib" and in *Eine Ausschweifung* but also the argument of "Ketzereien gegen die moderne Frau," which she wrote in the same year. In "Männerurtheil über Frauendichtung" (Men's Judgement of Women's Literary Endeavors,) Frieda von Bülow criticizes the use of the words "weiblich" (feminine) and "echt frauenhaft" ("truly feminine") as negatively loaded adjectives in the reception of literary works by women (565).[19] Lou Andreas-Salomé responds to her in "Ketzereien gegen die moderne Frau," arguing that what women produce *is* often "frauenhaft" (feminine), a document of the female self rather than an artwork of universal appeal. Insisting that women should be women first and foremost, she nonetheless does not plead with women to stop writing entirely. She merely advises them not to take their writing too seriously, to publish anonymously, if at all, and to cease competing with male authors for the praises of male critics:

> Sollen . . . die Frauen keine Bücher mehr schreiben? Das mögen sie thun, so oft es sie dazu treibt, wie sie überhaupt Alles thun mögen, wozu es sie treibt. . . . Nur so entsetzlich ernsthaft und wichtig sollen sie es nicht nehmen. Sie sollen ihre literarische Thätigkeit als das Accessorische, nicht als das Wesentliche an ihrer weiblichen Auslebung betrachten. . . . Wenn die Verleger es erlaubten, sollten sie am Liebsten noch anonym ihren Herzen Luft machen. Ungefähr so, wie man jauchzt oder weint, ohne den eigenen Namen darunter zu schreiben. Gerade das stofflich Persönlichere, das minder künstlerisch Geformte an ihren Werken sollte sie zum Entgelt dafür gleichgültig machen gegen die persönlichste Eitelkeit des Berühmtwerdens. (567–68)

> [So should women not write any more books? They may do so as often as they feel the urge to do so, just as they may do anything at all that they feel driven to do. . . . They just shouldn't take it so deathly seriously. They should regard their literary activity as supplemental rather than as a fundamental part of their expression of femininity. If their publishers allowed it, they would do better to just express whatever is in their hearts anonymously. Just as one rejoices or cries without signing one's name to it. It is precisely the more personal nature of the subject matter and the less aesthetically crafted form of their works that should make them indifferent to that most personal of vanities: fame.]

Her basic and repeated understanding of women's relationship to art emerges in this short passage, as does her understanding of the gap between a theoretical and aesthetically pleasing prescriptive discourse on woman and a more practical and descriptive discourse on real women. On the one hand, her reluctance to see women's writing as art surfaces in the parallel she draws between it and the physical and emotional reflexes of pouring one's heart out, whooping for joy and crying, and in her assumption that all women's writing is inevitably thematically more personal and formally less crafted than men's. On the other hand, the parallel she draws between writing and emotional reflexes suggests that writing is as fundamental a part of women's response to the world as it is of men's.

The points of similarity between Andreas-Salomé's argument about the term "frauenhaft" in "Ketzereien gegen die modern Frau" and the metaphor of a fruit tree she invokes in "Der Mensch als Weib" indicate the inevitable overlap between a theory of "das Weib," figurative though it may be, and real women. "Das Weib," she argues in "Der Mensch als Weib," is a tree whose fruit cannot be plucked and used for a variety of purposes without damaging the existential and natural beauty and strength of the tree. A wind may knock occasional pieces of fruit from the tree as part of an organic and natural process, but this fruit is merely something sweet to be consumed for pleasure. The fruit here represents art works that women might produce, but such products, she cautions, are not to be compared with the intellectual or artistic products of men, which are created in a very different fashion. What she envisages as the relationship between women and creative activity is an intensely natural process that yields works that do not alienate woman from her "natural" role of giving pleasure and comfort to others through her mere physical presence. Like many of her male contemporaries who threw themselves wholeheartedly into the project of denying women creative or artistic genius, Andreas-Salomé considers conscious concentration on artistic production to be distinctly unfeminine and considers it an anomaly for a woman to create a work of art.[20] Unlike her male counterparts (Schopenhauer, Möbius), however, she does not advocate preventing women from writing or painting. In fact, she depicts such production as inevitable. Her defense of woman's right and her organic need to produce creative works points again to the intersection of "das Weib" (woman) and "die Frau" (women).

That Andreas-Salomé's "Weib" is connected to real women is further suggested by the fact that her concept of the artist — something that "Weib" cannot be — is very clearly connected to real men. In the third part of the "Der Mensch als Weib" (20–29), the emphasis shifts to gender and its relationship to the figure of the artist. A couple of gendered continuums emerge on which "Weib" is to "Frau" as "Künstler" (artist) is to "Mann." If woman ("Frau") achieves an ideal state of being when she becomes "Weib," then man reaches his highest level of perfection when he becomes an artist. What an artist exercises in his art, a "Weib" exercises in her life. Through her very existence she offers beauty and transcendence. Though different from "das Weib," the male artist is very similar to it, embodying that form of masculinity that most closely approaches and best understands femininity: "Jedoch sicher ist dies, daß der männliche Künstler als solcher dem Weibe außerordentlich nah steht. . . . Nicht zufällig ist es, daß man Künstlern so oft weibliche Eigenschaften anmerkt oder daß sie den Vorwurf der Unmännlichkeit hören müssen" (21–22; This much, however, is certain: the male artist as artist is exceptionally close to "woman." . . . It is no coincidence that we often notice that artists have feminine characteristics or that they have to hear themselves accused of being unmasculine). Of equal importance as the proximity of "Weib" to artist however is the fact that "Weib" and artist are never the same. As man cannot become "Weib," so too woman cannot become "Künstler":

> Im Künstler lebt wohl all dies dunkle Drängen als schaffende Kraft in seinem Werke fort, aber herausgehoben in eigene Form und Klarheit, in ein neues Ding für sich, das die treibende Veranlassung zum ganzen Prozeß war; im Weibe andererseits leben wohl fortwährend primitiv künstlerische Anregungen sich aus, aber immer wieder und immer tiefer hineingezogen in das Erleben selbst, dessen Triebkraft sie durch ihre Wärme mitzeitigt ohne ihnen eigene Auswege zu öffnen. Im Weibe scheint sich alles ins Leben hinein, nichts aus ihm heraus, entladen zu sollen. (22–23)

> [In the case of the artist, all the dark striving lives on as creative force in his works, abstracted, however, into its own shape and vividness, into something new, existing in and of itself, something that was the impulsive motivation for the whole process; in the case of "woman," on the other hand, we see the expression of perpetually primitive artistic motivations, repeatedly and ever more deeply linked to experience itself. The momentum of these primitive urges is nourished by her warmth but denied an outlet of its own. In the case of "woman," it seems that everything should be invested in life with no expectation of a return.]

These parallel continuums intimate that "Weib" is a potential realization of woman, but not equivalent to woman, just as an artist is a potential realization of man but not equivalent to man. Having made this argumentative move, Andreas-Salomé then reinvests the term "Weib" with ambiguity. She valorizes literary discourses on women, claiming that in order to understand "das Weib," women must delve into literary texts about it by male artists. Thus she removes "das Weib" to the realm of the fictional again and points to it as something man-made, offering the possibility that one read the entire essay as an analysis of a literary invention and proffering yet another possibility of preserving distinctions between a model "Weib" and real women.

Since Andreas-Salomé sees art in similar terms to Freud, as aris-ing out of sublimation or lack, her concept of art *must* be diametrically opposed to her concept of "Weib": "Das gesamte Geistesleben [ist] selbst schließlich auch nur eine verwandelte, ins Feinste umgeformte Blüte aus der großen geschlechtlich bedingten Wurzel alles Daseins . . . — sublim-ierte Geschlechtlichkeit sozusagen" (16; The entire life of the mind is itself, after all, just a blossom transformed into something exquisite out of the great, sexually determined root of all existence . . . sublimated sexual-ity, so to speak,). Because man is a more differentiated being, he is fur-ther removed from nature than woman and lacks her sense of intimacy in and with the world. Homes and domesticity, for example, are primarily for men, not for women, she argues, because women, like snails, carry their homes on their backs. "Das Weib" emerges again here as a male creation. Men have created a notion of feminine identity that is a projec-tion of their own needs. Given Andreas-Salomé's basic understanding of the nature of "das Weib" and the nature of art then, a woman who con-sciously devotes herself to artistic production has necessarily either already damaged her femininity as thus defined or endangers it because such production demands self-reflexivity, and self-reflexivity threatens what Andreas-Salomé posits as woman's unmediated and direct relationship to life and experience. Art arises out of an agonized relationship to the world and such a relationship to the world is foreign to "das Weib."

Although Andreas-Salomé untangles "das Weib" from its traditional location in male-authored discourses in the first part of the essay, she rein-serts it into those discourses with a slight twist in the third part, turning it into a reflection of man's lack, that which man is not. It is something superior, subversive, the Other, that from which man fought his way free and to which he can never return. Real women then become the projec-tion screen for this imagined and original "Weib" but, as screens onto which something is projected, they can never actually be what is projected, just a copy of the original or a mapping of the original onto something else. She concludes that it is man who most needs "das Weib" in all of its incarnations: the literary ideal, their discursive projections based on lack, and real women who approach the ideal.

Employing irony and paradox repeatedly throughout the essay, she underscores how theoretical writings on gender function as a kind of science fiction, a fantasizing about how things might be rather than a description of how things are. Demonstrating the beauty of the theory of the feminine and of femininity, at the same time she reveals that it is not "truth." She appreciates theory and rhetoric and indulges in them for what they are rather than criticizing them for what they are not and can-not be. Andreas-Salomé at once demonstrates that figurative woman is not to be conflated with real women and yet can also never be completely free of its associations with real women because nobody is in control of the referent.[21] Thus "Der Mensch als Weib" is a challenging and immensely complex project for its author and its readers, who must struggle to dissociate "Weib" from its real-life referent in woman, yet must repeatedly encounter the impossibility of this task.

"Der Mensch als Weib," particularly when read in tandem with *Eine Ausschweifung,* suggests a reading strategy for theories of femininity that would limit the negative impact of such theories on the real lives of real women. This is not an essay on femininity as it is but an essay about discourses on femininity; Andreas-Salomé underscores that "femininity" as it has been described and constructed exists in discourse and may even exist in some women but should not be prescriptive, since prescription is a limitation of freedom. She explores discourses that seek to regulate femininity, but she does not seek to regulate. That may be the most important element of her essay: it demonstrates how theories can be circulated, examined, and even appreciated, without dictating behavior in the real world.

Artistic Woman as Decadent

Andreas-Salomé's qualifications of the applicability of theory, intellectually and aesthetically pleasing though it may be, are visible in her response to Frieda von Bülow as well as in her examination of the relationships between femininity and art in "Der Mensch als Weib" and *Eine Ausschweifung.* Pairing "Der Mensch als Weib" and *Eine Ausschweifung* on the themes of art and femininity reveals the author's interest in a third concept important to artistic discourses of the time, namely decadence. Though not explicitly addressed in either of the two texts under discussion here, decadence is summond by the coupling of femininity and artistic endeavor in female characters who struggle to be integrated, to find partners, and to have families. In *Eine Ausschweifung* we encounter an artist who claims to have paid for her commitment to her art with the loss of her sensual side, the loss of the potential of erotic fulfillment, and thereby the loss of serenity. In her assessment of her situation, Adine invokes the binary opposition between "Weib" and "Kunst" that we have seen in "Der Mensch als Weib": "Mir wurde plötzlich so klar . . . daß gleichviel was ich als Künstlerin erreichen würde, aus meinem Liebesleben, aus meinem Leben als Weib, der Ernst verlorengegangen war" (120; "Suddenly it all became clear to me. . . . As an artist, I might attain what I wanted; but my life as a woman, my love life, had lost its earnest and its meaning," 88). In the contrast between artistic woman and "Weib," decadence rears its head. If "Weib" is all that is wholesome, life giving, and vital in woman, then anything that causes women to deviate from their biological calling to be a "Weib" must be decadent. Here as elsewhere Andreas-Salomé raises a question similar to that of Rita Felski in her book *The Gender of Modernity:* what is the gender of decadence?[22] In several of her earliest texts at the turn of the twentieth century, Andreas-Salomé began formulating the tentative answer that decadence, though most often constructed as a dilemma faced by men, affected women equally, especially because of the changes ushered in by the women's movement.

In general, decadence has been discussed in relation to male figures in literature, both fictional characters and real authors, and women have figured in its engendering only to the extent to which they enabled it in men, as their companions, lovers, *femme fatales* and so on. Although it has often been associated with the feminine in the sense of that which is not the dominant masculine culture, and with effeminacy in men, it has been primarily conceived of as a man's mode of existence and as a literary style practiced by men. But Andreas-Salomé's jointly published 1898 novellas *Eine Ausschweifung*, whose very title suggests the theme of decadence, and *Fenitschka*, together with "Der Mensch als Weib," offer some answers to the question of what decadence might mean for a woman.[23] Both *Eine Ausschweifung* and "Der Mensch als Weib" present the woman who is an artist as incapable of being a realization of "das Weib." Artistic endeavor perverts femininity, the texts suggest; it renders woman decadent. Adine is a woman who departs from petrified bourgeois norms, seeks to exist otherwise, and thus risks losing any chance she has at a stable identity as a woman. Both the novella and the essay engage critically with the very self-conscious construction of the decadent in contemporary artistic and intellectual circles and begin carving out an aesthetic, theoretical, and cultural space for women's experience of decadence. Linked, like men's experience, to artistic endeavor, it nonetheless takes on different connotations for women. Andreas-Salomé's fictional explorations lend credence to Matei Calinescu's and David Weir's understandings of decadence as motion and transition.[24]

Drawing on nineteenth-century French and German attempts to define decadence, both Calinescu in *Five Faces of Modernity* and Weir in *Decadence and the Making of Modernism* remind us of Bourget and Nietzsche, who associated decadence with a cult of individualism, an overemphasis on the intellectual life, and an increasing distance from the natural in favor of the artificial. Both also address the main problem in dealing with the concept of decadence, namely the difficulty of pinning down exactly what it has meant and means in its various contexts. Weir argues that since decadence is frequently described in terms of its opposition to a variety of things, those oppositions can end up, when invoked in other oppositions, with connotations that were exactly the opposite of the connotations initially present (1–2). Decadence, for example, has been interpreted as at once anti-progress and as a symptom of progress. Calinescu similarly underscores "the dialectic complexity" of the relationship between modernity/progress and decadence, calling on Bernard de Chartres's image of dwarfs standing on the shoulders of giants (155). If the dwarfs are the decadents, then this image renders those who came before, the giants, superior, at least physically. Yet the dwarfs, despite their short stature, are higher up and can see further, rendering them superior. Both Weir and Calinescu conclude that decadence is not static but in motion: "a direction or tendency," to use Calinescu's words (155), "a dynamics of transition," to use Weir's (15).

In "Der Mensch als Weib," Andreas-Salomé praises motherhood as an incarnation of ideal femininity and, Kristeva-like, establishes motherhood as a model for human existence in general because it is "natural" and connects one to a more primitive and physical, a less-differentiated mode of being.[25] She constructs motherhood as an ideal of the relationship to the Other because it offers a positive alternative to contemporary problems of individualism and estrangement.[26] It is opposed to decay, death, and the end suggested by decadence, and, for Lou Andreas-Salomé, it represents in texts the renewal it enacts in life. In *Eine Ausschweifung,* Adine validates traditional women's roles but does not choose them.[27] Rejecting marriage, motherhood, and all of their potential to tie her more firmly to her family, her hometown, and her physical desires, she returns to Paris, her atelier, her art, and a potentially loveless life. She embraces decadence in that she is content to remain the last in a series, the last person in her family. Because of her commitment to a heady intellectual, artistic, "artificial" life instead of to a life determined by a "natural" feminine physicality that would inevitably lead to motherhood, Adine's line is about to be extinguished.

Central to Nietzsche's understanding of decadence is the notion of will, as Calinescu writes: "One can be sick or weak without being a decadent: one becomes a decadent only when one *wants* weakness. The distinction is that between actual sickness and *sickliness...*"(183). Extending the notion of will to the concepts of motherhood and reproduction that Andreas-Salomé includes in her exploration of decadence in women, I submit that it is Adine's conscious decision to privilege an artistic life over a life as a wife and mother that establishes her decadence. Adine chooses illness or weakness in her reaction to her engagement to Benno, practically starving herself and descending into semi-madness. Her illness functions as a substitute for the choice she wants to make but forces Benno and her mother to make for her instead.

Like Tonio Kröger, Adine herself is incapable of living the hale and hearty, traditional bourgeois life, but she values it and envies those who slip easily into it. Her return home reminds her that she is alienated from what is generally accepted as femininity: she is not married, she has no children, and she devotes her life to painting. By contrast, Mutchen, Gabriele's younger sister, follows every sexual urge and attraction she feels and does not reflect on her physical and natural urges. She examines neither their origins nor their potential consequences. Mutchen embodies the physicality of "das Weib" presented in "Der Mensch als Weib." She is completely at one with her physicality and so at peace with her desires that her only difficulty is the bourgeois restraints that would seek to contain those desires in heterosexual marriage. Mutchen is to Adine what Hans is to Tonio Kröger: a positive counterexample, a representation of what she wishes she were.[28]

Adine's will to sickliness manifests itself each time she is confronted with the possibility of a conventional life. When she returns to Brieg and feels attracted to Benno again, she wishes for Anna's madness and Daniela's physical deformity. As she did six years earlier, Adine creates the conditions for her freedom by lapsing into an unhealthy state. After enduring a sexual encounter with Benno that she did not want but to which she felt driven to submit, she leaves Brieg abruptly and returns to her life in the city as an artist, a life that causes Benno and her mother to worry because of its "'allzu-freie' Lebensgestaltung" (81; "'all-too-free' life style" 58). Adine's whole story is told in a letter to a friend and summarized as follows: "mich hat eine lange Ausschweifung zu ernster und voller Liebe unfähig gemacht" (71; "a long, passionate affair . . . has left me impervious to a serious and all-embracing love," 51).[29] Decadence in this text is linked to a refusal to marry, to submit to a husband, and to reproduce. As Andreas-Salomé intimates in *Eine Ausschweifung* and "Der Mensch als Weib," as in some of the novellas in *Menschenkinder*, to refuse motherhood is decadent, because it renders woman "useless" and "unproductive" in conventional terms and prevents her integration into normative society.

The title of the novella *Eine Ausschweifung*, together with this very early reference to Adine's own "Ausschweifung" (71) has provided for much discussion in the secondary literature. McGlashan and Haines have asked whether the "Ausschweifung" is Adine's commitment to art or woman's historical role as a self-effacing, submissive wife and mother. The various connotations of the German word "Ausschweifung" include wild excess, debauch, or aberration and thus might indicate the uncontrollable masochistically sexual urges to which Adine is prone, urges that for a man might well be considered decadent. "Ausschweifung," however, also includes the idea of a tangent or detour, a veering off from a beaten path, and thus might suggest instead Adine's commitment to art at the expense of a more traditional feminine role. Given that sexologists and psychologists considered masochistic behavior normal for women in erotic heterosexual relationships at the turn of the century, it would seem unlikely that the "Ausschweifung" Adine refers to has to do with the masochistic tendencies that establish her similarity to other women. Her explanation of the problems in her relationship to Benno as well as her valorization of her mother's and wet-nurse's relationships point to its being her devotion to art that renders her incapable of the only kind of true love she can thus far imagine.

During her engagement to Benno Adine abandons her art entirely, because it threatens to seduce her more than Benno can and to alienate her from him and real heterosexual love. Afraid that she cannot love him adequately if she does not give up her art, she ends up unable to love him adequately because she has given up her art. And now the opening pages of her retrospective narration read as a series of oppositions that differentiate her decadence from her addressee's complete involvement in life: "[Es] kommt . . . mir immer vor, als übte ich mit Kunstmitteln das ein wenig aus, was du mit dem ganzen Leben lebst, in deiner reichen Art, die Dinge voll und ganz zu nehmen und ihnen zu lebendiger Schönheit zu verhelfen" (71; "To me it always seems as if I were pursuing through my art a little of what you are achieving with your entire life, with your rich capacity to see everything in its totality and letting it realize its full potential and beauty," 51). She continues with a description of her art that calls to mind Calinescu's interpretation of Nietzsche's decadent as a gifted liar "who deceives by imitating truth and making the lie more credible than the truth itself":[30] "In meinen Bildern und Skizzen, denen niemand so fein nachgegangen ist wie du, schien dir mein ganzes Ich enthalten zu sein, und dahinter — ach dahinter lag nur eine alte Jugendschwärmerei, die kaum von der Wirklichkeit berührt worden ist" (71; "You thought my entire personality was contained in my pictures and sketches, which no one studied as thoroughly as you did. But there was nothing more behind them than an old youthful romance, barely touched by reality," 51).

Adine interprets her art as concealing as much as it reveals, as permitting insight into her identity that subverts insight into a more authentic self. She continues to explain how her recent experience in Brieg has opened her eyes to the role of unconscious impulses in shaping a life:

Unser Leben [hängt viel weniger von dem ab], was wir bewußt erfahren und treiben, als von heimlichen, unkontrollierbaren Nerveneindrücken, die mit unserer individuellen Entwicklung schlechterdings nichts zu schaffen haben. Seit ich überhaupt denken kann, seit ich von eigenen Wünschen, Hoffnungen bewegt werde, bin ich der Kunst entgegengegangen, habe ich mich an ihr entzückt oder um sie gelitten, und lange noch ehe ich mich ihr wirklich widmen durfte, in irgendeinem Sinne schon im Umkreis der ihr verwandten Sensationen gelebt. Und trotzdem würde jetzt, wollte ich dir mein Leben erzählen, von der Kunst kaum die Rede sein . . . riesengroß müßte in den Vordergund treten was doch in meinem individuellen Bewußtsein kaum existiert und was mir selbst immer schattenhaft undeutlich geblieben ist. (71–72)

[Our lives depend only to a minor extent on what we do and experience consciously. Secret and uncontrollable impressions on our nerves, which have no direct bearing on our development, play a much larger part. Ever since I began to think, ever since I was moti-vated by my own wishes and hopes, I was drawn towards art. I found joy in it, suffered for it; but even long before I knew that I would wholly devote my life to art, my sensations and experiences prepared me for it, and I lived on its fringes. And yet, if I now wanted to tell you about my life, I should mention art only very briefly. . . . With giant dimensions something else would occupy the foreground, something that has always loomed like a shadow and indistinctly in the back of my mind. (51–52)]

Differentiating between natural, primitive, innate drives that have to do with a collective women's history and her conscious desire to create art, she suggests a natural interference with the more artificial life she has chosen, a life that excludes marriage, subservience to a man, and mother-hood. In this attempt to explain and understand herself, Adine privileges a conservative lifestyle that she associates with a visceral happiness and a more organic, less differentiated mode of being in the world. David Weir draws our attention to French poet Théophile Gautier's description of decadence as when "artificial life has replaced a natural one," a descrip-tion that corresponds to Adine's understanding of her current position-ing.[31] Suffering from a tormented sensuality, from a conflict between an ingrained desire to submit to traditional woman's roles and a rationalized, individualistic desire for intellectual and artistic endeavor, Adine defines decadence for women as the abandonment of the traditional path to mar-riage and motherhood.

Questions about Adine's reliability as a narrator surface at this junc-ture. Is she seeking to emphasize her feminine (read: masochistic and sub-missive) side to her addressee who might, given her career choice and way of life, consider her a feminist (read: woman who is not interested in marriage and who is ending the relationship for this reason)? Why does she use the word "unwillkürlich" ("involuntarily") so often — a total of seven times — in reference to her actions? Why does she make a concerted effort in discussion with Gabriele, as well as in the narrative she writes, to deny agency for what she has become? Adine undermines the role her interest in art has played in her life in order to emphasize the importance of her masochistic tendencies. However, elements of her text, in particu-lar her description of her first months with Benno after her father's death, suggest another kind of unconscious urge, which she ignores or fails to see, namely the urge to be free, an urge that in the end wins out.

After the death of her father, Adine and her mother move with Benno to an apartment directly opposite both a prison and an insane asylum. It is no coincidence that Andreas-Salomé locates both of these institutions within Adine's view, for they come to represent her relation-ship to Benno. When Adine voices displeasure in the new surroundings and wants to move out, Benno's response emphasizes the role of sacrifice and submission in a woman's love for a man: "Von Rechts wegen und meinen Wünschen nach müßte Adine in goldenem Königspalast wohnen. Aber sie hätte mich nicht lieb, bliebe sie nicht hier" (77; "By rights Adine should be living in a royal palace. But she would not care for me very deeply if she did not want to stay here," 55). Only now does Adine begin to think about the future and to consider how what she wants for the future compares to what Benno wants. Her formulation of their joint wishes is not convincing: "Natürlich blieb ich auch jetzt schon, wo er war, natürlich wollte ich, was er wollte" (76; "Of course, I would stay where he was, even now. Of course, I only wished for what he desired," 55).[32] Her repeated use of "natürlich" ("of course") suggests in fact its opposite, an element of doubt. Indeed it seems that she is trying to convince herself as much as anyone else that his wishes are hers. Her uncertainty is revealed again in her description of her feelings as Benno takes her in his arms after their disagreement: "Aber unser gemeinsamer Zukunftstraum, der sich nun hier verwirklichen sollte, und etwas wie eine unverstandene Angst flossen seltsam ineinander über in einem schwachen Gruseln . . ." (76; "But these joint dreams for our future, which were to become reality here, flowed together in me with a feeling of fear, which I did not understand," 55). Although Adine seeks to emphasize the submissive element in her relationship to Benno, she discloses that it coexists with an element of resistance.

Curiously, Adine does not analyze in detail the behavior that follows this minor altercation, namely her newfound obsession with the prison and the prisoners across the street from her apartment. She spends hours staring at them, empathizes with their plight, and bemoans their lack of interest in other people, as if their incarceration has made them hate those who live close by:

Meine tiefste Aufmerksamkeit erregte das Zuchthaus uns gegenüber. Bisweilen konnte man zu einer bestimmten Morgenzeit einige Zuchthäusler sehen, die gefesselt schräg über unsere Straße zu irgendwelcher Arbeit in einen der Gefängnishöfe *hinübergeführt* wurden. Seitdem ich das bemerkt hatte, stand ich stundenlang mit müßig niederhängenden Armen am Fenster und wartete auf diesen Anblick. (77, emphasis added)

[But most of my attention was focused on the maximum security penitentiary across from us. Now and then you could watch, at fixed times in the morning, convicts in chains being *led* to the other side of the street to work in one of the prison yards. Since I had noticed that, I spent hours standing at the window, arms dangling at my side, just waiting for this occurrence. (55)]

Although Adine describes this obsession in detail, and although her first success as a painter is a "Sträflingskopf" ("portrait of a convict"), she fails to interpret her obsession as the fear of confinement and limitation. It is as if Adine wills herself to be masochistic. She does not draw an explicit parallel between the prison and her "domestic carceral," but the text begs the reader to do so.[33] She even repeats the verb "führen" (to lead), which she used to describe how the prisoners were led out every day to do their work, in her description of how Benno led her to do domestic chores: "die Beschäftigung, die Benno für mich im Sinne hatte, *führte* mich in die Küche und an die Nähmaschine" (77; "But the occupation that Benno had planned for me *led* me into the kitchen and to the sewing machine," 56; emphasis added). Just as the prisoners are led to physical labor as a form of rehabilitation, so too is Adine.

Adine reads her gradual transformation into a sickly, weak, and dependent woman as an attempt to make herself worthy of Benno's love.[34] But this transformation achieves the opposite of the intentions that motivate it and might be seen instead as her unconscious resistance to the limitations of her new home and her new role in life. Almost overnight Adine has gone from being her father's daughter and an artist to being Benno's fiancée and a housemaid. If she calls the reader's attention to the role of uncontrollable reflexes in shaping her life at the beginning of her letter, why does she not see the implications of her obsession with the prison and her period of self-imposed starvation? If the reader takes Adine's proclamation on "heimlichen, unkontrollierbaren Nerveneindrücken" (72; "secret and uncontrollable impressions on our nerves," 51) to heart, she will most likely develop a reading strategy that grants greater importance to those aspects of Adine's story that Adine herself does not appear to analyze or understand. Reading in this manner, we can see Adine's reactions to her relationship to Benno — her descent into illness/madness/masochism — as her physical response to an unconscious understanding of her situation as that of a confined prisoner or patient. As a patient, she must become ill, and as a prisoner, she must follow Benno's orders. She becomes both Benno's patient and his prisoner and awaits release.

Adine's debilitating masochism first manifests itself when her independence and her art are threatened, so it is perhaps not so much the immediate effect of that masochism that represents her "true" physical desires and needs but the delayed effect, namely the regaining of her freedom and her art. Her masochistic tendencies at once threaten her independence and her life as an artist and yet also secure her independence and her life as an artist. Whereas Adine concludes that an unconscious desire to submit threatens her conscious desire to be an artist, yet another unconscious desire appears in fact to be manifesting itself as illness, namely a desire to *not* submit. In the ambiguity surrounding what Adine refers to as "heimliche, unkontrollierbare Nerveneindrücken" (72; "secret, uncontrollable impressions on our nerves," 51), Andreas-Salomé resists adopting a definitive stance on woman's nature and exhibits ambivalence toward the arguments that characterize woman as either primarily submissive or primarily independent. Similarly, in "Der Mensch als Weib" she sees woman as both submissive and independent. She is independent and self-sufficient, carrying her home on her back like a snail, and yet submissive and self-subordinating because her independence is so definitive that nothing, not even submission, can threaten it.

The marginalized aspects of Adine's self-interpretation become very important in understanding how Andreas-Salomé develops what Brigid Haines argues is a consistent ambivalence toward feminine masochism. This ambivalence toward feminine masochism reflects her ambivalence toward feminism and the women's movement and also toward the limiting patriarchal structures that the women's movement sought to overcome. Haines points to the text's puzzling affirmation of masochism. But while the text may affirm — or at least refrain from condemning — the masochism of women of earlier generations, of women whom Adine represents as having found fulfillment in their domestic roles and in their subordination to men, it does not affirm Adine's debilitating masochism. Whereas Adine demonstrates that her own masochistic tendencies have become burdensome in her time because they conflict with other possibilities available to women, she presents those of her mother and wet-nurse as natural and fulfilling because the time, like Daniela's disability, offered them no choices.[35]

Adine represents herself then as a particular manifestation of masochistic woman, and the dilemma she elucidates seems precipitated by the historical moment in which the clash of patriarchal and feminist discourses occurs, making woman's "normal" masochism "pathological." It becomes pathological because the understanding of heterosexual love and its only socially acceptable form have failed to keep pace with new articulations of female subjectivity and identity and with new emphases in raising female children. In this regard Andreas-Salomé's treatment of masochism highlights aspects of woman's experience that feminists often neglect. I read *Eine Ausschweifung* as another example of her tendency to revel in being a devil's advocate and to say things that were provocative in their conservatism. She proposes in this novella, it seems to me, that like it or not and for whatever reasons, feminine masochism exists, and the desire to be subordinate, as it has existed for centuries, cannot simply be wiped away by a verbal demand for independence and freedom, and certainly not in one generation.

"Der Mensch als Weib" offers a complicated intersection of theory and playful rhetoric that proves difficult to pick apart or dissect. *Eine Ausschweifung* offers infinite perspectives on feminine identity, which are further complicated by an unreliable narrator. The contradictions and puzzles that each yields and that both yield when read together point to a complex historical understanding of identity and femininity that she sought to present even as she acknowledged the impossibility of an accurate presentation. Her works emphasize the turn of the century as a time of transition that gives rise to a sense of decadence, as a moment in which there is a lack of synchronization between newer modes of consciousness and ingrained structures of behavior. In this sense, the texts lend support to both Weir and Calinescu's notions of decadence as process. "What is crucial about the [organic] notion of decay," Weir argues, "is not so much the change from a greater to lesser state but the changing itself" (20). Both *Eine Ausschweifung* and "Der Mensch als Weib" underscore the process of change in that they offer us nostalgia for an easier and simpler time, a more primitive life tied to the organic processes of reproduction, and yet both make room for its opposite. Adine is deviant and decadent because she chooses the unfeminine, the artificial, something for which she believes she has to quell natural urges and tendencies. "Das Weib," on the other hand, is the archetype of feminine wholesomeness, a perfect human being whose sense of self is never threatened because she is so anchored in the natural. Whereas the decadent has been conceived of as feminine in that it is related to that wild otherness beyond a masculine, dominant culture, it takes on new connotations here in its connection with real women and their understanding and experience of decadence. Not unlike many other writers on decadence whom she precedes and follows, Andreas-Salomé conceives of the decadent/regenerative opposition in terms of a rivalry between nature and drives on the one hand and culture and thought on the other, whereby the former is life affirming and outside ideology and the latter is lived ideology, in this case feminist ideology. Thus feminists and women who choose not to reproduce, women like Adine, are decadent because they endorse individualist rather than organic/holistic ("das Weib") behaviors. The numerous overlaps between Andreas-Salomé's essayistic treatment of figurative woman's ("das Weib") relationship to art and her narrative investigation of Adine's relationship to art yield productive contradictions and demonstrate the complexity of Andreas-Salomé's relationship to the feminist, artistic, and scientific discourses of her time. Making a case for plural feminine identities rather than an overarching feminine identity, she engages in the impossible, yet vitally important project of disentangling figurative woman from women.

Notes

[1] For other readings of "Der Mensch als Weib" in tandem with a fictional work (in these cases with *Fenitschka*), see Gisela Brinker-Gabler, "Renaming the Human: Andreas-Salomé's 'Becoming Human,'" *Seminar* 36:1 (Feb. 2000): 22–41, as well as Agata Schwartz's "Lou Andreas-Salomé and Rosa Mayreder: Femininity

and Masculinity," *Seminar* 36:1 (Feb. 2000): 42–58; see also Lorraine Markotic, "Andreas-Salomé and the Contemporary Essentialism Debate," *Seminar* 36:1 (Feb. 2000): 59–78.

[2] Caroline Kreide, *Lou Andreas-Salomé: Feministin oder Antifeministin? Eine Standortbestimmung zur wilhelminischen Frauenbewegung* (New York: Peter Lang, 1996), 43.

[3] Except where noted, translations from the German are my own.

[4] I use "real" here not to claim that there is a realm of existence free of narratives and fictions but to differentiate between the words on the page that attempt to describe but also end up prescribing behavior, and the acting-out or working-through of such narratives/fictions in the illusion we accept as the real on a daily basis.

[5] Although Andreas-Salomé here develops models of the male and female psyches as rooted in biological differences, Biddy Martin tells us that she "argued explicitly and implicitly for the relative autonomy of human psychic life from its basis in biology" in a review of Bölsche's *Das Liebesleben in der Natur* (Love Life in Nature, 1898). Biddy Martin, *Woman and Modernity: The (Life)Styles of Lou Andreas-Salomé* (Ithaca, NY: Cornell UP, 1991), 148.

[6] Martin, *Woman and Modernity*, 90.

[7] Michel Foucault, *The History of Sexuality, vol. 1: An Introduction,* trans. Robert Hurley (New York: Vintage, 1990); originally published as *Histoire de la sexualité 1: La volonté de savoir* (Paris: Gallimard, 1978).

[8] See Uta Treder and Martin for a discussion of Adine as an "Übergangsfigur" (transitional figure) caught between a female tradition of submission and a feminist projection of the future.

[9] See Brigid Haines, "Masochism and Femininity in Lou Andreas-Salomé's *Eine Ausschweifung*," *Women in German Yearbook* 8 (1993): 97–115.

[10] Translations for *Eine Ausschweifung* are taken from Lou Andreas-Salomé, *Fenitschka and Deviations: Two Novellas,* trans. Dorothee Einstein Krahn (Lanham, New York, and London: UP of America, 1990).

[11] See Caroline Kreide for a detailed discussion of the bourgeois women's movement at the turn of the century and its differences from the proletarian women's movement.

[12] Both Krafft-Ebing and Freud believed that masochism represented an essentially feminine and natural mode of behavior. Krafft-Ebing does offer a couple of examples of pathological masochism in women but sees it primarily as a male affliction. See chapter 5 for a detailed discussion of masochism.

[13] Adine's distinction between generations reveals a further simplification. Her father devoted himself to her and encouraged her to channel all of her energy into the development of her artistic talents, but this was not necessarily representative of child-rearing for her generation. In *Unerhört: Die Geschichte der deutschen Frauenbewegung* (Unheard Of: The History of the German Women's Movement), for example, Ute Gerhard talks of the "Liberalität des Elternhauses" (liberalness of the home) in which the eldest girl was educated along with her brothers in the early part of the twentieth century. Ute Gerhard. *Unerhört: Die Geschichte*

der deutschen Frauenbewegung (Reinbeck bei Hamburg: Rowohlt Taschenbuch Verlag, 1990), 176.

[14] See Dale M. Bauer and Susan Jaret Mckinstry, "Introduction," in *Feminism, Bakhtin, and the Dialogic,* ed. Bauer and McKinstry (Albany: State U of New York P, 1991), 1–6.

[15] See Andreas-Salomé, "Gedanken über das Liebesproblem," "Der Mensch als Weib," and "Ketzereien gegen die moderne Frau" (Heresies against Modern Woman, 1898). "Gedanken über das Liebesproblem" appears in *Die Erotik: Vier Aufsätze* (Eroticism: Four Essays), ed. Ernst Pfeiffer (Frankfurt am Main: Ullstein, 1985).

[16] See Martin's *Woman and Modernity,* particularly chapter 1, "Questions of Self-Representation" (24–60).

[17] Hedwig Dohm, "Reaktion in der Frauenbewegung," *Die Zukunft* (18 Nov. 1899): 279–91.

[18] Rose-Maria Gropp, "Das 'Weib' existiert nicht," *Blätter der Rilke Gesellschaft* 11–12 (1984–85): 46–69.

[19] Frieda Freiin von Bülow, "Männerurtheil über Frauendichtung," *Die Zukunft* 7.26 (1898–99), rpr. in Erich Ruprecht and Dieter Bänsch, *Literarische Manifeste der Jahrhundertwende, 1890–1910* (Stuttgart: Metzler, 1981): 562–65.

[20] See McGlashan's discussion of the late-nineteenth- and early-twentieth-century discourse on the relationship of woman to art in *Creating Women: The Female Artist in Fin-de-Siècle Germany and Austria* (PhD diss., Indiana University, 1996). She traces "the efforts to define woman as non-artist from the late Enlightenment to the Fin-de-siècle" (10) and shows how "scientific, sociological, and philosophical texts of the late nineteenth-century emphasized the physical, mental, and creative inferiority of woman" (11). She summarizes her examination of turn-of-the-century tracts on woman's relationship to art as follows: "Male creativity was bolstered in its validity by the new sciences of sexual difference, psychology and psychoanalysis, by the ever-increasing importance of the public, hence male, sphere of influence, and by a tradition of male elitism reaching back to Goethe and beyond . . . women's artistic attempts went against scientific "fact," against social norms, and against an idealized literary and artistic image of their sex" (10).

[21] Although Andreas-Salomé focuses on woman as a figure in "Der Mensch als Weib" (that is, on "das Weib"), she also talks about "die Frau." Despite Rose-Maria Gropp's argument to the contrary, however, she does not always distinguish clearly between the two, conflating them as language does.

[22] Rita Felski, *The Gender of Modernity* (Cambridge and London: Harvard UP, 1995).

[23] Chapter 6 discusses *Fenitschka* at length. I will just mention a couple of ties to decadence here. *Fenitschka* chronicles Max Werner's attempt to understand a woman whose life choices leave him repeatedly perplexed. His bewilderment at Fenia's choices, choices that fit no rubric he is familiar with, emphasizes how unusual it is for a woman to remain single, intellectually active, and celibate all at once. While Max's understanding of women can account for the unmarried and

intellectually active elements of Fenia's lifestyle, it cannot account for them in combination with celibacy. Fenitschka further puzzles Max because of her simultaneous personal resistance to and theoretical elevation of traditional women's roles and the dynamics of traditional heterosexual relationships. Fenitschka embodies that sense of the decadent that David Weir describes, namely the submission to a series of desires that one recognizes as contrary to the greater human good, rebirth, and regeneration. She is devoted to intellectual pursuits and has, for a long time, engaged only in what Werner sees as "artificial" relationships to men. That is, she has enjoyed friendships with them but has not had a love/sexual relationship with any of them. Werner's inability to understand how male/female non-sexual relationships can exist points to Fenia's life choices as beyond a realm of the natural or normal. She represents a decadent woman because she decides on a lifestyle made possible only by feminism and what might be interpreted as an overly cultivated or refined, overly artificial society.

[24] See Matei Calinescu, *Five Faces of Modernity* (Durham, NC: Duke UP, 1987); see also David Weir, *Decadence and the Making of Modernism* (Amherst: UP of Massachusetts, 1995).

[25] I am thinking here of the interpretation of motherhood in Julia Kristeva's "Stabat Mater," in *The Kristeva Reader,* ed. Toril Moi (New York: Columbia UP, 1986), 160–86.

[26] Compare with Tracie Matysik's "The Interests of Ethics: Andreas-Salomé's Psychoanalytic Critique," *Seminar* 36:1 (Feb. 2000): 5–21. Matysik offers an excellent discussion of Andreas-Salomé's "Narzißmus als Doppelrichtung," arguing that the author undermines understandings of ethics as arising out of and guaranteed by object love: "The responsibility of the love object that may arise from a desire to preserve the object always entails as well the danger of irresponsibility in the form of excess if the finitude of the object is not recognized. Thus love for the other, which enables responsibility to that other, is logically inseparable from — because it produces — the counter-tendency to annihilate the other in its specificity. This paradox prompts Andreas-Salomé's dismissal of an ethics of love for an other as adequate grounds for an ethics of responsibility. As an alternative she offers an ethics of self-articulation in the form of an ethics of sublimation" (10).

[27] It is not at all unusual to find characters in texts of decadence who at once embrace what they perceive to be a decadent lifestyle and yet long for or valorize its opposite. Thomas Mann's Tonio Kröger is a more canonical example.

[28] Adine ignores, however, the potential problems that Mutchen will face if her sexuality is not quickly contained in a monogamous marriage. Again she simplifies the psyche and life of another woman, refusing to acknowledge the potential for psychic splits in their situations too.

[29] I find the translation of "Ausschweifung" as "affair" to be problematic because it refuses the ambiguity of the original text. Some form of deviate or deviation would have been a better choice in my opinion.

[30] Calinescu, *Five Faces of Modernity,* 80.

[31] Weir, *Decadence and the Making of Modernism,* 12.

[32] Given the general subject matter of the novella — woman's experience of love, marriage — the choice of "natürlich" ("naturally") in this context is interesting, because it emphasizes a contemporary assumption that a woman should share her husband's dreams, and that automatic submission to his needs and desires constituted an integral part of woman's nature.

[33] "Domestic carceral" is the phrase used by Paul Morrison in his essay "Enclosed in Openness: *Northanger Abbey* and the Domestic Carceral" to argue that Austen's heroine is imprisoned in her home. See *Texas Studies in Literature and Language* 33:1 (Spring 1991): 1–23.

[34] It is interesting to compare Gitta of *Das Haus* to Adine here, because they each have preconceived notions of what a wife should be based on their experiences of their own mothers. Gitta too thought that her marriage to Markus should entail sacrificing everything she had valued up until then, including her dog and her writing. After a series of minor conflicts, however, Markus manages to convince her that she should cling to her old hobbies and to the things that are important for her, explaining marriage to her as the coming together of two individuals who repeatedly recede into their individuality and their selves only to find each other again and become one. His understanding of marriage is possibly what saves his relationship to Gitta and can be contrasted to Benno's initial reaction to Adine's lack of interest in domestic matters. Later, of course, Benno regrets having reacted as he did.

[35] In Daniela, masochism is the thing that allows her to make Benno into a God and gives meaning to her life.

2: Marriage and Science: Discourses of Domestication in *Das Haus*

THE AMBIVALENCE, AMBIGUITIES, AND dialogic style that dominate "Der Mensch als Weib" and *Eine Ausschweifung* also play a significant role in the other works that Lou Andreas-Salomé wrote at the end of the nineteenth and beginning of the twentieth century. Although she did not write *Das Haus* (*The House*) until 1904, it reveals a similar engagement with feminist ideologies. As in *Eine Ausschweifung*, Andreas-Salomé weighs the pros and cons of the changes in women's and men's lives in this time of transition to new roles. Whereas *Eine Ausschweifung* (and the co-published *Fenitschka*) examines these changes in female characters who do not follow traditional paths in life and in the men they befriend, *Das Haus* explores the domestic domain and woman's changing role in marriage. Adine of *Eine Ausschweifung* envies her mother's marriage and regrets that what she presents as a kind of pathology prevented her from entering into a similar marriage, but she is not naïve enough to believe that marriage to Benno would have automatically brought fulfillment: ". . . hätten wir uns rasch heiraten können, so wäre wohl für mich die Enttäuschung auf dem Fuße gefolgt, oder aber es würde die Mutterschaft mich vielleicht in meinem ganzen Wesen stark verwandelt haben" (75; "If we had been able to get married soon, I would have had a quick and sudden disappointment. Or maybe motherhood would have changed my entire being completely," 54). The two options Adine presents here summarize what happens to Gitta and Anneliese in their marriages in *Das Haus*. Gitta's overpowering attraction to Markus wanes after they marry, and she leaves him twice before managing to resign herself to the domestic life their marriage appears to require. Anneliese, a boyish, independent girl who was devoted to playing piano before marriage, quickly lost sight of everything but her duties as a wife and a mother once she became pregnant. *Eine Ausschweifung* suggests that Adine's failure to develop a satisfactory sexual relationship leaves her unfulfilled, yet it does not present marriage as a panacea. The ambivalence that Adine shows toward marriage in her feelings of confinement and fear when she first moves in with Benno is fleshed out in Gitta's and Anneliese's negotiations of marriage and domestication in *Das Haus*. These works complement each other and, read in light of each other, cast new light on Andreas-Salomé's understanding of woman, man, feminism, and the relations among them at the turn of the twentieth century.

Published in 1919 by Ullstein, *Das Haus,* together with several other theoretical and fictional works by women on women then appearing on the market, including other works by Andreas-Salomé, testified to the increasingly topical nature of the "woman question" in early twentieth-century Germany, as well as to the shifting tendency on the part of publishing institutions to target a specifically female audience.[1] Various cultural impulses in the late nineteenth and early twentieth centuries spurred this wide-ranging interest. While the emphasis on racial improvement that dominated the reception of evolutionary theory in nineteenth-century Germany foregrounded issues of motherhood, marriage, and family, as Janssen-Jurreit points out, an emerging interest in female sexuality among sexologists and psychologists such as Krafft-Ebing and Freud drew attention to sexually differentiated behaviors, woman's social status, and the effects of one upon the other.[2] Concurrently a growing women's movement at once substantiated and complemented male interpretations of woman and her role by encouraging women with varied convictions to participate in their own sexual, social, and legal definition. *Das Haus* presents us with Lou Andreas-Salomé's contribution to such debates and discourses and represents its female characters' micro-contributions, contributions, that is, in the domestic and private sphere, to the same debates and discourses.[3] Reading *Das Haus* in terms of these particulars of the cultural context reveals Lou Andreas-Salomé's interest in the difficulties facing women in the changing environment of late-nineteenth-century Germany and in her strategic use of dialogue in literary texts to challenge and complement dominant ideologies of the day.

Presenting a complicated and subtle demystification of the oppressive patriarchal foundations of the domestic sphere, of family life, and, by extension, of society as a whole, *Das Haus* nonetheless reflects Andreas-Salomé's ambivalent position vis-à-vis the project of woman's emancipation. In this novel she embraces both conservative and progressive perspectives on women, and attempts to reconcile the traditionally contradictory characteristics of femininity and autonomy in the interests of her own understanding of "woman." Published in a traditional women's genre, *Das Haus* had the potential to reach far beyond limited groups of female intellectuals into the homes and lives of women who might be alienated or threatened by the political articulations of champions of the German women's movement but could still be influenced by feminist notions of emancipation in popular fiction.

In the Afterword to the 1987 edition of *Das Haus,* Sabine Streiter argues that the ideal of femininity presented in the novel is a submissive, subservient, and self-dissolving one (250–53) — an image of woman affirmed by the more conservative elements of the German women's movement.[4] Streiter's reading suppresses textual difference, the cracks and fissures that Andreas-Salomé clearly exposes in that image of woman and femininity. The details Streiter invokes are important and interesting, and, in isolation, support her conclusions, but countless textual details and moments of resistance and self-assertion offer critical insights into, and an alternative to, the traditional and stereotypical images of woman Streiter criticizes. Andreas-Salomé manipulates contemporary concepts and stereotypes of woman, sexuality, and marriage, in order to examine the basis for the self-dissolution of woman in marriage and criticize the notion of its inevitability. The stereotypes she invokes are by no means solely abstractions but comply with the social reality of many women's lives at the time; nevertheless her depiction of these stereotypes does not valorize them but rather challenges them and the boundaries they impose.[5] Andreas-Salomé portrays woman's subordination and self-dissolution in marriage, but she does not advocate it: she depicts it in combination with moments of woman's resistance in order to suggest compromises, forms of marriage and parenting that would neither suppress women's autonomy nor force that autonomy too hastily upon them. Her exploration of patriarchal abuses extends beyond the domestic sphere to the problematic relationship of women to science and scientific discourse, and indeed, even beyond biologically sexed women: her treatment of masculinity suggests that patriarchal oppression also affects men whose racial, physical, or intellectual difference is perceived as effeminacy.

Women, Masculine Authority, and the Domestic Sphere

Das Haus records the events in the lives of the Branhardt family — Frank, Anneliese, and their two children, Gitta and Balduin — over the span of approximately one year. Frank Branhardt stands at the center of the novel as the patriarchal authority around whom the other figures revolve, and in reaction to whom they define themselves. His initial authority and centrality are underscored by the narrator's references to him exclusively as Branhardt. He embodies the traditional Western, industrialist father whose primary familial responsibilities involve financial support and the enforcement of patriarchal law. Showing a minimum of concern for the emotional well-being of his children, he relies on his wife for information regarding them and then often dismisses her perspective as negligible in decisions affecting their lives. However, Branhardt's privileging of institutionalized social and authoritative codes over the individual desires and needs of his family members increasingly isolates him. This isolation and the disparity between how he perceives his authority and how his wife and children perceive it serve as a critique of his stifling attempts to completely orchestrate all of their lives. The opposition of his family contests what he and the society he lives in assume to be his superiority as a doctor and a man.

Branhardt's dealings with his daughter and his wife reveal his traditional understanding of his duty, privilege, and status as the head of the family and a community doctor. Yet the details of the familial interactions question his understanding, namely what he perceives as the superiority and legitimacy of his monologic and exclusive authority.[6] Branhardt's concerns about his daughter, Gitta, are associated primarily with her developing sexuality and consequent relationships to men but ultimately translate into worries about his own public persona and his relationships to these same men. From Branhardt's perspective, Gitta corresponds to the female of Eve Sedgwick's homosocial triangle. She is an enabler for relationships between men, which involve not simply one man's (Branhardt's) demonstration of his authority over woman (Gitta), but also, via that woman, the exhibition of his superiority over her male friends (Markus or Helmold).[7] While Sedgwick deals specifically with cuckoldry, which is not an issue in the triangular constellation in *Das Haus,* her observations offer an illuminating approach to the relationship between Gitta's father and her suitors. Conversely, applying Sedgwick's model to *Das Haus* illuminates the weak point of the homosocial triangle, the point at which it can be subverted.

Twice Gitta unwittingly foils Branhardt's attempts to maintain his public image as an authority figure, once by rejecting one of her father's colleagues as a suitor and later by running away from her husband, another of her father's colleagues. Helmold, a student of Branhardt's with whom Gitta establishes a tenuous relationship, presents Gitta with an alarm clock as a token of his affection. He implies that she will either share the clock with him some day in the future or return it as a sign that they will have no future together. Having forgotten the terms of the gift, Gitta returns it one day. Although unintentional, her rejection of Helmold as a companion complies with her actual wishes. Branhardt witnesses Helmold's devastation and arrives home that evening angered and indignant. He severely chastises Gitta and reminds her that her secondary status in society as a woman, and her required deference to men, should prevent her from behaving as she did: "Daß er [Helmold] sich's zu Herzen nehmen konnte — er — ! Daß du ihm was damit antun konntest . . . , — einem ganzen Mann! Daß du dich nicht scheutest, so einen zum Narren zu machen! Zum Himmeldonnerwetter! Achtung vor Männerwert und Männersachen! Mit deinen Frauenzimmerfingern fort davon!" (31; That he could take it so much to heart — him — ! That you could affect him so much with that . . . — a complete man! That you weren't afraid to make someone like him look like a fool! For God's sake! Have some respect for a man's worth and for men's affairs! Get your little female fingers away from those things).[8] His reaction is explained by the narrator as ". . . die Empörung des Mannes für den Mann" (31; the indignation of one man on behalf of another) indicating the primacy of male-male over father-daughter relations. His contemptuous differentiation of men's and women's roles denies Gitta agency.

A short time later, Branhardt focuses his ill will on Helmold, albeit in a manner that continues to vilify his daughter: "Helmold ist selbst schuld: wie kann er sich nur eine Minute darum grämen! Zu bemitleiden ja nur der, der mal so ein launisches Ding freit" (34; It's Helmold's own fault: how can he be upset about it for even a minute! Someone who courts such a moody young thing is only to be pitied). Gitta provokes Branhardt's anger in a similar manner much later in the novel, when she temporarily runs away from her husband, Markus. At first Branhardt sees Gitta's behavior as his personal failure to adequately domesticate Gitta: "Es kränkte ihn irgendwie von sich selber, Markus keine bessere Musterfrau herangezogen zu haben" (183; He was somehow mortified that he hadn't raised a better model wife for Markus). As in the case of Helmold, however, Branhardt later directs his animosity toward Markus, calling him a "Schlapphans" (189; an impotent fool) and criticizing him for not subduing Gitta well enough: "wenn ihm aber jemand sein Kind nähme, so habe er es so zu nehmen, daß es ihm nicht in Unarten verdürbe; wessen Hand nicht sicher genug dafür sei, der hätte seine Hand gefälligst ganz davon lassen sollen" (189; If someone was going to take his child, then he'd better make sure she didn't develop all sorts of bad habits; he whose hands weren't steady enough to ensure that should kindly keep his distance). Andreas-Salomé presents Gitta's challenges to masculine domestic authority in a manner that both makes evident and criticizes Branhardt's understanding of her as a less than autonomous individual. His sense of personal insult in each case is dependent on his perception of women as essentially the wards of men, first of their fathers and then of their husbands. For Branhardt, Gitta's resistance to these two men is public testimony to his inability to control her. In both instances his immediate response to his threatened authority is to vilify Gitta and identify with the two rejected men. However, realizing that such a response suggests weakness on his own part, he reassesses both situations, deflecting blame away from Gitta and thereby from himself. By deflecting the blame onto the other male, by relocating the fault in the other male's emotional (Helmold) or authoritative (Markus) weakness, Branhardt can restore his faith in his own superiority and in patriarchal authority.

The reader's faith in that authority is, however, not restored. On the contrary, the narrative links the Helmold and Markus episodes in a manner that comments ironically and humorously on the disparity between Branhardt's perception of his authority and its actual efficacy. When he angrily reprimands Gitta for having left Markus, she vaguely recalls a previous similar exchange: "Ihr [Gitta] kam es vor, als ob mit ähnlicher

Gründlichkeit der Vater nur ein einziges Mal sie ausgescholten habe . . . , obwohl sie sich seltsamerweise nicht darauf besinnen konnte, was das gewesen sei. Denn das wenigstens stand doch fest, daß sie zum erstenmal einem Mann fortgelaufen war" (183; It seemed to her that her father had only scolded her this severely once before . . . although, oddly enough, she couldn't remember when or why. This much was certain, in any case: this was the first time she had run away from a man).

In this vague memory of a single comparable exchange, Gitta reminds the reader of the Helmold affair, thereby unwittingly associating Branhardt's rage with very specific circumstances — her relations with men. She thus focuses the reader's attention on Branhardt's self-interested motivations and his authoritative fatherly role. At the same time, Gitta's inability to clarify for herself the connection between the two events — she cannot even recall that the first one involved another man — undermines Branhardt's authority, because she not only disregards the conventions with which he is preoccupied but is also naïvely oblivious to his reproaches, as becomes clear in her justification of her actions to her mother: "Selbst wenn der Vater damit recht behalten sollte, daß ich nichts tauge, — denke dir, so schrecklich es ist, mir ist's eigentlich viel, viel wichtiger, daß die anderen Menschen möglichst vollkommen sind, als ich. Wenn sie so sind, daß ich mich an ihnen entzücken kann, dann bin ich ganz glücklich! (186; Even if father were right about the fact that I'm a good-for-nothing, — just think, bad and all as that is, it is much more important to me that other people are as perfect as possible. If they are such that I can take pleasure in them, then I'm quite happy). Through the figure of Gitta, Andreas-Salomé exposes Branhardt's almost pathetic insistence on his authority in the face of an indifferent resistance. Gitta has failed to internalize the concept of woman endorsed by her father — that of the obedient, devoted, domestic, and dutiful daughter/wife. She is too conscious of her own desires, with the result that her ambition is not to please but rather to be pleased. The attraction she feels for men is based on the same premise. In a reversal of traditional male and female roles, she is the viewer, the subject who admires the beauty of the male.[9] Since she is concerned chiefly with her own pleasure in viewing and in interacting with men, she can muster little respect for Branhardt's authority, which would deny her these pleasures.

Gitta's reaction to her father's admonitions betrays a healthy narcissism. Karla Schultz discusses Andreas-Salomé's concept of narcissism in her article "In Defense of Narcissus: Lou Andreas-Salomé and Julia Kristeva," explicating it as an only seemingly paradoxical mixture of self-abandonment and self-assertion: "In both cases, we enact our 'natural egoism,' expanding it by compassion and vicarious joy in one case, and concentrating it to assert our individuation in the other. Self-assertion and abandon are not far apart" (186). For Andreas-Salomé, Schultz tells us, narcissism is a positive phenomenon that manifests itself as the root of love in all sexes, a paradoxical wish to be all and, at the same time, to have all. Tracie Matysik argues similarly in "The Interests of Ethics: Andreas-Salomé's Psychoanalytic Critique."[10] "To be all" implies a sense of complete unity with the whole; "to have all," on the other hand, suggests a subject-object relationship and thus a sense of separation from the whole. "Love, then," argues Schultz, "is poised on the threshold between undifferentiation and the first outline of a division" (186). Gitta's words express this conflict precisely. She both distinguishes herself from others — she does not need to be perfect as they do ("individuation") — and at the same time finds her happiness in their perfection and self-development ("compassion and vicarious joy"). She demonstrates that mixture of self-abandonment and self-assertion that Andreas-Salomé sees as fundamental to all love.

Not solely the object but very much the subject of desire, Gitta is just narcissistic enough to thwart, albeit it unconsciously, the smooth functioning of the gender and authority dynamics of the homosocial triangle.[11] Her actions expose its weak point, demonstrating that if homosocial relations depend on woman's yielding to one male authority over another, then the refusal, conscious or otherwise, to take account of masculine authority at all effectively subverts the homosocial relation. Gitta's narcissism precludes complete conformity to her father's patriarchal image of woman, and Andreas-Salomé celebrates Gitta's internal drive toward autonomy and her consequent comic lack of sensitivity to Branhardt's anger, engendered as it is by his patriarchal principles.

While Gitta's subversion of masculine authority occurs on an almost unconscious level, her mother's resistance is conscious and verbal but lacks much of Gitta's healthy narcissistic impulse and conviction. Anneliese is initially quite passive and frequently defers to Branhardt's authority. Although she mentally notes points of divergence between herself and Branhardt from the very beginning of the novel, she only openly admits a certain dissatisfaction with her submissive role when her friend Renate, a "Frauenrechtler" (feminist), comes to visit. In a discussion about Anneliese's children, Renate begs Anneliese not to treat Gitta as "nur ein Mädchen" (just a girl), not to let her marry too early (65). Anneliese's response betrays a subtle dissatisfaction with her own marriage, in which she has failed to develop the freedom of expression she hopes her daughter will experience: "Ich gönn' es ihr [Gitta] wahrlich, so ihren Ausdruck zu finden für alles, was auf dem Herzen sitzt, — mehr davon sagen zu können als etwa: 'Ach Frank!' Bei mir ist es leider bei dieser einen Kundgebung geblieben" (65; I wouldn't begrudge it to her at all, if she were to be able to express whatever is on her mind, — able to say something other than: 'Oh, Frank!' Unfortunately I never got beyond this single enunciation). Anneliese's discussion with Renate marks a turning point in her relationship to her husband and children. Although she continues to occasionally fall back on her conciliatory "Ach Frank" (Oh, Frank), she now begins to develop the ability to stand up to him about issues that she considers important.

Anneliese's initial acts of resistance to Branhardt occur primarily on behalf of her son who, like Gitta, is allowed little room for self-definition within the familial structures erected by Branhardt. Her first significant stand against her husband occurs when, in a decision involving their son's future, Branhardt claims superiority and exclusive legitimacy for his male and professional knowledge, rejecting her input. Branhardt is relentless in his demand for a son who follows in his footsteps as a rational and productive man of science. He insists that his refusal to allow Balduin to abandon his formal studies in order to pursue his poetic talents is the rational, male, and therefore correct decision: "Glaube mir, so poetisch-fatalistisch lassen Kinder sich nicht erziehen. Daß ich als *Mann* und als *Arzt nüchterner* darüber denke, sollte dir eigentlich nicht erstaunlich sein (138; Believe me, you can't raise children with that poetically fatalistic attitude. That I, as a *man and a doctor,* have a more *sober perspective* should not come as a surprise to you, emphasis added). Branhardt marks his authority as residing in two areas traditionally valorized by patriarchy and fundamental to its epistemological system, namely masculine gender and science. Both masculinity and scientific training lend him a "sobriety" (read: objectivity) that guarantees the superiority of his knowledge.[12] He cannot conceive of a realm in which these would not constitute the tools of truth, because they have been culturally and historically validated as such. It is ironic, however, that he invokes his masculinity, professionalism, and scientific expertise as tools in a context in which he is forced to deal with what have traditionally constituted their opposites — femininity, home, and art respectively. Not attempting to engage in dialogue, to offer his knowledge as an alternative or supplement to Anneliese's and his son's, Branhardt simply discounts their knowledge completely as "poetischfatalistisch" (poetically fatalistic), and elects himself the only source of actionable understanding. His treatment of Anneliese's compassion and intuition in the text mirror the dismissal of the non-empirical in scientific discourse.

Men, Masculine Authority, and Scientific Discourse

Given the context in which this novel was written and Lou Andreas-Salomé's documented interest in the bias of scientific discourse, it is not insignificant that Branhardt is a doctor, a man who believes in science and its unique ability to unveil truth. At the turn of the century, in the wake of evolutionary theory, medical science claimed a monologic access to truth, the truth about women, race, and biology.[13] In the figure of Branhardt, Andreas-Salomé emphasizes and criticizes the leveling effects of any discourse of such a totalitarian nature. The words Andreas-Salomé puts in Anneliese's mouth in response to Branhardt critique the monologism of scientific discourse and its attempts to exclude knowledge grounded in other experience: "Frank, ich könnte recht haben, selbst dann, wenn du mir gegenüber als dem Laien im Recht wärst. Dinge gibt es doch, die man nur erfaßt, wenn von mehreren Seiten" (138; Frank, I could be right even if your expertise were to make you right. There are things that you can only understand if you look at them from many sides). Anneliese's response establishes her as the representative of a contrasting and more inclusive epistemological system, one apparently sanctioned by Lou Andreas-Salomé herself, as Biddy Martin indicates when she draws our attention to Andreas-Salomé's resistance to the concept of *the* truth in her discussion of "Der Mensch als Weib." As I have argued in chapter 1, Andreas-Salomé exposes the fictionality of the scientific description of the sperm/male as active and the egg/female as passive in this essay. She complicates this paradigm, appropriating legitimized scientific discourse to validate her newly proposed characterization. She does not, however, set out to erect her model as "truth." Rather she suggests that both it and the model it seeks to displace are fictions that manipulate scientific terminology in order to give themselves the semblance of truth. In doing so, Andreas-Salomé challenges the absolute legitimacy with which scientific discourse invests itself, revealing its patriarchal bias and thereby the multiplicity that it seeks to exclude.[14]

In *Das Haus* Andreas-Salomé also addresses the patriarchal bias of scientific discourse, albeit it more implicitly. The dispute about Balduin's future culminates in Anneliese's obstinate resistance to what Branhardt perceives as his objectivity. Branhardt responds to her discomfiting challenge to his authority with the charge that her voice is not her own but that of her son.[15] Denying her subjective agency, he patronizingly accuses her of an overly exuberant sympathy with their son and of being no more than a cipher for Balduin's words. Anneliese briefly doubts herself, considering the potential legitimacy of Branhardt's accusation, namely that her oppositional stance may indeed be a symptom of her "Überschwang . . . denn in allem glaubte sie sonst doch an die Überlegenheit ihres Mannes" (139; ardor . . . for she otherwise always believed in the superiority of her husband). But when Branhardt continues to try to exclude her, insisting on his patriarchal privilege as the father, the one person endowed with the totality of power, Anneliese, provoked to anger, forcefully defends the need for plural perspectives on all issues, arguing that anything less constitutes rape: "Nein, nein! Nicht einer! Niemals einer! Selbst das weiseste Urteil kann Unrecht werden, Willkür, Anmaßung, gemessen am Leben. Und das Ärgste, — siehst du, — das Ärgste, was es unter dem Himmel gibt, das ist *die Vergewaltigung des einen durch den anderen*" (139–40; No, no! Not one! Never just one! Even the wisest verdict can become unjust, arbitrary, arrogant in a real life situation. And the worst thing, — see, — the worst thing under the sun is *the rape of one by the other,* emphasis added). Anneliese criticizes patriarchal authority and tries to hollow out a space for her own participation in decision-making, at least in the domestic sphere. Her word-choice (*Vergewaltigung*/rape) suggests her awareness of the gender bias, perhaps suppressed in her but very conscious in Andreas-Salomé, at work in what Branhardt, supported by a long cultural tradition, can defend as his rational and scientific/objective approach to knowledge. Not only does she speak here in terms of a binary system — "die Vergewaltigung des einen durch den anderen" (the rape of one by the other) — which is a conventionally invoked characteristic of patriarchy, but her use of the word "Vergewaltigung" implies the masculine/feminine binary opposition, rape generally, though certainly not always, denoting a violent violation of the feminine by the masculine. On the one hand, Anneliese's word-choice indicates the violation of real women in a patriarchal structure; on the other, the non-gendered subjects and objects of this rape suggest the feminization of everything that patriarchy, represented here by Branhardt's exclusive authority, violates or attempts to suppress. By expanding the circle of those marginalized by patriarchy to include more than just biologically sexed women, Andreas-Salomé attracts attention away from masculine/feminine as solely biological categories here in *Das Haus,* as in "Der Mensch als Weib."

Andreas-Salomé's palpable concern throughout the novel for the obstacles that two of the male characters face in their attempted assimilation into patriarchal society supports the argument I make here for an implied challenge to the bias of scientific discourse and, in particular, to what one might call discourses of female domestication. Balduin, son and poet, is portrayed as the antithesis of Branhardt, physically weak, sickly, and romantic. His mother wishes he were more masculine, more like his father, and the narrator compares him to a young girl because of his neatness.[16] Like his sister and mother, Balduin rebels against the authority of his father and is, in this respect, textually feminized: he occupies the same subordinate and defensive position as his mother and sister and is at least as oppressed as Gitta and Anneliese by his father's insistence on his exclusive privilege as familial authority. Markus, Gitta's Jewish husband, is similarly textually feminized in his deviation from Branhardt's accepted patriarchal norms, in his friendship and identification with Balduin, and in his laissez-faire attitude toward Gitta in their marriage.[17]

Tania Modleski's argument in "Time and Desire in the Woman's Film" proves fruitful in analyzing the role of the feminized male in *Das Haus:* "The feminized man is attractive, then, because of the freedom he seems to offer the woman: freedom to get in touch with and to act upon her own desire and freedom to reject patriarchal power" (545).[18] To be sure, Andreas-Salomé represents Gitta's resistance to patriarchal authority as almost innate, but she also emphasizes the encouragement Gitta gets from Markus to develop her sense of an independent self separate from him and her parents. Anneliese, on the other hand, develops an awareness of her own need for some level of autonomy only through identification with her feminized son, Balduin. In her struggle for his freedom, she simultaneously begins her own somewhat limited, but nonetheless significant, push toward independence. Through her son-in-law, Markus, she arrives at a new understanding of marriage, one that further persuades her to allow herself room in her marriage for self-determination and self-fulfillment. Andreas-Salomé promotes the feminized male in *Das Haus* as one source (along with the women) of a new social and familial order. Both Balduin and Markus play a significant role in Anneliese's changing attitudes toward marriage and her rights as an individual, as well as in her awakening ability to challenge the authority of her husband. Markus becomes the cornerstone of a new definition of marriage and woman's role in the domestic sphere within the text, a definition that deviates from, and is ratified over, Branhardt's traditional and patriarchal concept of marriage, and one that accommodates the existence in both woman and man of Andreas-Salomé's love-paradox, as explicated by Schultz.

Evolving Gender Relations

A comparison of the two marriages in the novel, specifically of each husband's philosophy of marriage and his wife's attempts to adapt to them, suggests that Andreas-Salomé saw the prospects for the success of the women's movement as residing in "evolution rather than revolution."[19] For Branhardt, marriage implies the perpetual unity and agreement of both parties, based on woman's acceptance of her husband's authority. For Markus, on the other hand, marriage can accommodate the preservation of individuality, divergent opinions, and, at the same time, a sense of unity and togetherness. Anneliese's progress from a completely submissive and subordinate wife to a woman who recognizes the validity of her own viewpoint and the necessity for her occasional stance against her husband represents a reverse of Gitta's situation. Gitta, a young woman interested primarily in the satisfaction of her own desires, has great difficulty in the early stages of her marriage because of her inability to become the wife she thinks she must become — her mother, submissive and self-dissolving.

Anneliese's argument with Branhardt about their son's future demonstrates her otherwise suppressed sense of self, independent of her husband. Up to this point Anneliese has seen marriage as a series of willing sacrifices on her part, a submission to Branhardt's will, and a form of self-dissolution — she and Branhardt are one. Indeed, even this confrontation veers toward a solution located in her submission. When Branhardt argues that her conflict with him has destroyed the unity that he sees as the basis of a good marriage, he reduces her to "Ach Frank" (Oh, Frank), that characteristic surrendering response for which she earlier criticized herself. He withdraws his affection, dropping the "Liebesname" (pet name) with which he generally addresses her and aloofly explaining that her dissent on the issue of their son affects them not only as parents but as husband and wife, "als zwei" (141; as two). At the very moment in which Anneliese asserts herself, she is faced with a threat to the oneness that constitutes love and marriage for her. As in the conflict over differing types of knowledge, Branhardt insists on binary structures that allow no room for double directionalities. He and Anneliese are either one or two, but they cannot be both. We see here what Schultz calls "dual orienta-tion" and what Martin calls the "double directionality of self-assertion and self-dissolution" timidly emerging in Anneliese and challenging the limits of Branhardt's comprehension.[20]

Despite initial setbacks of this sort, by the end of the novel Anneliese has brought about significant changes in her marriage. During a vacation at an old haunt on the Danish coast, memories of past times there and the "natural" order suggested by the fisherman and his wife with whom they stay threaten to recontain Anneliese's awakening powers of resistance.[21] But a letter from Balduin addressed only to her interrupts this idyll. Bran-hardt feels betrayed by his wife's collaboration in what he perceives as a plot to exclude him. He concludes that the closeness in which they have lived is incompatible with these new tendencies to indulge her autonomy and indi-viduation and symbolically sets her free. Although she attempts to discuss this decision with him, he cuts her short, opens the door, and directs her out of the room. Initially paralyzed by the freedom forced upon her, she realizes that it marks a significant change in their relationship:

> Anneliese ging über die steinerne Diele, nur eben aus dem Haus, und blieb stehen. . . . Was war ihr geschehen?! Ein Fremder, Zuschauen-der hätte denken können: Streit — Stimmungssache! Sie wußte, daß es das nicht war. Sie wußte es aus der zitternden Kühle, die ihr den Nacken hinunterstrich, lähmend, bleiern in jedes Glied fiel. Keine Stimmungsgelegenheit — eine Wendung. (197)

> [Anneliese crossed the stony entryway, just to get out of the house, and stopped in her tracks. . . . What had happened to her? A stranger, an observer might have thought: an argument — just a mood! She knew that this was not the case. She knew from the chilly shiver that ran down the back of her neck, paralyzing every limb, as if lead. Not a matter of mood — a real change.]

While the narrative is sympathetic toward Branhardt's disillusionment with regard to his son, it is also critical of his behavior toward his wife, and exposes his double standard. In the same moment that he accuses

Anneliese and his son of having dismissed the importance of his judgment and understanding, he refuses to engage in dialogue with Anneliese,
to acknowledge her judgment and understanding. In hindsight, looking
back on these life-altering moments, Anneliese characterizes Branhardt in
a way that leaves no doubt about her disapproval of the monologic and
totalitarian manner in which he exercises his masculine privilege: "Selbst
sein Entschluß auf Balduin erwuchs ja noch aus diesem Boden, aus dieser
einmaligen inneren Handlung, die da war wie eine endgültige äußere Tat-
sache: und einfach weiterwirkte. So wies er auch jetzt auf einen solchen
erledigten Vollzug hin: "Nimm es, wie es ist" (198; Even his decision
about Balduin was grounded in the same method, in this one-off, inner
act that appeared as a definitive, external fact and just continued to take
effect. Now he presented her too with an already completed maneuver:
"take it or leave it"). While Anneliese mulls over Branhardt's inflexibility,
he congratulates himself on his flexibility: "Beinah wurde er stolz auf diese
aufrichtige Duldsamkeit" (195; He was almost proud of this sincere fore-
bearance). He sees his personal coming to terms with his wife's emerging
sense of autonomy as a gift that he bestows upon her. The irony of the
situation is twofold. First of all, he believes he magnanimously allows his
wife a privilege that she has, in fact, already claimed for herself. Second,
what he perceives as his newfound magnanimity and tolerance is simply,
as Anneliese interprets it, his usual prescriptive and oppressive practice.

Anneliese does not attempt to challenge Branhardt's conclusion that
their former closeness is no longer an option in their marriage, but what
appears to be her passivity in this instance can be read as silent agency.
The freedom she sought is thrust upon her in a manner that gives her
some cause for regret and indecision, but she realizes that the result corresponds to her wishes: "Ein wenig Freiheit im Handeln, — persönli-
chem Spielraum, — Gewährenlassen — Selbstbestimmung. Sie rang sich
klar zu machen: was sie gewollt hatte, wurde nun durch ihn zur Wirklichkeit. Wollte sie es denn nicht mehr?" (198; A bit of freedom in her
actions, — personal latitude, — a hands-off approach — self determination. She struggled for clarity: what she had wanted, he had made a reality. Did she no longer want it?) She soon works through her dilemma,
adapting to the new circumstances of their marriage. After returning from
their vacation, they begin to live more separate lives. Branhardt, who
once rushed home at lunchtime to see his wife, and who kept his office
bare, now visits his daughter for lunch and introduces personal parapher-
nalia into his office. He also gathers together a group of students whom
he treats as sons, compensation, the reader suspects, for his disappointment in his own son and son-in-law. Anneliese enjoys being alone and,
reflecting her increasing independence from Branhardt, regularly receives
personal letters from Balduin without feeling guilty. When Branhardt
apologizes for the excess of work that forces him to leave her at home "wie

eine Wittib" (like a widow) she dismisses his concern by playfully intimating that he is dispensable to the family:

> "Tu dich nur nicht so wichtig!" warnte sie; "im Gegenteil trifft es sich ganz ausgezeichnet, daß die großen Kinder dich nicht vermissen, — und was das Klimperkleine in seiner höchsteigenen Villa anbetrifft, so hat es von deinem Dasein noch überhaupt nicht Notiz genommen. . . . Wer weiß, ob ich ihm den Vater nicht einfach unterschlage? (230–31)

> ["Don't try to make yourself so important!" she warned. "On the contrary, it's perfect that the grown children don't miss you and as far as the iddy-biddy one in his exceptionally private villa is concerned, you don't even exist yet. . . . Who knows whether I'll reveal his father to him at all?"]

Anneliese's joking suggestion that she might keep the recently conceived child in the dark about its father reminds the reader of the autonomy she has achieved through her now grown-up children. Certainly her independence is limited, based as it is in her understanding of the selflessness of motherhood. Nonetheless, the acts of resistance to Branhardt's authority that have led her to this point highlight the problematic nature of Streiter's claim that Andreas-Salomé's representation of Anneliese corresponds to her representation in theory of the ideal woman as passive and submissive. While Anneliese has been submissive for a great deal of her life, her underlying displeasure with this situation and its final emergence and enunciation are the actual foci of the novel.

The double directionality rejected by Branhardt forms the theoretical basis of marriage for the next generation, namely for Markus and Gitta. At first Gitta intends to emulate her mother, to live the concept of marriage that she has experienced at home: "das war ja eben gerade 'die Ehe,' daß man nichts privat besaß, — wie die Mumme ja auch nichts für sie allein gehabt" (122; that's just the way it was with marriage; nothing was yours alone, — just as Mom had never had anything to herself). The example of her mother that springs to mind points to the personal pronoun of Gitta's sentence, "man" (one), as anything but ungendered. Based on her internalized and, as of yet, unquestioned understanding of marriage as a loss of personal space and possessions, Gitta denies herself a room of her own in her new home. This renunciation of private space constitutes a fundamental and necessary sacrifice for a good marriage and for her acceptance of her place within a "natural" order: "Ich werde das Zimmer symbolisch abschließen als meine hingeopferte Mädchenstube. Man muß sich den weiblichen Existenzbedingungen eben anpassen" (122; I will symbolically lock the door, make it the childhood room that I have sacrificed. One just has to adapt to the conditions of a wife's life). Despite Gitta's good intentions, her idealistic concept of marriage proves incompatible with her personal needs and, as in Anneliese's case, the novel dramatizes the slow progression of her dissatisfaction with this limited and limiting model of marriage.

Although Markus praises Gitta's sacrifices at first, a series of problematic encounters that culminate in her running away lead him to discuss his own understanding of marriage openly with her, an understanding of marriage that differs substantially from that of his in-laws. When Gitta runs away, Markus patiently sits out her absence and welcomes her back in a manner that shows more insight into Gitta than she herself seems to possess at this moment. She returns apologetic, ready to try again and ready to give up her "Schreibsucht" and "Selbstsucht" (204; an addiction to writing and selfishness).[22] Markus is now wary of her persistent belief that she must make sacrifices in order to be a good wife: "Aber freuen konnte ihn das nicht, denn dabei [beim Aufgeben von Allem] war sie ja miteins auch ihre Liebe zu ihm losgeworden" (204; But he couldn't be happy about her giving up everything because it also cost him her love for him). His unwillingness to reproach Gitta for having run away and his encouragement of her "Schreibsucht" und "Selbstsucht" intensify Branhardt's and Anneliese's impression that he is problematically passive. Since his laissez-faire attitude appears threatening to them because of their inability to accept Gitta's self-sufficiency and independence, Anneliese, finding Markus at home alone one day, advises him that, as man and husband, he needs to wield a firmer hand: "Aber Markus! Dann mußt du es eben nicht dulden! An dir ist es dann! Endlich muß sie doch heraus aus Halbheiten und Kindereien, — muß sie opfern lernen wirklichem Glück und wirklicher Pflicht!" (214; But Markus! You just don't have to put up with it! It's simply up to you! Eventually she has to grow out of half measures and puerility — has to learn to sacrifice them for the sake of real happiness and real duty).[23] Denying that a woman's happiness in marriage is linked to sacrifice and duty, Markus offers Anneliese and the reader an alternative definition of marriage and partnership. He condemns the firm hand recommended by Anneliese, acknowledging that his approach to marriage subverts the traditional masculine approach. Reminding Markus that the aim of marriage is a "Zueinanderkommen" (coming together), Anneliese criticizes him for not achieving such a union with Gitta. Although he agrees that marriage involves a "Zueinanderkommen," he redefines its terms. For Anneliese, marriage means that two people become and remain one. For Markus, on the other hand, the "Zueinanderkommen" is a never-ending process. Two people forever remain separate, remain individuals and forever reenact a "Zueinanderkommen": "Zueinanderkommen — ja! Aber das heißt ja doch: jedesmal wieder von sehr fernher, — aus der Einkehr in sich selbst jedesmal wieder" (215; A coming together, yes! But that means every single time from a long way off — emerging each time from a retreat into oneself). To borrow Martin's terms, then, marriage for Markus is a series of necessary self-assertions and self-dissolutions for both women and men.

This discussion between Markus and Anneliese announces a new stage in Gitta and Markus's marriage, as if the mere articulation of an alternative aids in its realization. Since her return Gitta has spent a lot of time alone, wandering in the hills, writing, and enjoying a newly found, guilt-free independence. This phase of their marriage culminates in what is ambiguously marked as the first time they have sexual intercourse:

> Dann weckte sie [Gitta], aus den Hinterhöfen, ein Hahnesschrei. Mit hochgezogenen Knien fand sie sich, Markus in den Schoß geschmiegt, und sofort wußte sie wieder: etwas war geschehen, — ein Glück, — . . . Denn nun meinte sie: dies werde es am Ende wohl gewesen sein, wofür sie so lange aufgeblieben waren. . . . Gitta, die so viel auf Namen und Nächte gab, nannte dies später ihre Hochzeitsnacht. (224)

> [Then she was wakened by the cock crowing in the backyard. She found herself nestled into Markus's lap, her knees drawn up, and she immediately knew that something had happened, — something serendipitous — . . . And then she thought that this must have been what she had stayed up so long for. . . . Gitta, who put a lot of stock in names and nights, called this her wedding night.]

Though not explicitly a description of sexual intercourse, the combination of their physical positions in the morning, the name Gitta gives this night, and earlier textual references intimating Gitta's virginity (even after their honeymoon) suggest that this is, at the very least, their first meaningful sexual encounter. The success of Gitta's marriage, it would appear, will depend not on sacrifice as Anneliese believes but on negotiations of independence and unity between two partners.

Streiter contends that Anneliese, a submissive and self-dissolving wife, is the model wife in the novel and that Andreas-Salomé's ideal of femininity is defined in terms of the man: "Die Weiblichkeitsideal Lou Andreas-Salomés ist definiert in Bezug auf den Mann. Die Frau erhält ihre Existenzberechtigung nur durch das, was sie ihm ist: Kind, Mutter und Hausfrau" (Lou Andreas-Salomé's ideal of femininity is defined in relation to man. Woman's existence is justified by what she is to him: child, mother, wife).[24] But in order to make this argument, she must stress Anneliese's masochistic tendencies to the exclusion of her self-assertive ones, and she must level Anneliese and Gitta into representative stages of "Woman," whereby Gitta will one day become like Anneliese.[25] Masochism, self-effacement, and subordination are all significant elements of Anneliese's character; however, they constitute the limits of neither her character nor Andreas-Salomé's idealized woman. Each woman in this novel struggles with the discrepancy between her desire to measure up to a socially and culturally sanctioned image of woman and her desire for a level of personal freedom that this image ignores. Each woman negotiates the inner conflict between self-assertion and self-dissolution that Biddy Martin identifies as intrinsic to all of Andreas-Salomé's women. While this conflict indeed seems to form the basis of Andreas-Salomé's woman, it is differently constituted in each of the female characters of *Das Haus,* indicating generational differences and thereby the potential of historical change in woman's condition. Whereas in Anneliese the submissive self is more pronounced, in her daughter, Gitta, the self-asserting self is dominant.

Living Happily Ever After

The final chapter of the novel locates both married couples together at Anneliese's and Branhardt's home, in an idyllic country setting suggestive of harmony and happiness. Gitta and Markus have gone for a walk together in the hills, a space that previously represented a means of escape for Gitta, someplace where she could be alone and feel autonomous. Anneliese runs about inspecting the house and garden, pregnant once again, and enjoying the sense of unity with nature and the world that impending motherhood affords her. The stereotype that Andreas-Salomé invokes here, namely that sex and motherhood tame women, put them in touch with their "natural" selves, seems dubious from a present-day feminist perspective, as does the compromise she suggests between patriarchal order and the impulse of the women's movement. As in melodrama, everything in this novel unfolds in the domestic space, and the issues addressed are those traditionally seen as bearing on women — love, marriage, and family. Andreas-Salomé might be criticized for the same tentativeness and timidity of which Ute Frevert accuses the turn-of-the-century women's movement in Germany, whose arguments left women "with a role in life which was slightly broader in scope than before but still essentially 'feminine.'"[26] Nevertheless, the narrative's valorization of some stereotypes does not erase resistance, squelch woman's independence, or attempt to resolve conflicts, but rather emphasizes resistance and irresolvable conflict. This is in keeping with Martin's argument that for Andreas-Salomé, "the relationship of feminine and masculine was a conflict at the heart of culture and subjectivity, not a problem to be solved once and for all."[27] While the novel ends with an idealistic patriarchal image of women who have come to terms with their rightful social function as wives, the moments of resistance to patriarchal structures and authority that otherwise permeate the novel undermine any definitive definition of marriage and woman's role in it. Gender issues, conflicts of authority, and women's struggles to achieve and maintain agency are not resolved in the closing pages. On the contrary, the narrator hints at the impossibility of such resolution, at the uncertain and always fluctuating nature of woman, gender, and marriage. The moments of resistance are not subsumed, as Streiter and Angela Livingstone suggest, by what I contend is merely a pseudo "they all lived happily ever after."

Occasional negative premonitions or ironic comments that disrupt the idyllic atmosphere indicate that this final chapter merely plays with traditional romantic closure, awakening expectations that it then unsettles. Despite Anneliese's overwhelming sense of unity with nature and the world, her delight in her motherhood is interrupted by a sinister inkling when she looks into what will be her future child's bedroom and feels overcome by a sense of emptiness and death: "Kahl stand, teilnahmslos vor ihr, das leere Zimmer, wie ein verödetes Haus, wie ein entleertes Dasein. Mörtel lag zu ihren Füßen, sie atmete grauen Staub. Und Vergänglichkeit rührte sie an mit dem Stachel des Todes" (229; The empty room in front of her looked bare and uninviting, like a desolate house, like a hollow presence. Plaster lay at her feet and she breathed in grey dust. And she was struck by a sense of transitoriness that felt like the barb of death). This sense of emptiness and death recalls Anneliese's earlier misgivings when Branhardt introduced the idea of having another child. Her last experience with childbirth had proved unpleasant and painful, and the child died at the age of eight.[28] Branhardt too has a negative premonition in this final chapter. After Anneliese visits him in his study, he nostalgically recalls the young Anneliese and looks forward to the sound of children filling their house again. As he is about to be reabsorbed in his work, he is suddenly struck by a sense of foreboding: "Ganz dumpf und dunkel nur glitt ein Gefühl ihm nach, — eine beinahe körperliche Empfindung, — als ob etwas irgendwo nicht stimme . . ." (232; A dark and suffocating feeling took hold of him — almost a physical sensation — as if something somewhere were not right). Although these premonitions point toward nothing definite in Anneliese's and Branhardt's future, they do link the family idyll to anxiety and death and thereby serve to inject an ominous tone into the otherwise idyllic mood of the narrative.

The abiding nature of marital happiness is called into question in Gitta's case, and the level of compliance in Anneliese's. The narrator's comments on Gitta's and Markus's present state remind the reader of the many merely temporary reconciliations they achieved before, and underscore the potentially similar transience of their current harmony: "Die beiden waren so herrlich ernst und so herrlich froh miteinander! Sie [Anneliese] konnte sich kaum daran sattsehen. — Ob es aber so blieb? Das wußte Gitta wohl selbst am allerwenigsten" (230; They were both so wonderfully serious and so wonderfully happy with each other! She couldn't get enough of it. — Would it remain so? Gitta herself knew that least of all). As Branhardt approaches Anneliese in the garden, she is described from his perspective in terms of a framed image, an idyll: "Einen Arm, scheinbar vor der Blendung, ein wenig hochgehoben, inmitten der sich lichtenden Obstbäume, die Frucht getragen hatten und in später, zweckloser Schönheit farbig sie umrahmten: so wurde Anneliese von Branhardt gesehen, — und doch nicht gesehen" (237; One arm apparently raised to shield her from the sun, standing in the middle of the thinning fruit trees that had borne fruit and that now framed her colorfully with their later, aimless beauty: thus was Anneliese seen by Branhardt — and yet not seen). The simple paradox at the end of this passage undermines Branhardt's perspective, not least because it is a paradox and represents, on the part of the narrator, a challenge to the binary logic Branhardt has upheld throughout the novel. It also recalls Anneliese's personal reflections after a discussion with Markus on love and marriage, in which she admits to herself that she has conformed to Branhardt's limiting image of her throughout their marriage and that this has cost her much freedom: "Wenn sie sich ehrlich fragte, so hatte sie im Grunde dem Bilde nachgelebt, das ihr Mann sich von ihr gemacht; hatte dieser feinsten aller Schmeicheleien, die in solchem Ideal steckt, erst ihre beflügelteste eigne Kraft entnommen? Und hatte auch ihn vielleicht auf ähnliche Kosten gesteigert? — Hilfe und Fessel wurden da eben kaum unterscheidbar eins" (215–16; If she were honest with herself, she had to admit that she had essentially mimicked the image that her husband had created of her; had the most subtle of flatteries inherent in such an ideal robbed her of a personal, invigorating strength? And had the ideal perhaps built him up as it robbed her? Support and constraint became almost indistinguishable in this case.) The contradictory " — und doch nicht gesehen" (and yet not seen) tagged on to Branhardt's last image of Anneliese, together with the emphasis of the last several chapters on Anneliese's growing independence, points to an Anneliese who is more than Branhardt's projections. Her transition from a state of absolute compliance with her husband's wishes to one of greater self-sufficiency is signified by her association with a dog in the closing lines. This dog, a female dog with a masculine gendered name (Salomo), is associated only with the women of the novel. When Gitta marries, she renounces her "Mädchenstube" (girl's room) and Salomo as a symbol of her absolute devotion to Markus. In the course of the novel, she sporadically reclaims the dog, indicating an alternating need for self-sufficiency and submission. Throughout the novel, the dog, an animal that is at once domesticated and yet outside culture, has represented woman's resistance to total assimilation into the patriarchal order of the man. At the beginning, Salomo is associated primarily with Gitta, while she is Anneliese's companion at the end. This switch of associations suggests that Anneliese has at least partially realized that part of her that has always been more pronounced in Gitta: the need for independence.

In her depiction of both Anneliese's and Gitta's constant vacillation between submission and self-assertion, Andreas-Salomé confronts her reader with the conflict feminism represented for women, then as now. On the one hand, women were (and often still are) socialized to be wives and mothers. On the other, the women's movement articulated their need for recognition as individuals who would not be defined solely in terms of sexuality, husband, and child. Andreas-Salomé psychologizes this social conflict in the figures of Anneliese and Gitta. In the context in which she writes, she cannot create a romantic novel to which marriage provides a happy and unproblematic ending. She also does not present the reader, however, with a seamless transition for women from a state of subordination and submission to one of emancipation. In a manner that reflects the social reality of women's lives, Andreas-Salomé's female characters in *Das Haus* vacillate between the two poles. While I would agree, then, with Martin in her claim that Andreas-Salomé "never suggests that the oscillation between self-loss and self-assertion would cease to exist in a 'new' world," I would also emphasize that Andreas-Salomé neither places woman beyond the possibility of historical change nor accords scientific discourse an ahistorical claim to truth (*Woman and Modernity*, 190).[29] Anneliese's daughter does not face the same obstacles her mother faces. Although conflicts remain, Gitta lives in a time that, thanks to a heightened awareness of the patriarchal oppression of women, facilitates woman's individuality and self-assertion.

Notes

This chapter is a revised and lengthened version of an article entitled "Authority and Resistance: Women in *Das Haus*," published in *The Women in German Yearbook* 14 (1998).

[1] See Patrice Petro, *Joyless Streets: Women and Melodramatic Representation in Weimar Germany* (Princeton. NJ: Princeton UP, 1989); see also Lynda J. King, *Best-Sellers by Design: Vicki Baum and the House of Ullstein* (Detroit, MI: Wayne UP, 1988). King discusses Ullstein's marketing strategies in the case of Vicki Baum, drawing some general conclusions about women's publications and female authors' audiences, and Petro discusses the awareness of a female audience on the part of the popular press in early twentieth-century Berlin.

[2] See Marielouise Janssen-Jurreit, "Nationalbiologie, Sexualreform und Geburtenrückgang — über die Zusammenhänge von Bevölkerungspolitik und Frauenbewegung um die Jahrhundertwende," in *Die Überwindung der Sprachlosigkeit: Texte aus der Frauenbewegung*, ed. Gabriele Dietze (Frankfurt am Main: Luchterhand, 1979), 139–75; See also Richard von Krafft-Ebing, *Psychopathia Sexualis*, trans. Franklin S. Klaf (New York: Bell, 1965).

[3] Binion, *Frau Lou: Nietzsche's Wayward Disciple* (Princeton, NJ: Princeton UP, 1968), characteristically reads the text as biography, connecting each character

in what he refers to as this "plotless" novel to real people in Andreas-Salomé's life (316). Caroline Kreide, *Lou Andreas-Salomé: Feministin oder Antifeministin? Eine Standortbestimmung zur wilhelminischen Frauenbewegung* (New York: Peter Lang, 1996), analyzes the construction of gender in the novel and argues: "Männerwelt und Frauenwelt werden also als entgegengesetzte Pole verstanden, wobei die erstere die letztere beherrscht, und wenn nötig sogar die Idylle und vermeintliche Leichtfertigkeit der Frauenwelt zerstört" (108; Man's world and woman's world are thus understood as opposite poles, whereby the former dominates the latter, and, if necessary, even destroys the idylls and supposed levity of woman's world). Although she recognizes an ambivalence in the novel toward Branhardt's masculine paternal authority, she, like Sabine Streiter in her afterword to *Das Haus,* concentrates on the aspects of the novel that comply with Andreas-Salomé's relatively traditional theoretical writings on woman. This approach, namely the search for coherence between Andreas-Salomé's fictional representations of woman and her theoretical models, numbs the reader to the complementarity of her works and imposes consistency where, as I argue, none exists. See Sabine Streiter, "Nachwort," *Das Haus: Eine Familiengeschichte vom Ende vorigen Jahrhunderts,* by Lou Andreas-Salomé (Frankfurt am Main: Ullstein, 1987), 239–53.

[4] See Janssen Jurreit, *Nationalbiologie,* again for a provocative discussion of conservative elements of the German women's movement. See also Ulrike Prokop, "Die Sehnsucht nach Volkseinheit: Zum Konservatismus der bürgerlichen Frauenbewegung," in Dietze, *Die Überwindung der Sprachlosigkeit,* 176–202.

[5] In her chapter "Middle-Class Women and Their Campaign in Imperial Germany," Ute Frevert explains that the majority of middle-class women remained housewives well into the twentieth century despite legal reforms that granted them access to education and paid work. Ute Frevert, *Women in German History: From Bourgeois Emancipation to Sexual Liberation,* trans. Stuart McKinnon-Evans (Oxford: Berg, 1989).

[6] It is important to note that it is not only the women who have difficulty with and challenge Branhardt's authority in the novel. Branhardt's son Balduin and his son-in-law, Markus, also find themselves at odds with him, the former because of his poetic aspirations, the latter because of his Jewishness and what Branhardt interprets as his genetic passivity.

[7] Eve Kosofsky Sedgwick, *Between Men: English Literature and Male Homosocial Desire* (New York: Columbia UP, 1985).

[8] Unless otherwise noted, all translations are my own.

[9] Compare Treder's discussion of the objectification of the male in Andreas-Salomé's novella *Eine Ausschweifung* as a "Vertauschung der üblichen männlich-weiblichen Wertskala" (inversion of the usual masculine-feminine value scale, 77). Treder argues that within patriarchy beauty is an attribute of the feminine to be admired by the male. As in *Eine Ausschweifung,* Andreas-Salomé shifts the emphasis here to masculine beauty admired by a woman.

[10] Tracie Matysik,"The Interests of Ethics: Andreas-Salomé's Psychoanalytic Critique," *Seminar* 36:1 (Feb. 2000): 5–21.

[11] Gitta's overly honed sense of her own desire leads to her marriage, for example. Her first attraction to Markus was purely visual, and in a crisis moment before their

wedding she regrets the passing of their courtship as a "Wunderwelt, die alles noch enthielt, *ungesagt,* ungemessen, unfaßlich" (107; magical world that still embodies everything, *unspoken,* unmeasured, unintelligible, emphasis added). When her parents deny her the opportunity to go to a dance one evening with Markus Mandelstein, a Jew of whom they disapprove, she visits some friends and stares too long at a Greek man who reminds her of Markus. This newly wed man follows her, jumps on her train, and spends some time with her. Her parents, apparently scandalized by this public display of awakening sexuality, suddenly consent to her seeing Markus. Gitta's ease with her own desire and her insistence on acting on it lead her parents to seek ways to contain it and, when that fails, a legitimate way for her to express it, namely to one man to whom she is promised in marriage.

[12] In "Gender and Science," Evelyn Fox Keller discusses the traditional association between the sets of categories masculine and objective, masculine and scientific, and scientific and objective. She examines how these associations have lead to the belief that facts and truth are "hard," reliable, and masculine, while feelings and intuitions are "soft," capricious, and feminine. See Evelyn Fox Keller, "Gender and Science," in *Discovering Reality: Feminist Perspectives on Epistemology, Metaphysics, Methodology, and Philosophy of Science,* ed. Sandra Harding and Merrill B. Hintikka (Dordrecht, Netherlands: D. Reidel, 1983), 187–205.

[13] See Janssen-Jurreit's discussion of science, evolution, and the bourgeois feminist movement (*Nationalbiologie*). Biddy Martin also makes reference to the hegemony established by the field of biology in her introduction to *Woman and Modernity: The (Life)Styles of Lou Andreas-Salomé* (Ithaca, NY: Cornell UP, 1991), 15. Finally, see Sander Gilman's *Difference and Pathology: Stereotypes of Sexuality, Race, And Madness* (Ithaca, NY: Cornell UP, 1985) for a discussion of how medical and scientific discourse lent authenticity/legitimacy to stereotypes at the turn of the century.

[14] The gender bias of science that Andreas-Salomé suggests and implicitly criticizes in her essay "Der Mensch als Weib" and in her novel *Das Haus* becomes, of course, a major concern later in the century with the institutionalization of feminism as an academic discipline. In "Feminism and Science," Evelyn Fox Keller articulates explicitly what Andreas-Salomé's works as a whole gesture toward, namely "the powerful influence of ordinary language in biasing our theoretical formulations" (591). Keller underscores the predominance of the male perspective in scientific descriptions and challenges the "truth and necessity" of the conclusions of natural science that have excluded women and women's perspectives (592). See "Feminism and Science," in *Feminism and Science,* ed. Evelyn Fox Keller and Helen E. Longino (New York: Oxford UP, 1996), originally published in *Signs: Journal of Women in Culture and Society* 17:3 (1982): 28–40.

[15] Flax speaks of male development and assimilation in patriarchy as rooted in "a need to deny the power and autonomy of women" (245). Branhardt must deny Anneliese's autonomy if he is to preserve his patriarchal right to authority. See Jane Flax, "Political Philosophy and the Patriarchal Unconscious: A Psychoanalytic Perspective on Epistemology and Metaphysics," in Harding and Hintikka, *Discovering Reality,* 245–81.

[16] Streiter points out the connection between the character Balduin and Salomé's poet friend Rilke ("Nachwort, *Das Haus*," 242). This constitutes an interesting association from the perspective of Balduin's feminization, given that Rilke's mother dressed him in girls' clothing for some time. Rilke also supposedly changed his name from René to Rainer at Lou Andreas-Salomé's request, because she found the former too feminine. Livingstone, *Lou Andreas-Salomé: Her Life and Work* (New York: Moyer Bell, 1984), 100.

[17] As is the case in her portrayal of the female characters in her novel, in portraying Markus Lou Andreas-Salomé does resort to some stereotypical images of Jewishness. However, she does not reiterate negative stereotypes unconsciously but engages with them in a critical manner. Although she aligns Markus with the women in the novel, for example, she is very careful to preserve Markus's professional authority (read: masculinity). He emerges, then, as the most positive model of masculinity in this novel in his well-balanced approach to his own authority as a man and a husband. The shared experience of oppression on the part of the women and the younger men introduces an interesting constellation and set of associations, particularly when one considers the historical, social, and cultural contexts in which the novel was written, namely the constellation woman, Jew, and poet. In *Difference and Pathology,* Gilman has examined the ramifications of this constellation in detail, discussing the systematic and disparaging feminization of "the Jew" in turn of the century European scientific discourse. I do not argue that Lou Andreas-Salomé responds directly in *Das Haus* to authors who perpetuated this tradition, but there can be no doubt that she was acutely aware of negative assessments of Jews, given both her personal association with several Jewish men and the incredible success of Otto Weininger's *Sex and Charakter,* published a year before *Das Haus* was written, and its repeated reprintings by the time the novel was finally published. Weininger, *Geschlecht und Charakter: Eine prinzipielle Untersuchung* (1903; repr., Berlin: Kiepenheuer, 1932).

[18] Tania Modleski, "Time and Desire in the Woman's Film," in *Film Theory and Criticism,* ed. Gerald Mast, Marshall Cohen, and Leo Braudy, 4th ed. (New York: Oxford UP, 1992), 536–48.

[19] Thanks to Karla Schultz at the University of Oregon for this pithy and accurate formulation.

[20] Karla Schultz, "In Defense of Narcissus: Lou Andreas-Salomé and Julia Kristeva," *The German Quarterly* 67:2 (Spring 1994): 185–96, here 186; Martin, *Woman and Modernity,* 36.

[21] The fisherman goes out to sea every day while his wife remains at home and mends the nets, knits, and takes care of the household. The narrative describes their arrangement as follows: ". . . so wuchtig selbstverständlich sprach in diesem Außen und Innen der Geschlechtergegensatz sich aus wie Naturgeschehen" (178; gender polarity was articulated in such a powerfully self-evident way in this outside/inside binary that it seemed a natural occurrence). Although Anneliese and Branhardt are overwhelmed by this simple lifestyle and its suggestion of the "Urwelt" (original world), Andreas-Salomé's rhetorical use of a simile to compare gender difference with a natural occurrence indicates her awareness that gender

difference is as much culturally defined as innate. Anneliese and Branhardt's one-sided perspective on a "natural order" is qualified by the narrator's simile.

[22] Interestingly these two things, the desire to write and selfishness, are paired here in the figure of Gitta as they are often in Andreas-Salomé's works. Writing, the production of narrative, is once again closely associated with the development of a personal identity and with a certain consciousness of subjectivity.

[23] Anneliese's advice echoes Branhardt's earlier criticism of Markus as incapable of ruling with a firm enough hand. At first she allows Branhardt's views to override her own, but by the end of this particular conversation with Markus she comes to a new appreciation of his brand of marital wisdom.

[24] Streiter, "Nachwort," *Das Haus,* 249.

[25] Streiter, "Nachwort," *Das Haus,* 250–51.

[26] Frevert, *Women in German History,* 126.

[27] Martin, *Woman and Modernity,* 6.

[28] Anneliese is overcome by negative feelings in their earlier discussion of this matter. She suppresses a shiver when he broaches the subject, telling her that there is no reason for her to sacrifice the further possibility of motherhood. Anneliese is disturbed by his stance on this issue, although she does not tell him this: "Verzichten nannte er das! Hätte er — er also wirklich wünschen können — er, der sie so entsetzlich, unmenschlich leiden gesehen. . . . War sie denn feige, — war er brutal in seinen Wünschen? Liebte er sie denn nicht zu sehr für eine solche Wiederholung . . . ?" (18; He called that a sacrifice! Could he really have wished — he who had seen her suffer so inhumanely . . . Was she cowardly — Were his wishes violent? Did he not love her too much to see a repeat of that?).

[29] Martin, *Woman and Modernity,* 190.

3: Untamed Woman: Talking about Sex and Self in *Jutta*

A
MBIVALENT TOWARD FEMINISM, fearing that women would lose sight
of their sensual and erotic sides in their pursuit of careers, Andreas-
Salomé also recognized that patriarchal society had not been particularly
successful at encouraging women to accept their sexuality and sensuality unless it could be channeled into and tamed within marriage. In *Das
Haus,* as we have seen, Gitta's flirtation with a Greek man strikes fear
into the heart of her parents, who immediately consent to her marriage
to Markus, a Jew of whom they had previously disapproved. The fear of
the untamed or inadequately domesticated woman and her uncontained
sexuality that Andreas-Salomé touches on in *Das Haus* forms the focus of
Jutta.[1] Written at about the same time as *Fentischka* and *Eine Ausschweifung* (1898), *Jutta* too reflects both its era's intensified public discourse
on women's issues and that period's challenges to narrative convention
and tradition. It resembles *Eine Ausschweifung* and *Fenitschka* in that it
too demonstrates the subtlety with which Andreas-Salomé manipulated
narrative structure to expose the limitations imposed on women's psychological and sexual development by conventional definitions.

Critical interest in Andreas-Salomé has concentrated on *Fenitschka*
and *Eine Ausschweifung* and focused above all on the theme of female
sexual identity that they address, often indicating as it does so how those
texts employ literary structures in sophisticated and interesting ways in
order to explore and criticize prevailing images of woman and prevailing ideologies having to do with woman's nature and sexuality. Julie Doll
Allen, for example, shows how dialogue and narrative perspective interact in *Fenitschka* to undermine and criticize the quantitatively dominant
male perspective and grant qualitative dominance to the perspective of
the female protagonist, while Brigid Haines argues that Andreas-Salomé
employs a "masochistic aesthetic" in *Eine Ausschweifung,* thus placing the
reader in a position that mirrors the dilemma of the first-person narrator
Adine.[2] The reader, she posits, "while standing outside the masochistic
scenario, … is… also constantly invited to identify with it" (108).[3] On
close scrutiny, *Jutta* proves to involve yet another variation on this inter-
relationship of narrative structure and ideological criticism, and thus yet
another counter to Julia Kristeva's claim in "Kein Weibliches Schreiben:
Fragen an Julia Kristeva" that women's texts are conspicuous for their

lack of interest in composition, that they do not possess the art "die Sig-
nifikanten zu orchestrieren, wie man es mit Noten macht" (of arranging
the signifiers as one does with notes in music).[4] In *Jutta*, Andreas-Salomé manipulates narrative structure in a subtle and clever way in order
to expose the limitations imposed on women's psychological and sexual
development by culturally sanctioned definitions of women based on
binary oppositions and to show how such definitions affect the representation of female sexuality in texts and narratives.

The narrative structure in *Jutta,* much like that in *Eine Ausschweifung,* awakens expectations that the entire text eventually refutes, thus
fostering a critical awareness of the inability of conventional outlooks and
forms to grasp women. In *Eine Ausschweifung* the opening promises a
conciliatory confession from which Adine's narrative ultimately deviates
when she ends her story with episodes that defy prevailing expectations of
moral behaviour and narrative closure. Similarly, *Jutta* awakens hopes that
the entire context refutes — albeit this time with the woman not breaking
free from but rather dominated and confined by conventional moral outlooks and narratives of her world. The narrative structure is initially such
as to awaken hopes of youthful confusion explained and clarified — with
an older, wiser title-heroine coming to terms narratively with a past mis-
step. Yet the entire text in fact reveals the reductive effect that the mature
Jutta's struggle for moral and narrative control have on the fullness of her
past experience.

The novella is a fictive diary entry in which the title-figure tells retrospectively of a Whitsun vacation that proved a turning point in her life.
Thus there are two Juttas: the older, wiser narrating Jutta recalling the
naive and inexperienced younger Jutta, who once set out to spend a few
days in a mountain village with her brother Herbert and a number of his
fellow students, only to discover upon arrival that her brother had been
detained by a sprained ankle. Her brother's six friends rejoiced in Jutta's
presence and entertained her with their banter and antics, many of which
were sexually loaded. The retrospectively narrating Jutta insists, however,
that naive, narrated Jutta understood nothing of the sexual innuendo,
even if she occasionally had an uneasy feeling about the situation and
certain obscure conversations and jokes. Out of a sense of duty to her
brother, a wish to avoid insulting his friends, naive Jutta was duped into
embarking alone on an excursion with Florian, one of the group members. One evening, a little suddenly but with the unspoken consent of
both parties, their relationship became sexual. Because of an understand-
able ambivalence, Jutta soon concocted a complicated plan forcing herself
to leave Florian, and the affair ended as abruptly as it began. Because
her premarital sexual encounter is incompatible with her understanding of
herself as a respectable middle-class daughter, narrating Jutta is confused
and suffers an identity crisis.

Presented in the form of a diary entry, a confession, *Jutta* (both the title Lou Andreas-Salomé gives the story and the title our first person narrator gives her diary entry) is a private text, an act of self-representation intended only for Jutta herself. The novella represents the act of talking about sex and self as Jutta cannot yet imagine talking about them to another person. By writing about herself in this way, the first person narrator transgresses against two prohibitions: she has not only been sexually active but dares to talk about it in personal rather than scientific terms.[5] Narrating Jutta's crisis of identity becomes evident in the first sentence, in which she identifies with the narrated Jutta while at the same time distancing herself from her.[6] Despite her attempt to do otherwise, she introduces a divided self: on the one hand the first-person Jutta, "ich," on the other hand the third-person Jutta, "die Jutta": "'Jutta' schrieb ich erstmal groß über dies Pfingsttagebuch. Denn nicht nur heiße ich so, sondern ich will mich ja mit dem, was hier steht, durchaus zu mir selbst bekennen — das was hier hineinsoll, das ist eben die Jutta" (29; I started out by writing "Jutta" in capital letters as the header for this Whitsuntide journal of mine. That's my name, of course, but I also really want to admit my responsibility for what I've written down here — what I am about to write here, well, that *is* Jutta").[7] This division of Jutta into two cannot be explained simply by the temporal difference within the narrative between the time of narration and the time narrated. Rather it exists in the present of the narration as, among other things, the superego and the id. The narrating Jutta represents the superego in her constant justification or criticism of narrated Jutta's actions, which she depicts as instinctive, unwitting, and involuntary. The divided self also corresponds to the two incompatible poles of traditional vamp and virgin images. Narrating Jutta's attempt to understand and account for herself as a woman is determined by such internalized stereotypes: women are either "Bürgertöchter" (daughters of bourgeois families) or "Studentinnen" (female students), whereby these categories signal certain moral codes — the former are wholesome and virginal, the latter deviant and seductive. Such limited possibilities of self-categorization did not pose a problem for Jutta until the events she is about to recount transpired. Now, through the narrative process, Jutta confronts this self-representational dilemma, seeking to reconcile her image of herself as basically moral and wholesome with the undeniable reality of her premarital sexual encounter. She would like to be able to accept the narrated, sexually vital Jutta (id) from whom she distances herself in the opening sentence as a part of her self. By creating a Jutta who is an unreliable narrator, however, Andreas-Salomé insists on the impossibility of such a task for a woman whose dilemma is both caused and complicated by a moral code of which she is at once a victim and a proponent.

The private character of the embedded genre (diary) and Jutta's purpose in writing it (attempting to come to terms with herself) would normally imply an honest unfolding of the events that inspired the sexual encounter, as well as an analysis of her feelings and desires leading up to it. But Andreas-Salomé subverts reader expectations by creating a Jutta whose desire to be honest with herself is impeded by an equally strong desire to retain control of the narrated material and her image in the face of a potentially judgmental readership. Although Jutta's narration is a diary entry intended predominantly for herself and forcing readers into a voyeuristic role, she not only welcomes potential voyeurs but frequently addresses them directly, responding to imagined interjections and criticisms on their part. While she projects a potential reader at the beginning of her narration — a person who like herself became entangled in a set of events she would never have imagined for herself — her rhetoric and her persistent justification of her self-representation hint at a somewhat different audience. Her fervent desire to make believable that she never intended to engage in premarital sex and her defense of her academic background suggest that she writes not with this compassionate reader in mind but with a relatively hostile and judgmental one akin to her own well-developed superego.

Throughout the narrative, Jutta is at pains to emphasize her honesty, frequently interrupting the narrative to defend particular representations of her younger self or to reflect on the writing process. Her greatest concerns are that a reader will find the narrated Jutta's naivety exaggerated, will question the narrating Jutta's precise memory of certain events and conversations, and will therefore doubt the authenticity of her self-representation. Having related a fairly bawdy conversation full of sexual innuendo that took place among her brother's six friends in her presence, for example, she immediately justifies her memory: "Daß mir aber die einzelnen Gesprächsbrocken so genau im Gedächtnis blieben, als seien sie gestern gesprochen worden, geschah dadurch, daß ich sie wiederholt hintendrein mit Herbert besprach und ihm hersagte" (34; If I have been able to recall the exact details of these individual snatches of conversation as if it had been only yesterday, it's because I recited them to Herbert afterwards and went over them with him again and again). Such interruptions underscore her efforts to control her self-representation after she has relinquished control to some degree by writing everything down. Ironically, in her attempt to control the narrative, to influence the reader's reception of her story, Jutta loses control of her self-representation. Her metanarrative takes on a life of its own and becomes more than her controlled and manipulative commentary on the narrative. Rather than dictate the reader's interpretation of the narrative, Jutta inadvertently reveals her self-doubts and arouses that very suspicion in the reader that her interjections are designed to avert — the suspicion that she may not be entirely sincere. Jutta's double bind suggests what Martin Escher's etching "Drawing Hands" illustrates. Escher's etching depicts a drawing hand being drawn in turn by the hand it draws. The represender and his or her representation, it infers, enter into a reciprocal relationship whereby each structures the other. Representation inevitably involves a loss of control on the part of the represender, because the media or tools used and the images drawn on in an attempt to make sense of experience for oneself and others have a long tradition to which precepts and expectations have accrued. As in Goethe's "Der Zauberlehrling" (The Sorcerer's Apprentice), the medium takes on a life of its own and reflects back on the user in unintended and uncontrollable ways. In the character of Jutta, Andreas-Salomé broaches this representational dilemma. Her treatment of Jutta, her exploration of the relationship between Jutta's intended narrative and the text she finally produces, prefigures the differentiation Kristeva makes between narrative and text in *The Revolution of Poetic Language*.[8] For Kristeva, narrative is the author's attempt in language to impose order, sense, and grammar on experience, whereas "text" is the ultimate product of this attempt, a product that is more than the narrative intended by its author. It is in comparing how Jutta intends to represent herself with how the text ultimately represents her that we become aware of Andreas-Salomé's critique of limiting cultural stereotypes and their effect on representation. Jutta has been co-opted and her attempted self-representation reveals this.

That Lou Andreas-Salomé should write a novella that articulates the complexities of representation is interesting, not least because of the criticism she herself has suffered at the hands of critics who have accused her of being duplicitous in both her fictional and autobiographical writings. Literary critics dealing with Andreas-Salomé's fictional texts have often read them solely in biographical terms, denying the sophistication of her texts and failing to employ their own sophisticated literary awareness in analyzing them. A commonplace in literary criticism, for example, namely that the author is not to be confused with the first person narrator of a fictional text, has frequently been ignored in Andreas-Salomé scholarship. In Rudolph Binion's summary of *Jutta*, he writes of the excursion on which she and Florian embark: "The others have chosen Florian to test her virtue: they see the pair off to the mountains with knowing glances" (201). In a footnote, he comments on the fact that Jutta noticed the knowing glances: "The literary effect of such passages is incongruous in that naïve Jutta is herself the narrator." In other words, if naïve Jutta is really as innocent as narrating Jutta claims, who saw these "knowing glances" that narrating Jutta is now able to relate? Indeed much of what the naïve Jutta must have remarked in order for narrating Jutta to be able to report it later seems at odds with that very naïveté. Retelling how she and Florian reserved hotel rooms on the first night of their outing, for example, Jutta recalls a smile that she did not see at the time: "*Ich sah nicht,* daß über seine Züge dabei ein flüchtiges Lächeln glitt — und zwar ein Lächeln bewundernder Anerkennung!" (50; *I didn't notice* the fleeting smile that crossed his face — a smile of surprised and admiring acknowledgement, emphasis added). The smile that Jutta "did not notice" was either in fact seen, implying a Jutta who was not quite as naive as the representation offered by her older counterpart, or it was added to the narrative later to emphasize Florian's questionable intentions toward her, implying a deceptive narrating Jutta. In either case, Jutta unintentionally undermines her own trustworthiness by transforming herself into an omniscient narrator, as it were. Binion's conclusion that such details result in incongruous literary effects is questionable. His undoubtedly correct grounding of this text in autobiographical experience leads him to confuse Jutta, a fictional character in a fictional text, with Lou Andreas-Salomé, the author of that fictional text. This error prevents him from reading what he perceives as incongruous effects for what they really are: Andreas-Salomé's construction of an unreliable narrator.

Basic oversights of this kind have contributed to the view that Andreas-Salomé lacked the textual subtlety and complexity that would have put her on a par with her modernist contemporaries. The discrepancy between what a naive Jutta would probably never have seen and narrating Jutta's account of events is not the result of mistakes on the part of Andreas-Salomé. Rather Jutta's confusion is a contrived textual function that contributes to the psychological development of a fictional character in a fictional text. Through her first-person unreliable narrator, Andreas-Salomé shows how internalized social and moral edicts breed a psychic split in woman that makes her complicit in her own sexual repression and obstructs the sincere and truthful discussion of her sexuality, even to herself. Jutta's inability to let the narrative stand on its own betrays her adherence to the conceptual framework that makes her dilemma insoluble. In this way, Andreas-Salomé's *contrived* text suggests that what has been called woman's insincerity about her sexuality is not necessarily purposeful and coy but rather a defense mechanism against public and moral outrage. If Jutta is insincere, she is so because of a formidable superego and her own belief in the moral code that would cause others to scorn her. In *Jutta* Andreas-Salomé presents us with a complex and contradictory image of a complex fictional character suffering under a multitude of stresses determined by a cultural context that limited women and undermined their self-esteem by providing them with only a limited number of defining rubrics with which to see and justify themselves.

To call Jutta an example of "weiblicher Selbstbestimmung" (female self-determination) is an exaggeration.[9] To see her as such implies that she consciously decides to have sex with Florian. Yet while she certainly engages in sex with Florian completely of her own accord, her description of the sexual encounter undermines the idea of conscious volition on her part. Everything just happens: "Es *geschah alles so selbstverständlich*, wie

Hände sich helfen beim Bergesteigen" (68; *It all just happened naturally,* just like one hand instinctively helps the other when you go mountain climbing, emphasis added). From the very beginning of the narrative, when she refers to the event "in das ich hineingeriet" (that I blundered my way into), Jutta seeks to emphasize the uncontrollable development of events, as if a force stronger than herself compelled her to have sex (29). Of course, Jutta is an unreliable narrator. Yet given her psychic dilemma, it seems overstated to describe her in terms of self-determination. While some level of volition is certainly involved, her psychic condition forces her to deny this volition later, undermining the notion of self-determination and the unquestioning acceptance of her sexuality that Kreide's characterization implies.

Reflecting the uncontrollable momentum that Jutta claims motivated her, her narrative, as she begins to describe her first sexual encounter, takes on characteristics that captivate readers and make them participate in the seduction. In stark contrast to the rest of the narrative, into which the narrating Jutta constantly intrudes with her self-doubts and her insistence on the narrated Jutta's naivety and passivity, the narration of the first sexual encounter is rhapsodic, exhilarating, and unbroken, celebrating female sexuality and sex even though it occurs in a context that defies prevailing moral standards. Up until now, narrating Jutta has gone out of her way to avoid anything that might be considered an endorsement of morally questionable behaviour. Here, however, the character of the language has changed from what has gone before, taking on a metaphorical and effusive dimension (68–71). The dominant punctuation mark in the narrative foreplay is the dash (68), suggesting the usurpation of the rational by a physical force that would interfere with a lucid and cerebral articulation of the events:

> Nach meiner eigenen heimlichsten Empfindung hielt er [Florian] mich aber gar nicht auf der Gangbrüstung sondern trug mich hinaus — Wohin — ? das wußte ich nicht, doch jedenfalls aus aller Fremde hinaus — in ein unerfaßlich Heimatliches. Denn das wußten für mich meine Hände, meine Arme, meine Glieder alle, in denen jeder einzelne Blutstropfen diesen Weg heimwärts zu kennen schien — und, bewegt von bergender Wärme, ihr allein entgegenzuströmen schien — um wieder in mich zurückzurinnen, bis tief ins Herz, das schlug, als schlüge es in Zweien. (69)

> [As far as I could tell from my own most private sensations, he was not holding me on the parapet at all, but carrying me off, out — to where? I didn't know, but I knew it was away from everything alien — toward an unfathomable sense of at-homeness. And my hands, my arms communicated this to me, and all of my limbs in which every single drop of blood appeared to know this way

home — and, stirred by a salvational warmth, seemed to just flow
toward that warmth — only to then flow back into me, deep into
my heart, that pounded, as if it would break in two.]

From "sondern" on, this passage is composed of short syntactical
units that are connected through rhythmical, structural, or lexical repetition. The effect is one of rapid forward movement as the reader is ushered
on to the next unit — the style thus linguistically mimicking Jutta's physical capitulation. The narrating Jutta appears to have lost all inhibitions
and her otherwise unremitting consciousness of a potentially judgmental
audience. She is consumed by her own narration, reliving the events as if
in the present, and crying out at the sweet memories of the relationship
as it neared its end: "O unnennbare Süße, unvergeßbare, alle Bitternis
durchdringend wie ein Laut aus einem Märchen — dies Gehörchendürfen" (86; Oh, unnameable, unforgettable, sweetness, penetrating all
bitterness like a tone from a fairytale — this permission to obey). Her
attempt to "narrate," in the sense of rationalizing her experience, is compromised by her "text," especially by this rhapsodic part of her text.

Jutta's images and language as she narrates this first sexual encounter
suggest a pre-cultural, natural, and wholesome world full of drives and
desires that cannot be accounted for by popular theoretical models that
would classify women as either virgin or vamp. Before Jutta begins to
describe it, she admits to having had Adam and Eve fantasies while wandering in nature with Florian, fantasies in which the brown-haired Adam
clearly corresponds to Florian. The Adam and Eve story represents both
the idyllic and originary relationship between one man and one woman
but also reminds the reader of the fall brought about by Eve, the temptress
and seducer. Jutta's identification with Eve, as the original woman, the
only woman, the virgin who seduced Adam, undermines the virgin/vamp
distinction, since Eve was neither strictly one nor the other; it implies that
while female sexuality can be mitigated by socialization, it already exists as
a powerful extra-cultural force. Jutta's depiction of the sexual encounter
as an overpowering physical and almost out-of-body experience similarly
emphasizes a natural, pre-cultural element. Although she does not know
where she is going, every drop of blood in her limbs knows the way home.
Her sexuality denies the appropriateness of the "Bürgertöchterchen/Studentin" distinction that she otherwise accepts, because this distinction is a
cultural construction that cannot account for the physical force that overcomes her, not only as she is having a sexual encounter with Florian but
also retrospectively, as she remembers it.

One could certainly take issue with the ideological implications of
imposing an essentialist reading on unfettered and uncontrollable female
sexuality. Yet more important is how Andreas-Salomé uses this image of
female sexuality rhetorically in her fictional text. The reader is brought to

sympathize with Jutta, the naive and virginal young woman, and then, through Andreas-Salomé's manipulation of language, to participate in her powerlessness as she is swept into a sexual experience. Only by invoking and having Jutta ratify the virgin/vamp binary opposition in the first place can Andreas-Salomé emphasize the inadequacy of such limited categories in accounting for woman's experience. By presenting Jutta as a virgin and a firm believer in the moral code that would require her to remain so until marriage, Andreas-Salomé makes her "fall" seem all the more unavoidable. Despite her best intentions, Jutta's awakening sexuality overpowered her. The inconsistencies in Jutta's narration — on the one hand her questionable sincerity because of her fear of a judgmental audience, on the other her apparently sincere admission of sexual fantasies and sexual exhilaration to this audience — reveal the juggling act she performs within her psyche and give expression to the critique of the cultural stereotypes that require such a struggle.

Despite Jutta's implicit and explicit affirmation of the sexual, sentient side of herself, the division in narrating Jutta has not been overcome. When she refers to "diese Jutta" (this Jutta), the Jutta who had Adam and Eve fantasies, as the Jutta "die [ich] ja nicht bloß *war,* nein, die ich *bin*" (who I not only *was,* no, but also *am*), she momentarily casts off the shackles of her superego, valorizing one term of the binary opposition, the sexual, over the other (66). This closure is merely temporary, since it cannot and does not account for a very significant part of Jutta's self-understanding, the traditional "Bürgertöchterchen," bound to the bourgeois moral code. This Jutta recedes after the narration of the sexual encounters, and although she occasionally interrupts the narrative again, she never resurfaces as the narrating, apologetic Jutta the reader had come to know. However, her regression to the then of her narration does not suggest that she has come to terms with herself, but rather that she is suffering from a trauma caused by the renarration of the events.

Jutta's lasting affirmation of herself as the sexual Jutta would require indifference to social and moral codes, but both narrating and narrated Jutta share a motivation that precludes such indifference. Jutta, both as the naive narrated Jutta and as the older narrating Jutta, is driven by a continual awareness of how people see and judge her and by her desire for acceptance and approval. Shortly after she first joins her brother's six friends, he warns her in a letter to behave appropriately — to be neither too innocent *(Bürgertöchterchen)* nor too intellectual *(Studentin)* in their presence. Her desire to comply with her brother's wishes, to present the image that will facilitate both her acceptance and the continued approval of her brother by the group, leads to her involuntary participation in a sexually loaded game and to her passivity in all situations where she has a vague sense that she has been slighted or mocked. After Florian shocks her on the first evening of their excursion by asking if he should ask for one room or two, she decides that she will leave the next morning. At breakfast, however, her concern about how their hosts might perceive and judge her interactions with Florian prevents her from telling him that she intends to leave: "Die Morgenkühle gab denn auch das nächstgelegene Gesprächsthema her, das schon wegen der Wirtsleute nicht zu auffällig stocken durfte. . . . Des Personals wegen wußte ich meinen Entschluß zu sofortiger Rückreise nicht energisch genug klarzustellen" (54; The morning chill gave us something we could chat about without halting and stumbling too noticeably, what with the hotel proprietors right near-by . . . With them there, I wasn't able to make it clear that I was planning to leave right away). Even in the privacy of her own diary, the narrating Jutta, like the narrated Jutta, is obsessed by the potential disapproval of an audience that she projects. She has internalized a moral code and an understanding of female sexuality that foil any conscious or open embrace of her experience.

In this sense Jutta's narrative is a failure. She set out to find an acceptable means of justifying her sexual experience to herself but arrived at a stalemate. In writing about her sexual experiences, she relives them in a positive manner. But in writing, she also recreates the judgmental public that fashions and is fashioned by her own superego, thereby thwarting her attempt to accept her sexual self. The writing process has in fact brought Jutta back to the beginning, back to the definitional dilemma that inspired the narration. She closes with the retelling of her leave-taking from Florian and with a description of herself in the departing train: "Da war nur Jemand, der litt zwischen Tod und Leben, litt wie ein gedrosseltes Tier, und Jemand, der auf dies Tier schweigend achtgab" (90; There was only someone who was suffering between death and life, suffering like a throttled animal, and someone who silently observed this animal). The juxtaposition in the final sentence of "Tier" ("animal") and "Jemand" ("someone") recalls the binary division into natural/instinctive/sexual Jutta and rational/intellectual/moral Jutta that formed the original point of departure for the narrative. Jutta has not made progress; she has come full circle, and the text ends where it began, or begins again where it ends, with the internal rift between the sexual and the moral.

Andreas-Salomé was involved both directly and indirectly in the debate on woman's sexuality. Apart from her essays on women and sexuality, which contributed directly to contemporary public discourse, she also had to tolerate criticism for her own "aberrant" sexual practices. Her ties to such prejudice are in many ways irrelevant to an analysis of the fictional text *Jutta,* which could have been written whether or not she had direct experience of the circumstances represented. But the fact that she experienced this kind of discrimination buttresses the argument for her awareness and critique of the limitations imposed on women's sexuality. *Jutta* celebrates woman's sexual nature and condemns the moral code that scorns this celebration. At the same time, it acknowledges the difficulties that arise when "respectable" women transgress against the stereotypes and ideologies that approve of their chastity. She reveals the inadequacy of a reductive binary categorization that limits the understanding and acceptance of woman in her entire range of possibilities. Through a series of narrative ploys, Andreas-Salomé emphasizes Jutta's dilemma of self-representation and self-acceptance, undermines the contemporary culture's understanding of woman and female sexuality, and criticizes its negative effects on woman's psychic life. By constructing Jutta as a first-person narrator who wants to come to terms with herself as a sexual and sentient being but who has internalized a moral code that conflates sexual woman with amoral/aberrant woman, Andreas-Salomé does not simply add to a multitude of literature already available — including her own essays collected in *Die Erotik* — that made apparently definitive or prescriptive statements on woman's sexuality.[10] Instead she examines the psychological stresses induced in women by the narrow definitions of their sexuality that the culture accepts.

Notes

This chapter is a slightly revised version of an article published in *Seminar.* See Muriel Cormican, "Female Sexuality and The Dilemma of Self Representation," *Seminar: A Journal of Germanic Studies* 36:1 (Feb. 2000): 130–40.

[1] Lou Andreas-Salomé, *Amor, Jutta, Die Tarnkappe: Drei Dichtungen,* ed. Ernst Pfeiffer (Frankfurt am Main: Insel, 1981).

[2] Julie Doll Allen, "Male and Female Dialogue in Lou Andreas-Salomé's *Fenitschka,*" in *Frauen: Mitsprechen, Mitschreiben: Beiträge zu Literatur- und sprachwissenschaftlichen Frauenforschung,* ed. Marianne Henn and Britta Hufeisen (Stuttgart: Akademischer Verlag Hans-Dieter Heinz, 1997), 479–89; and Brigid Haines, "Masochism and Femininity in Lou Andreas-Salomé's *Eine Ausschweifung,*" *Women in German Yearbook* 8 (1993): 97–115.

[3] Cf. also Uta Treder, *Von der Hexe zur Hysterikerin: Zur Verfestigungsgeschichte des "Ewig Weiblichen"* (Bonn: Bouvier, 1984); and Biddy Martin, *Woman and Modernity: The (Life)Styles of Lou Andreas-Salomé* (Ithaca, NY: Cornell UP, 1991).

[4] Julia Kristeva, "Kein weibliches Schreiben? Fragen an *Julia Kristeva,*" *Freibeuter* 2 (1979): 79–84, here 81.

[5] In *Dora,* Freud explains early on why it is acceptable for him to talk about sex with a young unmarried woman. He invokes science as his defense. Because he is a doctor, because they deal with sex and sexuality in a scientific discourse and with the appropriate vocabulary, he assures the reader that there is nothing prurient about his process or its written representation. See Sigmund Freud, *Dora: An Analysis of a Case of Hysteria,* ed. Philip Rieff (New York: McMillan, 1963).

[6] See Peter Gay for an overview of attitudes toward female sexuality at this time. Peter Gay, *The Education of the Senses,* vol. 1 of *The Bourgeois Experience: Victo-*

ria to Freud, 3 vols. (New York: Oxford UP, 1984–93). There was no consensus among "the experts" in the late nineteenth and early twentieth century as to whether women were or were not naturally sensual beings. Many argued against this notion, some argued for it — most of those arguing were male (Gay, *Education of the Senses,* 144–68). Women and men, medics and lay people alike sought to understand what Freud, in suitably colonial and metaphorical language, would later term the "dark continent" of female sexuality. Hysterics and interest in them abounded, and in literature sexuality was a common theme.

[7] Unless otherwise noted, translations from *Jutta* are my own.

[8] Julia Kristeva, *Revolution in Poetic Language,* trans. Margaret Waller (New York: Columbia UP, 1984), 101.

[9] Caroline Kreide, *Lou Andreas-Salomé: Feministin oder Antifeministin? Eine Standortbestimmung zur wilhelminischen Frauenbewegung* (New York: Peter Lang, 1996), 44.

[10] Lou Andreas-Salomé, *Die Erotik: Vier Aufsätze,* ed. Ernst Pfeiffer (Frankfurt am Main: Ullstein, 1985).

4: Motherhood, Masochism, and Subjectivity in *Ma: Ein Porträt*

. . . literature has not provided us with enough stories written from the mother's point of view.

— Shirley Nelson Garner

ANDREAS-SALOMÉ thought very highly of motherhood as a vocation in life and pointed to her own childlessness as one of her only regrets. A recurring theme in her works, motherhood generally constitutes a positive way of being in the world, and motherly feelings toward the Other translate into a laudably intense empathy with that Other. Motherhood takes on ethical dimensions as a model for interpersonal relations, because it binds the self to the Other through love. In *Das Haus* (1904) motherliness dominates Anneliese's relationship to her husband from the last days of her first pregnancy: "Da, in einer linden Sommernacht, geschah es . . . wo ihr plötzlich, in einem inneren Wunder, dies Heiligste aufging: er, der neben dir ruht, ist dein Herr und doch nun auch dein Kind, — du, sein Weib, bist ihm nun doch auch Mutter" (211; And then one soft summer night, it happened . . . suddenly, in what felt like an inner miracle, the holiest of realizations occurred to her: the man sleeping beside you is your master and yet also your child — you, his wife, are now also a mother to him). This combination of caring and self-subordinating sentiment represents Anneliese's first genuine realization of her femininity. A boyish, independent girl devoted to playing her piano before marriage, Anneliese loses sight of everything but her duties as a wife and a mother in this night. Toward the end of the novella *Eine Ausschweifung* (1899), Adine experiences similar motherly feelings for Benno: "Und während ich seinen unsinnigen Küssen nachgab, regte sich in mir etwas Wunderliches, ganz Zartes und beinahe Mütterliches, — die Hingebung einer Mutter, die einem weinenden Kinde lächelnd ihre nahrungschwellende Brust öffnet" (115; "And while I yielded to his insane kisses, something strange stirred in me, something very tender, almost maternal — like the loving devotion of a mother who offers her breast to her crying infant," 84).[1] Benno's position at Adine's feet is repeated in the final image of the novella, when Adine takes the same position at her mother's feet. Having decided to leave Benno for good, Adine entrusts him to her mother. This transfer of responsibility signifies her own refusal of

motherhood, but her brush with motherhood leads Adine to the conclusion that her love life, and consequently her life as "woman," has
been eternally marred. Anticipating Kristeva's essentialist concept of
maternity, Andreas-Salomé makes motherhood the basis of woman's
physical and psychical difference in both of these fictional works, as
well as in her essay "Der Mensch als Weib."

In her 1977 essay "Stabat Mater," Julia Kristeva laments the absence
of an adequate discourse on motherhood and then sets about offering
the beginnings of a more adequate one.[2] Ambling through summaries
of the place of the paradoxical virgin mother in Christianity and of her
own personal experiences with pregnancy, birth, and mothering, Kristeva
participates in the "jamming of the theoretical machinery," to borrow
Irigaray's phrasing, by resisting a linear and clear theoretical narrative.[3]
Finally, Kristeva arrives at the idea of a "herethics," an ethics based on
women's experience of motherhood, the mother's radical experience of
the Other as her child (185). Though stylistically not nearly as experimen-
tal as Kristeva's "Stabat Mater," "Der Mensch als Weib" seeks to jam the
theoretical machinery as well by, among other things, arguing through
implication and by ironically invoking contemporary scientific discourses
on femininity.

The figure "Weib" and her state of "Weiblichkeit" (femininity)
emerge in the first few pages of "Der Mensch als Weib" from a discussion
of the human reproductive process. Beginning with a biological description of conception and what she understands the egg, the embryo, and
the womb to represent, Andreas-Salomé derives a theory of the feminine.
Though she states that femininity precedes motherhood, her understanding of femininity rests on her understanding of motherhood, as if motherhood were a symptom of femininity. She discusses motherhood as a
mystical, organic union with the universe and mothers as paradoxically
self-absorbed and self-abnegating, capable of recognizing the significance
and wonder of the self and reconciling it to that of the Other. Describ-
ing the roles of both men and women in reproduction, she deduces the
major difference between the masculine and feminine principles. While
the man is the more aggressive, active person in the act of reproduction,
she argues, he is only momentarily involved in the process. He acts, but
that act does not consume him. It is brief and then over, and his being
is separated from the act performed. In the case of woman, however, the
act is literally internalized. The woman harbors the result of the act within
herself and releases it only when it is itself a complete Other, a discrete
human being. Although the concept of the feminine that Andreas-Salomé
develops here is dependent neither on real women nor on actual motherhood, it is predicated on the biology of reproduction and on a series of
traditionally accepted dicta on women and mothers, and, for that matter,
on men and fathers too.

Like Andreas-Salomé, Kristeva criticizes the reduction of femininity to motherhood. Like Andreas-Salomé, she then goes on to indulge in the same kind of reduction by elevating maternity to the level of purest interpersonal relationship. But whereas Kristeva claims to be able to disentangle the real from the ideal, insisting that her mother/woman is merely a figure, a non-essentializing metaphor, as it were, Andreas-Salomé acknowledges the difficulty of separating the figure "woman/mother" that she constructs from real women/mothers. In "Der Mensch als Weib," she suggests that femininity, maternity, and masochism can be pried apart and yet all exert a magnetic pull on one another such that the prying apart can be nothing more than temporary. In the novel *Ma* she broaches the subject of motherhood again. Here, however, she complicates earlier depictions of motherhood, qualifying her idealization of it through several divergent voices. Idealizing motherhood, invoking the cult of the virgin mother, and expounding on the beauty of Russian icons of the virgin, she nonetheless undercuts all of this in the end by pointing to these images as aesthetic constructions.

Set in Russia at Christmas, *Ma: Ein Porträt* is the story of a woman who, widowed early in life, must care and provide for two young daughters. Devastated by her husband's death, she is initially listless, withdrawn, and uninterested in her children. Tomasow, a doctor employed by her family to treat her, succeeds in coaxing her back from the brink of death. She enters a long friendship with him and a long period of utter devotion to her daughters. Realizing that someone must care for the children, she reclaims her life and becomes a working and dutiful mother. Much later, the wishes of Ma's daughters to go abroad and study threaten their intimacy and Ma's sense of her own identity that depends on that intimacy. The novel deals with the crisis induced by the imminent departure of Ma's second daughter, Sophie, who reminds her very much of her dead husband. Whether Ma will let Sophie go or not becomes the crux of the novel and the ultimate test of Ma's celebrated motherhood.

Motherhood and Subjectivity

After a trip to Russia with Friedrich Carl Andreas and Rainer Maria Rilke in 1899, Andreas-Salomé began work on *Ma: Ein Portrtät* in September. The threesome had arrived in Moscow in time to see the Easter celebrations of the Russian Orthodox Church, which fascinated both her and Rilke. Enamored of the religiosity of the peasantry and the pomp and circumstance with which they acknowledged and celebrated their belief in God and their adoration of the virgin mother, she romanticized the Russian psyche as primitive and naive. Her delight in Russian Orthodox rituals, in particular the relationship of the congregation to the virgin mother, finds its way into *Ma,* providing background material for both the opening and closing of the novel. Heidi Gidion draws our attention to word-for-word borrowings from descriptions of this trip in Andreas-Salomé's diary in the opening and closing pages of *Ma* and demonstrates how these appropriated diary entries provide a frame of reference for understanding the main character.[4]

Opening with a long description of a procession of the "iberische Mutter Gottes" (Iberian mother of God) — an icon of the virgin mother with her child — through the streets of Moscow, Andreas-Salomé emphasizes the magnificence of this icon and its great significance as an image of comfort and beauty.[5] Ma, the next mother figure we encounter, parallels the "iberische Mutter," representing comfort and beauty to her daughters and returning from her own daily route through the streets of Moscow. At the end of the novel, the "iberische Mutter" has disappeared and, in an action reminiscent of the images of the procession from the opening pages, Ma now descends from the Kremlin to go among the people of Moscow. Together with Ma's masochistic tendencies, the parallels drawn between Ma and the virgin-mother figure have long formed the basis for her reception as superhuman and too-good-to-be-true. Contemporary and more recent critics alike have argued that she is too wholesome a character, overdone in her self-sacrifice and her heroism in all grief.[6] Contemporary critics' objections to Ma on the basis that she is unrealistic reveals a lack of faith in the theoretical idealizations of motherhood of the time and educes Sylvia Bovenschen's argument in *Die imaginierte Weiblichkeit,* namely that the idealization of woman in theory and literature had little to do with the treatment of real women in history.[7] Three significant aspects of the novel modify an understanding of Ma as unconditionally positive, and this chapter brings them to light: the unspoken details of the relationship between Ma and her daughters that pass through her children's minds, Andreas-Salomé's implicit critique of the glorification of suffering in religious art in close proximity to Ma's alignment with religious and sacrificial figures, and the novel's thoroughgoing exploration of masochism in both Ma and her friend Tomasow.

When Rudolph Binion recommends *Ma* because it deals with a subject almost universally neglected by novelists — motherhood and renunciation — he touches on an important issue. Feminist studies of the 1980s and 1990s, such as Jessica Benjamin's *The Bonds of Love* (1988), Daly and Reddy's *Narrating Mothers: Theorizing Maternal Subjectivities* (1991), and Bassin, Honey, and Kaplan's *Representations of Motherhood* (1994), contend that motherhood, in its complexities, has long been ignored in literature and psychoanalysis.[8] Mothers, they argue, have been idealized, sentimentalized, and demonized, but the connection between motherhood and subjectivity has rarely been explored. In fact, some theories suggest that one excludes the other. It is telling, for example, that Freud regarded impregnation and motherhood as the solution to many women's so-called neuroses. Focused on a child, a woman would presumably lose the privilege of obsessing about her own identity and psychological difficulties. Read alongside her theoretical tracts on motherhood, the novel *Ma: Ein Porträt* represents yet another instance of Andreas-Salomé's reluctance to allow her theoretical models to limit accounts of individual experience. While *Ma* does not contradict the concepts of motherhood that Andreas-Salomé elsewhere articulated, it does qualify and complicate them. It also qualifies and complicates the image of mothers and motherhood presented by many of her contemporaries.

Andreas-Salomé's fictional texts rarely present a monologic view of the characters and issues they examine, and *Ma* also does not. It is populated by characters who function both as supporters and critics of Ma's understanding of motherhood as complete self-abnegation. The tension between varying opinions is significant. *Ma* explores the transformation of the parent-child relationship from a state of imagined oneness to a state of separateness and independence, emphasizing the mother's perspective — not, however, to the exclusion of the child's. Read against the backdrop of its time, a time in which conservative feminists and many of Andreas-Salomé's acquaintances idealized a very traditional, middle-class mother and a time in which Freudian psychology silenced mothers by concentrating on the male child's perspective in the mother/child relationship, the novel has to be acknowledged for its attempt to break with such monolithic discourses.[9] Motherhood, as a physical and daily reality and as a psychological phenomenon, was a widely talked about and significant issue for members of the women's movement, opponents of the movement, and, albeit from a different perspective, psychoanalysts.

Many turn-of-the-century antifeminists and feminists alike — including, in places, Andreas-Salomé herself — saw motherhood as woman's biologically ordained and highest calling. In Helene Lange's, Gertrud Bäumer's, and Helene Stöcker's writings about motherhood, for example, motherhood was frequently glorified, and mothers became godlike by virtue of the self-sacrificial and humanly transcendent characteristics that authors projected onto them and depicted as materializing of their own accord as soon as a woman gave birth.[10] Pointing to many turn-of-the-century writings about motherhood as preoccupied with personal experiences in an upper-middle-class society that assumed the help of nannies in raising children, Caroline Kreide argues that the mothers of such texts are inevitably theoretical idealizations that bear little resemblance to the lives of the real women and mothers to whom they refer or to the real women and mothers of the lower classes, whom they ignore.[11] And indeed, Hedwig Dohm, a contemporary and an impassioned feminist of the radical wing of the turn-of-the-century women's movement, does criticize such writings in *Die Mütter: Beitrag zur Erziehungsfrage* for their failure to account for woman's experience and for motherhood in realistic terms:

> Die Gegner der modernen Frauenbewegung freilich sehen in der Mütterlichkeit des Weibes die Verbürgung der Rechte des Kindes. . . . Daß alle seelischen und physischen Kräfte des Weibes nur der Mutterschaft zu dienen haben, daß auf der Mütterlichkeit ihre Genialität beruhe, wird immer wieder mit den Zeusgebärden souveränen Allwissens der Welt verkündet. Wie sich in Wirklichkeit das Leben der Frau als Mutter der Babies abspielt, will ich hier zu schildern versuchen. (1)[12]

> [Of course, the opponents of the modern women's movement see the guarantee of the child's rights in the motherliness of woman . . . Again and again, with the Zeus-like, sovereign authority of omniscience, they announce to the world that all of woman's spiritual and physical energy should be used in the service of motherhood, that the ingenuity of this energy is tied to motherhood. Here I will try to show what a woman's life, as a mother to babies, actually looks like. 1]

"Real" mothers — the poor and struggling mother, the unloving mother, the bad mother, the wealthy but negligent mother, the prostitute mother — are nowhere mentioned. Whatever the reality of motherhood might have been at the time, theoretical and fictional writings often romanticized the mother figure.

Ma, the main character of the novel under discussion here, is at once a product of her time and yet someone who exceeds the expectations for women and middle-class mothers of that time. Representing the point at which the traditional woman and the modern woman intersect, she values her motherhood above all else on the one hand but is, on the other hand, a working mother who must often be away from the household. Her life circumstances have forced her to adopt roles she might not otherwise have adopted, and she has been very successful in them. For her, going out to work is a matter of survival and not something to be chosen or rejected as it is for her daughters, Cita and Sophie. Although she fits neatly into the patriarchal system and has internalized the necessary ideology, her daily life undermines the ideology she embraces. She neither forces nor encourages her daughters to conform to her ideas, never even speaking to them about love, marriage, and motherhood. Despite her own believes and preferences, Ma has succeeded in offering her daughters alternatives to the conformist way of life she initially chose and still regrets losing. Uninterested in women's emancipation, and firmly convinced that a woman's truest happiness is to be found in marriage and motherhood, Ma is nonetheless an enabler for her daughter's emancipation.

By locating Ma at this particular intersection of values and roles, and by introducing characters who mitigate Ma's traditional views on woman and progress, Andreas-Salomé complicates the narrative perspective on Ma.

In opposition to both of her daughters, to her sister, and to Tomasow, Ma is firmly aligned with traditional Russia and with what it represents for Andreas-Salomé, namely a positive lack of progress in both the public (industrialization and alienation) and private (feminism) spheres.[13] While Tomasow criticizes the Russian people as unenlightened, Ma praises their lack of enlightenment, because it translates into a reverence that has long been lost in Western Europeans.[14] Arguing against progress, Ma defends the quality that annoys Tomasow about the Russians he sees around him — their "Zurückbleiben" (61; backwardness). Her preference for what she perceives as their tranquil and unquestioning way of life can be grounded in her personal experience of a hectic life running from job to job every day, something she associates with modernity and progress. Tomasow's perspective, his displeasure with the ignorance he regards as contributing to the impoverished conditions in which the Russian peasantry lives, qualifies Ma's romanticization of their lot and similarly qualifies the romanticized representation of Ma herself.

The criticism that the Russians are "zurückgeblieben" (backward) comes from two other characters as well, from Cita, Ma's eldest daughter, and from Ottilie, Ma's sister. Notably, both Cita and Ottilie are critical of Ma for certain aspects of her motherhood, and both represent a non-Russian, modern standpoint. Cita lives in and is heavily involved with the women's movement in Berlin, and Ottilie prefers the more European city of St. Petersburg to Moscow. Andreas-Salomé juxtaposes Russia to more advanced Western Europe and idealizes elements of a Russian present/Western European past that she believes are on the verge of extinction. Yet despite a heavy nostalgia for the past and for aspects of women's lives before the advent of feminism, she does not condemn the modern woman, the woman who wants to go abroad to study, who dismisses marriage and motherhood. In contrast to her idealization of Russia in *Ródinka,* as well as her nostalgia for Russia's traditional ways and for traditional aspects of motherhood, marriage, and woman's life in general, in *Ma* Andreas-Salomé demonstrates an awareness of the problems of her nostalgia.[15] Details of the novel point to nostalgia's dependence, for example, on a heavily romanticized view of the past that excludes negative experience. By representing oppositional voices in the narrative, voices that emphasize the negative aspects of tradition, of a reverence lacking in critical reflection, Andreas-Salomé acknowledges the flaws in Ma's, and by extension her own, idealized images of the Russian people and their lives. Her depiction of a "modern woman" as a good mother further emphasizes nostalgia's dependence on a blind spot, on the failure, unwillingness, or inability to see that changes in woman's social positions do not necessarily erase women's potential to be good mothers.

Ma's actions and decisions are determined by both selfless and selfish inclinations, and Andreas-Salomé explores the psychological struggle between the two. In her investigation of Ma's transition from being consumed by her motherhood to being independent, she treats maternal ties as inhibiting as well as supportive. By drawing attention to Ma's selfish impulses, she shows that behind Ma's acts of self-sacrifice a self-centered subjectivity coexists with a self-dissolving masochism. Treating Ma as an entity who, almost in spite of herself, can become independent of her children, she resists the equation of motherhood with self-abnegation. Ma's selfish streak manifests itself in her love for her children, which is based, at least in part, on a somewhat unhealthy and unfair dependency, and on an understanding of mother and children as a unit. Hating the daily separation from her nineteen and twenty-one year old daughters that her job necessitates, she wishes, when she sees a mare pulling a cart in the street with her foal trotting alongside her, that women's work could be arranged so as to allow for the same (59). Ma's heavy dependence on her daughters, particularly on Sophie, is implicitly explained by the loss of her husband. After he dies, the children gradually become her raison d'être, and Sophie's likeness to her father is emphasized throughout the novel, as is her surrogacy for her mother's dead husband. She looks like him and coughs like him, and Ma admits that letting Sophie go abroad would be like losing him all over again. Not simply her children, Sophie and Cita are also Ma's link to her lost husband, and, far from a simple and uncomplicated devotion based on complete selflessness, her love for them constitutes a crutch, along with Tomasow, that allows her to begin living again.

In the course of the novel, Ma is forced to clearly define the borders between self and child, so that she can acknowledge Sophie, her younger daughter, as an individual in her own right. Shortly after Sophie reveals her desire to go abroad for the first time, making all of Ma's worst fears an imminent reality, Ma arrives home to find Sophie with a tear-stained face, slumped over the books that represent familial discord, and ponders to herself:

> Konnte die Mutter denn gewähren, was ihr Liebling von ihr heischte? Konnte sie denn wirklich auch die letzte fortlassen? Ganz, ganz allein nachbleiben? Mußte das sein? "Nein! Nein!" schrie es in ihr. ". . . Nimm den Augenblick wahr, wo sie, sich selbst verratend, daliegt, als sei sie dir ausgeliefert. Mache sie zu deinesgleichen, hauche ihr dein Wesen und deine Wünsche ein. Sie ist ja dein." (95–96)

> [Could the mother grant what her darling was begging for? Could she really let the last child go? Stay behind utterly alone? Did it have to be? "No! No!": her whole being shrieked. "Take advantage of this moment in which she is prostrate before you, surrendering to you, ready to betray herself. Shape her in your image, fill her with your being and your wishes. She is, after all, yours."[16]]

Reminding the reader that Ma, despite her selfless devotion to her daughters, has not eradicated her own subjectivity, identity, needs, and desires, these thoughts reveal her inner struggle between selfish and selfless tendencies. In a manner that reflects the complexities and inconsistencies of psychic reality, Andrea-Salomé's female characters are embattled, insecure, inconsistent, and complex, and Ma is no exception.

Ma's dependence on her daughters and her self-interest in them do not just manifest themselves inwardly. Her daughters, in particular Sophie, are very aware of their mother's emotional investment in them, and Andreas-Salomé's treatment of their negotiation of the situation examines and critiques the negative side of a mother's all-consuming love. Although Ma has never explicitly limited Sophie, Sophie feels responsible for and limited by her mother's potential loneliness, as well as guilty about her own desire to go abroad. Her fears about going abroad are not for herself but for her mother. In fact, she criticizes both her own and her sister's ambitions, associating them with the failure to fulfill a debt to their mother: "Du und ich, wir sind undankbare Scheusale! Wir, mit unserm dummen Ehrgeiz" (14; You and I, we're ungrateful monsters. Look at us, with our stupid ambition). Sophie's criticism aligns her for the first time with her sister and discloses what she has so far attempted to conceal from her family: that, like her older sister, she wants to pursue an education in another country.

When Sophie eventually unburdens herself about feeling trapped at home and unable to pursue her goals, her general comments refer to home in the larger sense of Mother Russia but also implicate Ma and their domestic arrangements. A visit by a young man, Hugo Lanz, who fancies himself a poet but is forced by his family into a profession as a salesman, prompts Sophie's evaluation of her own situation. Identifying with him, she unwittingly reveals her sense of home as an oppressive and limiting environment:

"Auf die Art der Beschäftigung kommt es auch nicht an, sondern darauf, daß er [Hugo Lanz] *auch* hinausstrebt — fort, hinaus! Mit dem einzigen Unterschied, daß er das infolge von Gedichten tut. Das schadet aber doch nichts. Die Hauptsache haben wir doch gemeinsam. Auch ihm ist eng, auch er hat allerlei Träume, die er kaum zu Hause zu nennen wagt — auch seine Pläne lassen sich nun einmal nicht zu Hause verwirklichen. Und seine Familie — die hält ihn. Wie sollten wir da nicht sympathisieren?! Wie sehr kann ich ihm das alles nachfüh — ." Sie stockte jäh. (71)

["The particular motivating interest is not so important, just that he too wants to break out — out and away! The only difference is that he wants to do it because of poetry. But that doesn't matter so much. Our primary concern is the same. He too feels confined; he too has all sorts of dreams that he doesn't dare to mention at home. And his family — they're holding him back. How could we not sympathize? I can't tell you how much I can empath — ." She stopped short abruptly.]

Ma's concept of unity with her daughter is shattered by the disclosure of their conflicting wishes, and Sophie's ambition will threaten Ma's stability, whether she lets her go or not. If she does not let her go, her image of herself as a good mother is destroyed; if she does, she relinquishes the one thing that has given her a hold on life for years. Sophie's wish to go abroad creates a crisis for Ma and does not simply present her with another opportunity to do the right thing. Providing to the reader material that points to the dark underbelly of a mother's love and power, Sophie's dilemma underscores the oppressive side of Ma's codependence.

Jessica Benjamin's psychoanalysis of the separation and individuation process in the mother/child relationship provides a useful perspective on the relationship between Ma and Sophie.[17] Because Benjamin emphasizes the child as an independent subjectivity from the beginning, her model facilitates going beyond the mother-infant stage of development to examine the mother-teenage daughter stage as it arises in *Ma*. In *The Bonds of Love* Benjamin discusses the process by which the dependent child learns to separate from the mother. Contesting the notion that this process involves a linear movement from oneness to separateness, she instead sees the relationship between self (child) and other (mother), "with its tension between sameness and difference, as a continual exchange of influence" (49). "It focuses," she continues, "not on a linear movement from oneness to separateness, but on the paradoxical balance between them" (49). Benjamin argues that the independence of the child is achieved through a system of mutual recognition: two subjects, mother and child, must recognize each other as independent beings because, in order to receive the recognition that is necessary to see oneself as independent, one must grant that the other is also independent and capable of giving this recognition. Independence, she therefore implies, is never absolute, since the very recognition that makes it possible derives from a dependence. The paradoxical balance between dependence and independence that Benjamin speaks of is therefore unavoidable in the mother/child relation, but because paradoxes and contradictions can be painful, a normal balance between dependence and independence sometimes breaks down, resulting in a master-slave relation. Sophie's and Ma's relationship appears dangerously close to such a breakdown when Sophie expresses her desire to study abroad.

Without her mother's acknowledgement and approval Sophie cannot establish autonomy. Ma must use the authority she has gained over Sophie to skirt the master-slave relation and allow Sophie to develop a sense of agency. Sophie's older sister, Cita, intervenes, impressing upon her mother that it is clear what Sophie wants, but that she has not yet developed enough independence to articulate it: "Sophie ist doch noch sehr ein Kind. . . . Aber du kannst mir glauben, daß sie darauf brennt zu studieren. Man muß nur erst in ihr alles das klären und ordnen" (115; Sophie is still so much a child. . . . But believe me, she is dying to go to university. We just have to clarify and settle that for her). In the present situation, it is only in Ma's absence and with Cita's encouragement that Sophie can recognize herself as an agent. Like Cita, Tomasow is aware of the delicacy of the situation and, when Ma seeks advice from him, he instructs her to not only approve of Sophie's goals but to insist that she pursue them. Up until now, Ma has fed off Sophie and clung to the "oneness" of the mother-daughter relationship to Sophie's detriment. Now, however, she must come to terms with her youngest daughter's radical separateness from her if their relationship is not to descend irrevocably into a master–slave relationship. While such a relationship promises more immediate gratification for Ma, it would ultimately erase the positive aspects of her motherhood and limit Sophie's development.

The aftermath of Ma's initial and tentative approval of Sophie's goals makes clear that Sophie was teetering on the edge of independence. She suddenly gains the confidence to express her opinions more directly, so that when Ma proposes a compromise, she does not hesitate to laugh at it. She dashes Ma's hopes that they could live together in a small university town in Switzerland where, Ma suggests, they could both have what they wanted. Sophie has already developed a level of independence that allows her to better acknowledge and express her wants and needs. Although Ma does "the right thing," then, it is not second nature to her. She stumbles toward it and realizes it only with tremendous difficulty and pain. Drawing attention to Ma's dependence on Sophie and how that dependence threatens Sophie's individuality, Andreas-Salomé exposes the thin line between mothering and smothering.

Like Ma's dependence on her daughters and her concept of motherhood, the warm and loving environment that she has created for Sophie and Cita is ambivalently presented. Depictions of the three women together in their home abound in thoughts left unsaid and in constant attempts by one daughter to make amends to Ma for something the other has said or implied. On one of her first evenings back from Western Europe, for example, Cita regrets that her mother lacks both a sense for sarcasm and an understanding of the goals of the women's movement. When Ma worries that Sophie's helping out in the kitchen may be the cause of her lack of appetite, Cita considers making a sarcastic feminist remark about women's work in the household, but balks for fear of an overly serious response from Ma and of yet another sacrificial act:

Cita hatte auf den Lippen, zu äußern: "Die berühmte Haushaltungs-
arbeit ist eben lange nicht so gesund, wie ausposaunt wird." Aber sie
schwieg noch immer. Es war so entsetzlich schwer, in Mas Gegen-
wart ein spöttisch gefärbtes Wort mit dem nötigen Selbstbewußtsein
herauszubringen. Wie ein Unrecht wurde es gleich, denn die Mutter
hätte den Spott darin nicht bemerkt. Für Spott fehlte ihr das aufneh-
mende Organ. Sie wäre ihm gleichsam mit offenen Armen entgegengegangen und hätte sie versucht mit vereinten Kräften, mit Citas
eigener Hilfe, ausfindig zu machen, was zu tun sei, — und ob nicht
lieber Ma selber beim Heimkehren von den vielen Stunden jedesmal
erst noch kochen solle. (20)

[It was on the tip of Cita's tongue to say: "That famous house work
isn't nearly as healthy as it's made out to be." But she kept quiet. It
was so incredibly difficult to make a smart remark with the necessary
self-confidence in Ma's presence. It would immediately seem unjust
because her mother wouldn't catch the sarcasm in it. She lacked the
receptive organ for sarcasm. She would have embraced it sincerely
and would have invested all of her energy, with help from Cita, in
figuring out if something could be done — and if it wouldn't be
preferable for Ma herself to cook when she got home from her many
hours of work.]

While Cita's actual concern here seems minor, her critical thoughts
betray a subtle dissatisfaction with Ma's exaggerated concern for Sophie
and indicates that Cita, at least, does not always welcome her mother's
acts of self-sacrifice, even if she appreciates the sentiment behind them.
Home for Cita, Sophie, and Ma is not a simple and uncomplicated environment, and as the novel progresses, the reader grows increasingly aware
of the suppressed tension within the family.[18]
    Ottilie, Ma's sister, further muddies the water with her criticism of
precisely those aspects of Ma's motherhood that are currently causing difficulties for Sophie. Although Ottilie's criticisms of Ma are directly and
immediately undermined by Ma herself, they resonate throughout the
text and seem significant particularly after Ma declines Tomasow's marriage proposal. Ottilie argues that Ma loses herself so much in her motherhood that she retains nothing of herself. In her own defense, Ma claims
such self-abnegation to be the very basis of motherhood and feels sorry
for Ottilie's daughter, whom she perceives as requiring more affection
and attention than her mother gives her. Ma's and Ottilie's reflections
on motherhood undermine each other and offer the reader competing understandings of motherhood, including an understanding of it as
something that does not necessitate self-dissolution and self-subordination. This difference between Ma's and Ottilie's concepts of motherhood resurfaces shortly after Ma has granted Sophie leave to go abroad.

Still flirting with the idea that she can accompany Sophie, she ponders Ottilie's practice of motherhood, interpreting it as inferior to her own: "Wie konnte sie[Marianne] ihr[Ottilie] das deutlich machen! Dieses *Einsein* mit den Kindern, dieses Mutterglück und diese drängende Hingebung in allen Fasern. Dieses Auskosten der vollen Liebe bis auf den letzten Tropfen. Denn *jetzt waren sie zu Hause alle drei doch nur noch wie ein Mensch — nun erst ganz unzertrennlich*" (141; How could she make that clear to Ottilie? This *sense of oneness* with the children, this maternal happiness, and this surging devotion in every single fiber. This savoring of complete love right down to the last drop. For *right now, at home, all three of them were just like one person — for the first time now completely inseparable,* emphasis added).

Ma's belief in the unity of mother and child is an illusion soon to be shattered. Returning home from Ottilie's, she finds Sophie alone and takes the opportunity to mention the hope she has been nurturing that Sophie could study in a small town in Switzerland where Ma could direct a girls' boarding school. At first taken aback, Sophie laughs as at a joke: "Sophies Gefühl war so ganz unwillkürlich gewesen. Aber es verriet, daß Mutter und Kinder *ganz und gar nicht eins waren, eines Wesens, — daß das ein bloßes Trugbild war, ein Traum*" (149; Sophie's reaction had been so involuntary. But it betrayed the fact that mother and children *were not one at all, one being — that this had just been a mirage, a dream,* emphasis added). Ottilie's understanding of motherhood seems more applicable here, and her concept of woman as someone who should not accept self-definition solely in terms of husband and children comes closer to Andreas-Salomé's concept of woman as described in "Der Mensch als Weib" than does Ma's. *Ma: Ein Porträt* might be seen, then, as an exercise in unraveling the implications of the theories of motherhood developed in "Der Mensch als Weib."

Ma is not, to borrow a phrase from *Das Haus,* a "geborene Mutter" (a born mother) to whom everything comes easily (19). After her husband's death she must learn to come back to life in order to care for her daughters. Her love for her husband threatens her very existence, and she forgets her daughters for a while, only to then transfer an all-consuming, self-effacing love onto them. Now Sophie's imminent departure threatens to engulf Ma in the same self-destructive misery brought on by widowhood. Rather than present masochistic and self-sacrificing aspects of motherhood as "natural" in this novel, Andreas-Salomé points to them as the result of circumstances and to motherhood as a challenge, a series of negotiations, and a process of learning by trial and error. Ma struggles to overcome her own selfishness and to simply recognize that part of what appears to be selflessness is in fact its opposite. In characteristic fashion, Andreas-Salomé creates a character about whom the close reader can only feel ambivalent. On the one hand, she romanticizes Ma's great love for her children. On the other hand, she exposes the imperfections of such love.

The mother figure Andreas-Salomé idealizes is thus similar to and more complex than the virgin-mother figure that dominates the opening pages and sets the stage for understanding Ma. She qualifies the very positive religious imagery of the opening scenes by, among other things, associating Ma with Christ himself. Sitting on a church bench after realizing that she has lost Tomasow's companionship, and attempting to come to terms with the knowledge that she is now "ganz allein" (quite alone), Ma glances up and catches sight of a painting of Jesus: "Wo sie eben hereingetreten waren, blickte von der Tür ein großes dunkles Christusbild zu ihr nieder, die Züge kaum kenntlich, ein schwarzer Fleck, umhüllt und umkleidet von unendlichem Goldglanz. Sie starrte daraufhin, bis sie vor Tränen nichts mehr sah. Rätsel hinter Gold" (171; Right where they had entered, a large, dark image of Christ gazed down upon her, the features barely intelligible, a black spot, enveloped and enwrapped in an infinite golden luster. She stared at it until she could scarcely see anything else for tears. A mystery behind the gold). The painting, described from her perspective, conceals and disguises something. Both "umhüllt" and "umkleidet" suggest a covering up/shrouding, the obfuscation of something else with a golden gleam. The golden gleam distorts and obscures the features of the figure portrayed and conceals something of quite a different color: "ein schwarzer Fleck." Ma's contemplation of this image of Jesus implies that the idealization of self-sacrifice and the glorification of suffering obscure darker implications, complexities, and mysteries such as the pain and suffering that she is currently enduring. The artwork, an aestheticized form that is traditionally seen as celebrating beauty and capable of eliciting the sublime, must often conceal negative aspects of its subject in the name of beauty, thereby falsifying its subject to a degree. On the other hand, the artwork, as is the case in this instance in *Ma,* simultaneously gestures toward what has been concealed and reveals that an obscured puzzle exists — the "schwarzer Fleck" and the distorted features.

When read as referring to both *Ma* and the painting, the ending of the passage quoted above — "Rätsel hinter Gold" — offers the reader a critique of the idealization of self-sacrifice in religious imagery, as well as a reading strategy for *Ma,* whose subtitle — *Ein Porträt* — further supports the parallel I suggest. Andreas-Salomé appeals to her reader to look beyond the surface idealization of her subject, to discover a more complex set of motivations for Ma's actions, and to grapple with the puzzle of Ma's subjectivity and identity. This passage, whether intentionally or not, also offers a reading strategy for Andreas-Salomé's works as a whole, but in particular for her theoretical works. Just as the author admires the aesthetics of the artwork but can acknowledge its shortcomings, she admires the aesthetics of theory and yet acknowledges its shortcomings. Theory is no less a fiction than art, no less a story than a novel, and should be read as such. In the case of the combination woman/mother/masochist, theory, be it Andreas-Salomé's or Kristeva's, has promised final harmony but has provided not harmony but cacophony. The cacophony suggests, furthermore, that Julia Kristeva's bemoaning of the absence of an adequate discourse on motherhood in 1977 may be misguided. That is, if Andreas-Salomé is representative, and she certainly demonstrates significant overlaps with French feminist theory, then we may have an abundance of discourse on motherhood masquerading as a discourse on the feminine. Thus what we lack may not be an adequate discourse on motherhood but an adequate discourse on the feminine as separate from motherhood.

The final description of Ma echoes the description of the Jesus painting, which underscores how aestheticization obscures; the strength of self-sacrifice is emphasized to the practical exclusion of its negative implications. Ma does seem encouraged and helped by the idealized image of self-sacrifice, however, and while we have no direct access to her psychic ruminations at this juncture, she pulls herself together outwardly, puts on a positive front, and hides her pain as she walks away. Significantly though, our final image of Ma is from the perspective of an aspiring artist. As Hugo Lanz observes Ma walking away from the Kremlin, he sees a figure surrounded by beautiful colors, including gold — a picture, a work of art:

> Denn in ihm arbeitete sich irgendein Bild mit mächtiger Gewalt zu künstlerischer Klarheit hindurch — ein Bild, in dem er Ma vor sich sah — ein Bild, in dem ihr Glück lebte und ihr Vereinsamen und ihr Weh und ihr Sieg — ein Bild, in dem geheimnisvoll lebte, was in diesem Augenblick in ihr selbst wohl nur in dunklen Ahnungen rang. (174)

> [Because within him an image was forcefully materializing with artistic clarity — a picture in which he saw Ma in front of him — a picture in which her happiness was alive and her loneliness and her pain and her victory — a picture that gave mystical life to this vague internal churning that she was currently experiencing].

This closing image has long provoked criticism of Andreas-Salomé's romanticization of Ma's suffering and self-sacrifice, but seeing it as a romanticization necessitates ignoring the implications of the preceding pages, which are repeated in Lanz's image of Ma. He is not oblivious to the fact that part of what attracts him to this image is the almost invisible and thus mysterious inner turmoil. Even here, Andreas-Salomé stresses that a positive portrayal does not preclude attention to negative details. Treating Hugo Lanz's perspective on Ma as one that is heavily influenced by an artistic sensibility that she has already questioned, she creates space for the darker implications of Ma's current state. Given the body of work Andreas-Salomé produced, it would also appear that she points here to what I deduce is her own programmatic stance on art. Rather than ignore complexities, contradictions, and ambiguities for the sake of a unified picture, art, as she practiced and pondered it, attempts to represent life in all of its convolutions and inconsistencies.

Masochism and Subjectivity

In a number of her fictional works written between 1896 and 1904 (*Eine Ausschweifung, Das Haus, Menschenkinder,* and *Amor*), Lou Andreas-Salomé takes up the problem of woman's masochistic tendencies. Refusing to see masochism as an innate feminine quality, as woman's automatic response to the world, she examines and explores it as a feature of feminine subjectivity under patriarchy, and as one of the only legitimate channels for the expression of sexual desire open to women under patriarchy.[19] She presents it as a complex construct influenced by social and cultural conditions, expectations, and ideologies, and as a changing and shifting construct much different from Krafft-Ebing's and Freud's more universal versions of masochism.[20] Andreas-Salomé neither celebrates nor condemns masochism in women but investigates its effects on female subjectivity and identity in the changing context of late nineteenth- and early twentieth-century Europe, in which the women's movement had begun to articulate new models for feminine identity and subjectivity. Her treatment of masochism in *Ma* demonstrates how she interacted with, participated in, and contributed to contemporary discourses on women and psychology.

In *Ma* Andreas-Salomé undermines the assumption that feminine masochism is an essential female trait. She suggests that non-pathological masochism does not manifest itself exclusively in women as Krafft-Ebing believed, and, in response to contemporary feminists who disdained the masochistic tendencies that, from their perspective, patriarchal culture had imposed upon women, she maintains an ambivalence toward it, treating it as a phenomenon that at once threatens woman's autonomy and self-assertion and at the same time creates the basis for autonomy and self-assertion. In its refusal to condemn women's tendency to subordinate themselves, the paradox she embraces complicates not only traditional representations of masochism but also contemporary feminists' negative reactions to those representations.

Krafft-Ebing names masochism, a pathological, sexual disorder found primarily in men, in *Psychopathia Sexualis* (1886). He presents the reader with a series of case studies of men who have fantasies of being whipped and concludes that all such fantasies of flagellation are subsidiary to the idea of subjection to the will of a woman. Masochism, for Krafft-Ebing, is a manifestation in the male of particularly feminine instincts. Whereas he sees it as normal or inevitable that women develop instincts of subordination and subjection to their partners, he considers such instincts aberrant or pathological in men. Freud too saw masochistic tendencies as normal in women. Even as late as 1924 in "The Economic Problem of Masochism," he reminds the reader that feminine masochism is so called because its fantasies "place the subject in a characteristically female situation; they signify, that is, being castrated, or copulated with, or giving birth to a baby" (277). It follows from this that the "characteristically female situation" is essentially masochistic. Freud's analysis, like Krafft-Ebing's, makes it clear that what can be psychologically problematic when found in a man is characteristic of women. Concepts of woman as inherently self-sacrificing, self-abnegating, and self-subordinating were, of course, not novel for the time, but the solidification of such stereotypes in scientific, sexological, psychoanalytic, psychological, and medical literature under the rubric of masochism invested them with an authority that would prove difficult to undermine.

Women are "castrated"; thus they are inferior and their identity is based on a lack. Women are "copulated with"; thus they are dominated and passive. And women give birth; thus they exist beyond themselves in someone else. Ma demonstrates all of these characteristics. Although she works hard as a teacher, she does so only to make money to support her daughters, seeing her work as a necessary means to an end and regretting the amount of time it consumes. Returning home to her daughters, whose pleasure she enjoys vicariously, is her greatest joy. In fact, each time Ma asks Tomasow, her supportive male friend, to visit or to prolong a visit, she does so because she hopes his presence will please her daughters. Scoffing at Tomasow's desire to provide her with a spread of fruit so that he might view her pleasure, she simply responds: "Dummes Zeug" (64; silly stuff). In order to survive her husband's death, Ma must find a locus of self-abandonment and she does so in her daughters, eventually losing all sense of a self unconnected from them. Depicted as the complex psychic development of a woman destroyed by the loss of a deeply loved husband, masochism plays a defining role in the formation of Ma's new identity. Paradoxically masochism, which is associated with the suspension of identity and the promotion of self-dissolution, here forms the basis of a renewal of self. Ma's masochistic or self-sacrificing relationship to her daughters is not solely selfless. Her loss of self, her ability to overcome her self-absorption is the only thing that saves her from destruction after her husband's death. Her devotion to her children is a loss of self that saves the self, a defense mechanism against self-annihilation. Sophie's impending departure years later looms large as a threat to the stability of Ma's renewal, because it forces Ma back upon herself and out of the self-effacing and dependent relationship that has defined her for years. In *Masochism in Modern Man,* Theodor Reik underscores the paradox, what he calls the "impression of paradox," inherent in masochism, explaining how the masochist acts in a manner that appears to be self-defeating in order to gain an advantage: "The masochist is comparable to a person who 'intentionally' goes astray in order to reach his secret aim by a detour" (203).[21] While Ma's aim then may be self-preservation, her actions imply its opposite.

The ending of *Ma* offers an example of this "impression of paradox." Ma's rejection of Tomasow's proposal seems lamentable, the result of yet another act of subordination to her daughters and their desires. Yet this apparently masochistic decision results in the rejection of a masochistic marital relationship and in the acceptance of her ultimate independence. Ma understands the heterosexual marital relationship to be the cornerstone of a woman's happiness. More than anything else, she wishes that her daughters find the sort of love she enjoyed, even if it were to last only as short a time and end as tragically as hers did: "Wenn über meine Kinder *mein* Glück käme — ein so unfaßbares Frauenglück, das reicher und weiser macht, als alle Reichtümer und Weisheiten der ganzen Welt zusammengenommen — wenn ihnen das geschenkt würde! — — Und wären es auch nur acht kurze Jahre, wie bei mir, gleichviel. Und käme auch selbst dahinter — wie bei mir" (54; If my children were to experience my happiness — such an incomprehensible female happiness that makes you richer and wiser than the cumulative wealth and wisdom of the entire world — if they were to have that bestowed upon them! — And even if it were only for eight short years, as in my case. And even if it were followed by — what happened to me). Despite her overt masochistic tendencies, the relationship Ma describes between herself and her husband does not suggest a master–slave relationship in which she played slave. Looking at a picture of her dead husband, in which he seems particularly young, Tomasow expresses surprise at the success of the marriage, because he has always seen Ma as a woman who needed someone above her and he cannot imagine this young man in a dominant role: "Mir hat es doch immer scheinen wollen, als ob in Ihnen ein starkes Bedürfnis ist nach einer Überlegenheit neben Ihnen — nach jemand, zu dem Sie aufblicken" (36; It has always seemed to me that you have an irrepressible need for a superior presence next to you — for someone you can look up to). Ma responds: "Oh über uns beiden war ja so viel — über uns beiden! . . . Wozu noch eine andre Überlegenheit? Wir wandelten, ineinander geschlungen, gemeinsam unter so hohen Träumen, so hohen Zielen entgegen" (36–37; Oh there was so much above us both — above us both! . . . Why bother with another superiority? Entwined in one another, we strolled along together amidst such lofty dreams and toward such lofty goals). Ma's description of her relationship to her husband differs significantly from the relationship that both she and Tomasow imagine would develop between them were she to accept his proposal. He sets great store in the companionship and strength he can offer her after Sophie's departure: "Nur wissen, — wissen, daß Sie keineswegs so *selbstherrlich* allein dastehen werden . . ." (161; Just know, — know that you will not have to endure a life of *mannish self-reliance,* emphasis added). The use of the word "selbstherrlich" is interesting because the combination selbst/Herr suggests Ma's position at this point — lord and master over herself. Tomasow, in marrying Ma, would take this solitary independence away from her. He imagines himself as the lord and master on whom Ma would depend, to whom she would look up: "Ja, Hütte oder Palast, das war fast das gleiche: in beiden Fällen ward der Mann der Fürst, der Herr vor seinem Weibe, das von ihm sein Leben empfing" (164; Yes, whether one lived in a shack or a palace, it was practically the same: in both cases, the man was the prince, lord over his wife, who received life through him). The vocabulary employed to describe Ma's reaction to Tomasow's proposal suggests a force, a compelling authority, one to which Ma begins to succumb, but which she then ultimately resists: "Es war gerade, als *risse* Tomasow mit ein paar *gewaltsamen Griffen* den Vorhang von irgendeiner fremden Landschaft zurück, so daß sie plötzlich bewußt werden *sollte:* nur ein Vorhang scheide sie davon" (161; It was just as if Tomasow had, with *a couple of violent tugs, torn open* a curtain to expose some kind of unfamiliar landscape that suddenly made her aware that only a curtain separated her from it, emphasis added). The lead-up to Ma's rejection of Tomasow's marriage proposal focuses on the masochistic nature of the relationship that would evolve.

Given Haines's analysis of Adine's masochistic tendencies in *Eine Ausschweifung* — she treats masochism as a pathological desire to subordinate oneself to a man — it is surprising that she would see Ma's reluctance to accept Tomasow's marriage proposal at the end of this novel as problematic because of its masochistic origins. After all, an acceptance of the marriage proposal would also have been traceable to her masochism. To be sure, Haines rightly argues that masochistic tendencies push Ma toward the rejection of the marriage proposal and that Ma sees self-sacrifice as intimately linked to motherhood. If Ma were to lose the pain she feels, to give in to a promise of pleasure unrelated to her daughters' pleasure, it would cost her her motherhood, because she equates motherhood with sacrificial acts made in the name of her daughters. This equation (motherhood = sacrifice/suffering) constitutes an internalized and personal psychological reality, and its specificity to Ma can be gleaned from Andreas-Salomé's failure to explain exactly why Ma sees marriage to Tomasow as distancing her even further from her daughters than their emigration will. Logical explanations of Ma's thought process here would simply serve the purpose of generalizing a concept of motherhood for all women, something Andreas-Salomé seeks to avoid. Something within and specific to Ma, whether learned or natural, makes the denial of her own pleasure the proof of her true motherhood, and by not explaining the reasons behind it, Andreas-Salomé represents it as an arbitrary psychic phenomenon whose arbitrariness makes it no less compelling for the person who experiences it. By resisting the rationalization of Ma's decision, she indicates that alternatives exist, that Ma is not necessarily representative. Andreas-Salomé depicts Ma as at once a victim of a society's idealization of maternal self-sacrifice and yet also as a willing participant in her own victimization. But regardless of the reasons for her rejection of Tomasow, ultimately she rejects a marriage based on self-subordination and the acceptance of Tomasow as her lord and master. Ironically, then, the masochistic tendencies that have resulted in her absolute devotion to her daughters save her from her masochistic tendencies now and force greater independence upon her.

In her essay on *Eine Ausschweifung* Brigid Haines refers to *Ma* in an aside, arguing that Andreas-Salomé glorifies "the masochistic sacrifices involved in motherhood . . . without problematizing what this means for the women involved" (98). However, in her treatment of religious imagery and paintings in the narrative, in her inclusion of voices that undermine Ma's perspective, and in her comprehensive treatment of masochism, Andreas-Salomé does precisely what Haines accuses her of not doing: she acknowledges the negative aspects of glorifying suffering. Ma's self-sacrifices are not exclusively elevating, and she suffers for her decision to reject Tomasow's marriage proposal. If she appears at the end of the novel as an envoy from some higher religious being, she does so from the perspective of a young and inexperienced artist whose tendency is to privilege the aesthetic at the expense of a somewhat more complicated reality. Neither celebrating nor condemning maternal masochism, Andreas-Salomé investigates its effects on female subjectivity and identity. Her treatment of masochism, as something that threatens woman's autonomy and self-assertion on the one hand but that also creates the basis for autonomy and self-assertion on the other hand, complicates her representation of it, revealing both positive and negative implications. Masochism becomes, paradoxically, both the cause of woman's desire to be subordinate to a male partner and the power to withstand that desire.

A locus of the complex intersection of a variety of masochistic and other tendencies, Ma is neither "naturally" masochistic nor "naturally" a good mother. Her mothering instincts, her particular and personal understanding of motherhood and its masochistic tendencies, have developed within specific social contexts and have been determined by personal circumstances. Her brief elation at the prospect of marrying Tomasow, for example, is based on the thought that marriage would allow her time to rise above the daily tasks and responsibilities that now consume her:

Führte er sie nicht hinauf auf einen Berg und zeigte ihr der Welt Herrlichkeit — jene Herrlichkeit, die man zu eigenem Genießen haben kann, in der man sich selbst leben kann, sich sättigen in allem Angenehmen und Erfreulichen des Daseins? Führte er sie nicht hinweg aus der Alltagsniederung mit ihrer einseitigen, bitteren Mühsal, mit der armseligen paar Aufgaben, die ihre Kraft aufgesaugt, sie gedemütigt und unfähig gemacht hatten zu eigener, breiterer Entfaltung? (165)

[Was he not leading her out onto a mountain to show her the splendor of the world — that splendor that one can enjoy all to oneself, in which one can be oneself, satiate oneself with all the pleasures and joys of existence? Was he not leading her out of the indignity of the everyday, with its one-sided, bitter hardship, with those miserable few tasks that sapped her energy, humiliated her and made her incapable of her own broader self-fulfillment?]

Focusing on the personal and real circumstances that make masochistic submission attractive to a woman, Andreas-Salomé undermines "natural" female masochism. She depicts a complex network of ambivalences in cultural terms as a telling counterexample to essentialist feminine stereotypes of the time. Denaturalizing supposedly feminine characteristics, she shows them to be influenced and motivated by cultural and discursive aspects of the contemporary cultural imagination.

Andreas-Salomé's investigation of masochism in *Ma* is not confined to the title character, since Tomasow too exhibits masochistic tendencies. Brigid Haines argues convincingly that Andreas-Salomé examines masochism in *Eine Ausschweifung* in order to suggest that contrary to contemporary popular belief women can suffer from pathological masochism.[22] In this novel she complements *Eine Ausschweifung*'s treatment of masochism in women, because her depiction of Tomasow challenges an understanding of masochism in men as exclusively pathological. For years he participates knowingly and willingly in a relationship in which he plays second fiddle to Ma's daughters and in which he is primarily Ma's counselor and a source of strength and amusement for her daughters. On one occasion when Tomasow meets Ma in the street buying grapes to take home to Cita and Sophie and delighting in the pleasure they will give her daughters, she invites him home for the same reason: "Aber wir sind wirklich gleich zu Hause! Wollen Sie nicht ein wenig mit hinaufkommen? Die Kinder würden so froh sein" (64; But really, we're almost at home. Don't you want to come up for a little bit? The children would be delighted). Partially in jest, partially seriously, Tomasow accuses her of treating him like a bunch of grapes. He becomes something she can take home to her daughters to make them happy: "Ein klein wenig garstig waren auch Sie. Daß Sie mich Ihren Kindern mitbringen wollten, — gleichsam eine zweite Tüte, neben den Trauben" (65; You were a little bit mean yourself too, wanting to bring me along to your children, — a second goody bag, so to speak, like the one with the grapes).

The terms of Tomasow's oral contract with Ma force him to help her in ways that postpone his wishes. Having fallen in love with her very soon after their first meeting, he hopes that he might one day marry her and believes that if she fails to find her feet financially and otherwise she will be thrown into a relationship of dependency on him. Creating the conditions for his wishes to remain unfulfilled by promising Ma to help her overcome her limitations and to support her in bad times, so that she can become an independent supporter of her two children, he subordinates his wishes and desires to hers:

> Ein so starker Appell an seine eingreifende, planvolle Kraft ging von diesen ruhig vertrauenden Augen aus, — *eine so starke Freude* an der ihm auferlegten Verantwortung weckten sie in ihm, als spannten sich alle Fähigkeiten seiner Seele auf ein Ziel hin. Und seltsam: *gleichzeitig empfand er es noch nie so bitter* wie in der Stunde, nicht selber zwiespaltlos und einheitlich, mit voller Tatkraft, im Boden seiner Heimat zu wurzeln. (45–46, emphasis added)

> [There emanated from these quiet, trusting eyes such an appeal to his intervening, strategic strength, — they awakened *such healthy pleasure* in him, pleasure in this responsibility placed upon him; it was as if all of the faculties of his soul were straining toward one goal. And, oddly, *at the same time, he had never had such a painful awareness* of the fact that he himself was not firmly rooted in his native country, unconflicted and integrated.]

The combination of contradictory feelings — joy and bitterness — that Andreas-Salomé describes in Tomasow at this moment further evokes masochistic leanings, as does his friend Wera Petrowna's suggestion that in his relationship to Ma he makes himself a patient (125). Furthermore, Tomasow uses the adjectives "unversiegbar" and "sieghaft" (irrepressible and victorious) to describe Ma, implying her superiority and unattainability, attributes that he has enabled: "Was sie so schön und sieghaft aussehen ließ, führte stets irgendwo auf einen Einfluß, ein Zureden, einen Rat von ihm zurück: und bei ihrer ganzen Art, so tief und inbrünstig zu leben, lag in dieser Mitarbeit daran etwas, was seinen Ehrgeiz wunderlich erregte"(123; Everything that made her appear so beautiful, so triumphant could be traced back to some influence, cajoling, or advice from him. And his contributions to her whole manner of living so intently and fervently excited his ambition in a whimsical way).

In Andreas-Salomé's repertoire of characters Tomasow represents something new. A middle-aged doctor, he is, unlike Branhardt in *Das*

Haus, not authoritarian, and he promotes a reversal of the traditionally gendered scenario by accepting his role as a great man behind a great woman. His choices in this regard are not portrayed as perverse or inappropriate. In fact the relationship between Ma and Tomasow approximates what Jessica Benjamin calls mutual recognition: the constant vacillation between dependence and independence that does not dissolve into the master-slave relation that both he and Ma envision in positive terms as marriage. Tomasow's fantasies about marriage as a relationship of mastery over a woman, demonstraes that he is not solely masochistic. He endures his relationship to Ma as a subordinate in hopes of a final reward but must face disappointment instead in the infinite deferral of desire that accompanies her rejection of his marriage proposal.

Tomasow and Ma parallel each other. While Ma lives for her daughters, looks forward to seeing them, enjoys their pleasure, and subordinates her own desires to theirs, Tomasow is committed to Ma, looks forward to seeing her, enjoys her pleasure (gives her gifts and wants to provide her with fruit as she wants to provide her daughters with fruit), and subordinates his own desire to hers. A dream of perfect unity motivates both relationships, but the "masochists" in each relationship, whether consciously or otherwise, continually work against the possibility of this perfect unity. Ma encourages her daughters to value and pursue an education, and Tomasow helps Ma to find paid work that makes her independence from him possible. Tomasow and Ma's relationship relies, then, upon the masochistic dynamic set forth by Gilles Deleuze in *Coldness and Cruelty.*[23] It is based on an oral contract in which the satisfaction of Tomasow's sexual desire is always deferred. Indeed, in trying to characterize Tomasow's desire, his friend, Wera Petrovna, speculates that he seeks in a relationship "ein Leben, das mehr verführt als befriedigt" (a life that seduces more than satisfies), further suggesting Deleuze's interpretation of masochism as the endless deferral of the satisfaction of desire (126). As in *Fenitschka,* Andreas-Salomé strays from the conventional culmination of the male/female relationship in sexual or marital union, dashing not only Tomasow's desires within the narrative but, in all likelihood, the learned desires for the "happily ever after" shared by many readers of the narrative. Despite his desires and interests, Ma's and Tomasow's relationship remains platonic. Eager to continue with a platonic relationship, Ma loses Tomasow, who cannot maintain his side of the relationship without at least the anticipation of erotic fulfillment.

Not only in this novel, but throughout Andreas-Salomé's fictional corpus, the reader is confronted with ambiguities and contradictions that make it impossible to determine what her ideal woman, mother, man, or marital relationship was. Her ambivalence allows for an investigation of psychological phenomena in women that does not deny women's own complicity in their subordination and that neither condemns nor glorifies such complicity. Dealing with stereotypes in a productive way, she acknowledges the reality of some aspects of stereotypes while stressing that to grant a stereotype or theoretical model absolute accuracy is to fail to account for the complexity of individuals, to limit individuals socially in a problematic way, and to inhibit their self-development. Ma is certainly a very positive figure, and her descriptions of traditional women's roles are indeed infused with nostalgia, but arguments that she is merely idealized and that Andreas-Salomé portrays her positively because she is self-sacrificing and masochistic detract from the complexity and interest of the text. If Ma represents some ideal of motherhood, she does so not because she is completely self-sacrificing and revels in self-effacement but because she is a mother who, in the end, pushes herself toward the independence that frees her children to do what they want to do.

Notes

The epigraph at the start of this chapter is from Shirley Nelson Garner, "Constructing the Mother: Contemporary Psychoanalytic Theorists and Women Autobiographers," in *Narrating Mothers: Theorizing Maternal Subjectivities*, ed. Brenda O. Daly and Maureen T. Reddy (Knoxville: U of Tennessee P, 1991), 76–93, here 76.

[1] Lou Andreas-Salomé, *Fenitschka and Deviations: Two Novellas*, trans. Dorothee Einstein Krahn (Lanham, NY, and London: UP of America, 1990).

[2] See Julia Kristeva, "Stabat Mater," in *The Kristeva Reader*, ed. Toril Moi (New York: Columbia UP, 1986), 160–86.

[3] Luce Irigaray, *This Sex Which Is Not One*, trans. Catherine Porter with Carolyn Burke (Ithaca, NY: Cornell UP, 1985), 78.

[4] Heidi Gidion, "Nachwort," in *Ma: Ein Porträt*, by Lou Andreas-Salomé (Frankfurt am Main: Ullstein, 1996), 189.

[5] Gidion explains that this icon was of such importance that it was driven through the streets of Moscow on an almost daily basis in the late nineteenth- and early twentieth-centuries (189).

[6] For contemporary reviews see Eduard Platzhoff, "Ma," *Das literarische Echo* 4 (1901): 1573–74. Platzhoff concludes in his short review that Andreas-Salomé should perhaps concentrate on something other than her fiction for a while: "Der Verfasserin sagen wir: auf Wiedersehen. Vielleicht giebt sie uns nun erst ihre gesammelten Aufsätze über religiöse und sexuelle Probleme, die vermutlich noch von anderen als mir ungeduldig erwartet werden" (1574; We'll bid goodbye to the author. Perhaps she will soon present us with her collected essays about religious and sexual problems for which, I assume, others are waiting as impatiently as I). See also Arthur Eloesser, "Neue Bücher," *Neue Deutsche Rundschau* (1901): 652–62. Eloesser's review is not particularly negative but takes issue with the religious affect of the final pages and the practical beatification of Ma. See also Rudolph Binion's *Frau Lou: Nietzsche's Wayward Disciple* (Princeton, NJ: Princeton UP, 1968), 251–52; Angela Livingstone's *Lou Andreas-Salomé: Her Life and*

Work (New York: Moyer Bell, 1984), 213–14; and Brigid Haines, "Masochism and Femininity in Lou Andreas-Salomé's *Eine Ausschweifung*," *Women in German Yearbook* 8 (1993) for more recent criticisms of the character. Haines similarly sees Ma as too wholesome and adds that her masochism is affirmed without adequate consideration of its negative implications (98).

[7] Silvia Bovenschen, *Die imaginierte Weiblichkeit: Exemplarische Untersuchungen zu kulturgeschichtlichen und literarischen Präsentationsformen des Weiblichen* (Frankfurt am Main: Suhrkamp, 1979).

[8] Jessica Benjamin, *The Bonds of Love: Psychoanalysis, Feminism, and the Problem of Domination* (London: Virago, 1988); Brenda O. Daly and Maureen T. Reddy, "Introduction," in *Narrating Mothers: Theorizing Maternal Subjectivities,* ed. Daly and Reddy (Knoxville: U of Tennessee P, 1991), 76–93; and Donna Bassin, Margaret Honey, and Meryle Mahrer Kaplan, *Representations of Motherhood* (New Haven: Yale UP, 1994).

[9] In *Beyond the Pleasure Principle* (1920, so even much later than *Ma*), for example, Freud's focus is on the child's coping mechanisms as evidenced in the *fort/da* game. Sigmund Freud, *Beyond the Pleasure Principle*, trans. James Strachey (New York: W. W. Norton, 1961).

[10] See especially Helene Lange, *Kampfzeiten* (Berlin: F. A. Herbig, 1921); Gertrud Bäumer, *Die Frau und das geistige Leben* (Leipzig: C. F. Amelangs, 1911); and Helene Stöcker, *Die Liebe und die Frauen* (Minden, Germany: Bruns, 1908). Kreide offers an excellent summary of the Wilhelmenian Feminists' stance on motherhood in *Lou Andreas-Salomé: Feministin oder Antifeministin? Eine Standortbestimmung zur wilhelminischen Frauenbewegung* (New York: Peter Lang, 1996), 98–104. Of course, the idea that motherhood involves an automatically loving devotion to one's child and the transformation of any woman into a self-sacrificing individual whose own needs and desires are subsumed by the needs and desires of her children persists today and is perhaps a necessary part of the myth of motherhood with which society attempts to produce good mothers.

[11] Kreide, *Lou Andreas-Salomé: Feministin oder Antifeministin,* 103–4.

[12] Hedwig, Dohm. *Die Mütter: Beitrag zur Erziehungsfrage* (Berlin: S. Fischer Verlag, 1903).

[13] See, for example, Andreas-Salomé's poem *Altrußland* (Old Russia)in *Lebensrückblick,* ed. Ernst Pfeiffer (Frankfurt am Main: Insel, 1968. In the first verse, she writes: "Du (Rußland) scheinst in Mutterhut zu ruhn, Dein Elend kaum noch zu begreifen, So kindhaft scheint all Dein Tun, Wo andre reifen" (73; You seem to rest as in a mother's safe-keeping, your misery is scarcely to be fathomed, your activity seems so childlike, whereas others are maturing). Ma is related to Russia in her defense of the Russian people and their unenlightened nature and in her association with the strongly honored virgin mother figure, "d[er] iberische[n] Mutter Gottes." She is praised by the other staunchly Russian women in the novel for her commitment to her motherhood, and each regrets the fact that the family will be split up.

[14] In general, Andreas-Salomé associates reverence with the lack of critical thought and enlightenment and waxes nostalgic about it. She tends to idealize a certain kind of primitiveness and to project onto the simple life a greater unity with nature

and the world and an acceptance of one's lot, including one's biological lot. She believes that reverence and the direct relationship to nature that it indicates are being destroyed by progress in Western Europe.

[15] Lou Andreas-Salomé, *Ródinka: Russische Erinnerung,* 1923 (1923; repr., Frankfurt am Main: Ullstein, 1985).

[16] Unless otherwise noted, translations from *Ma* are my own.

[17] Benjamin, *The Bonds of Love.*

[18] The depiction of the home environment is far more complicated and interesting, for example, than the heavily romanticized home environment of the immensely popular *Little Women* by Louisa May Alcott. A much more traditional Bildungsroman, which valorizes integration into society and the sublimation of woman's autonomy in the name of motherhood and marriage, *Little Women* must have appealed to a wider, conservative audience. A comparative study of the two novels, their genesis and reception, would undoubtedly yield productive insights.

[19] See Haines, "Masochism and Femininity in Lou Andreas-Salomé's *Eine Ausschweifung.*" In this essay she offers a wonderfully complex reading of Adine's masochistic tendencies, emphasizing the probable development of masochism into a unique path of feminine desire.

[20] See Sigmund Freud, "The Economic Problem of Masochism," in *Essential Papers on Masochism,* ed. Margaret Ann Fitzpatrick Hanly (New York: New York UP, 1995), 274–85; and Richard von Krafft-Ebing, *Psychopathia Sexualis,* trans. Franklin S. Klaf. (New York: Bell, 1965).

[21] Theodor Reik, *Masochism and Modern Man* (New York: Farrar & Rinehart, 1941).

[22] Haines, "Masochism and Femininity in Lou Andreas-Salomé's *Eine Ausschweifung,*" 97.

[23] Gilles Deleuze, "Coldness and Cruelty," in *Masochism,* trans. Jean McNeil (New York: Zone Books, 1991), 9–138.

5: Returning the Gaze: Uppity Women in *Menschenkinder*

IN 1899 LOU ANDREAS-SALOMÉ published a collection of ten short stories called *Menschenkinder*, some of which had already appeared in magazines and journals, some of which would appear in magazines and journals in the first years of the twentieth century.[1] The collection comments interestingly on the historical and cultural phenomena of woman's negotiation of identity at the turn of the twentieth century in Europe. Although it is evident that men and women negotiate the terms of their identity all the time, the turn of the twentieth century brought revised social expectations for women and a shift in the conceptualization of women's roles, sexuality, and psyches. Andreas-Salomé's repeated thematic commentary on the dilemma of woman's self-definition, her formal decisions about narrative perspective, and her repeated explicit treatment of men and women looking, both surreptitiously and otherwise, amount to a theory of the gaze, even if she was unacquainted with this late-twentieth-century terminology. Prefiguring Laura Mulvey's 1975 article on visual pleasure and the narrative cinema, *Menschenkinder* examines in narrative the relationship of gender to the gaze, how the gaze operates in relation to power, and how the gaze triggers both objectification and identification.[2] *Menschenkinder's* treatment of looking and being looked at even prefigures later critiques of Mulvey's theory and indicates, among other things, how the gaze might be challenged and destabilized. Thus this collection raises questions that Mulvey, De Lauretis, Doane, Irigaray, and other feminist theorists, and in particular feminist film theorists, have been concerned with over the past forty years:[3] Is representation possible without objectification? Can a woman be the subject of the gaze even if she is also its object? And vice versa, can a man be the object of the gaze even if he is primarily its subject? Is the gaze the privilege of the male subject? Can or how can the gaze be destabilized? Revealing both women's and men's subjection to prevailing categorizations of gendered sexuality and identity, the novellas in *Menschenkinder* do not merely illuminate the problems of female identity but also touch on corresponding difficulties for men.

Repetition in *Menschenkinder:*
Thematic Considerations

Each of the ten novellas in *Menschenkinder* features a young woman coping with her awakening sexuality and a heterosexual relationship. Like the women in *Das Haus, Jutta, Ma, Fenitschka,* and *Eine Ausschweifung,* each woman struggles to adapt to the social and ideological environments in which she lives and to accept the limitations they impose on her. In this collection as elsewhere, such limitations are frequently represented as the projections and expectations of a male suitor, but the society and women themselves prove complicit. All interfere with and complicate a relatively innocent personal situation or desire. Andreas-Salomé does not investigate the vicissitudes of identity at the expense of men,; on the contrary, she refrains from depicting them as intentionally overbearing and eager to keep women in their place. She is careful to indicate that men similarly negotiate the terms of their identity within their own set of restrictive, if more generous, social regulations. She reveals too that the limitations encountered by women and men, and the manner in which each gender deals with them, systemically inhibit and define the other one. Erwin of "Inkognito" explicitly addresses the relationship between masculinity and femininity in his harangue on feminism and his idealization of Russian men to Anjuta, for example. His impression is that Russia has not yet experienced much of feminism's changes, and he assumes, since Anjuta is Russian, that she must similarly have little or no experience with feminism and emancipation: "Wie männliche Männer muß das geben. Und solche Männer — wie weibliche Frauen müssen sie ergeben" (245; "What masculine men such an attitude must produce. And such men — what feminine women must inspire them" 135–36).[4]

Though each woman's essential conflict in *Menschenkinder* revolves around the difficulty of reconciling what is conceived of as feminine with independence and self-sufficiency, the female characters of the various novellas differ substantially from each other in terms of desire, ambition, and ideological conviction. In "'Ja, so würde ich es heute auch noch sagen': Reading Lou Andreas-Salomé in the 1990s," Brigid Haines criticizes *Menschenkinder* for being repetitive, but that repetition serves an important purpose.[5] By repeating conflicts and themes, Andreas-Salomé can underscore the similarity in women's situations and contexts, while emphasizing the differences among the women themselves. And by emphasizing difference, she shows, as in *Fenitschka,* that the ubiquitous and unquestioned practice of categorizing others first and foremost in accordance with preconceived gender notions seriously limits the scope of identity formation and leads to psychic and social discord. *Menschenkinder's* subtitle, "Novellencyklus" (Novella Cycle), even draws attention in advance to the repetition the reader encounters in the collection, as well as to the concept of a constant return to similar issues shaped slightly differently by new circumstances.

The first story in the collection is entitled "Vor dem Erwachen" ("Before the Awakening") and deals with the relationship between a young woman, Edith, and her uncle, Klaus. The final story, "Zurück ans All" ("At One, Again, with Nature") also deals with the relationship between a young woman, Irene, and her uncle. Each woman is a creature of nature and loves the rural setting in which she lives, the animals and crops she tends, and yet the outcome of each novella is radically different. The structural devices employed here, the cycling back to the beginning and the paralleling of circumstances in the women's lives, emphasize difference. Paradoxically, the repetition allows Andreas-Salomé to underscore divergence. The recurrence of themes, of ambivalence toward both feminism and tradition, and of a lack of narrative closure hammer home that for all the commonality among human beings (*Menschenkinder*), there can be no uniform or clear-cut feminine and masculine identities.

A sampling of the ten different female protagonists in *Menschenkinder* can serve to illustrate Andreas-Salomé's manipulation of content to impress on the reader how minor differences in context make for an inassimilable diversity to which the reduction that is representation can only do violence. The four novellas "Inkognito," "Ein Todesfall," "Ein Wiedersehen," and "Zurück ans All" ("Incognito," "A Death," "A Reunion," and "At One, Again, with Nature") present us with four central characters who share experiences of being looked at, shaped, and judged by men, and who struggle with the conflicting emotions to which these experiences give rise and the conflicting directions in which they feel pulled by them. Despite similar psychic dilemmas, each acts differently and with varying amounts of attention to masculine authority and the look trained upon them.

In "Inkognito," Anjuta is a newspaper editor who, on a short vacation in the mountains near Innsbruck, is attracted to a man who despises feminists and feminism. Knowing nothing about her life and contrasting her to feminists, working women, and female students, the kind of woman she, in fact, is, Erwin tells her that she is an ideal woman, a real woman. That he can see in her everything that she is not underscores the nature of femininity as a construct or projection and of woman as a site or screen for that construction and projection. Because Anjuta has rarely received attention of this kind from a man and enjoys Erwin's flattery, she quickly becomes self-critical and wonders if her life up to now does not amount to a "perverted" femininity. Erwin's conception of Anjuta and his self-assured presentation of that conception to her shake Anjuta's groundings and points to the fragility of atypical feminine identity. Worried about the torn hem of her skirt, she stays up and freezes half the night in order to present herself differently the next day. At first she thinks of this as adorning herself, presenting herself as something more beautiful to be seen, but she realizes sorrowfully that it corresponds instead to "etwas verdecken — etwas verhüllen. Und vielleicht am meisten gerade das, worauf sie bisher am stolzesten war" (258; "cover[ing] up something — [hiding] something. And perhaps most of all that of which she had previously been most proud," 143). She later also wishes for a coat "der sie ganz bedeckte und auf immer unkenntlich machte in ihrer ganzen Vergangenheit für den Mann ihrer Liebe und Sehnsucht" (265; "that would cover her entirely and make her whole past invisible forever to the man of her love and her desire," 147). Anjuta associates her own understanding of her identity with an embarrassing nudity. She wishes to cover it up so that it cannot be seen and feels completely exposed when she discovers that Erwin, on a trip into Innsbruck, has found out how she really lives: "Ihr wurde dann, als risse ihr jemand das Kleid vom Leibe und stelle sie irgendwo an den Pranger" (269; "She felt as if she had been stripped and pilloried," 150). In the aftermath of this discovery Anjuta never sees Erwin again. She does not wait for him to return but takes matters into her own hands, deciding to simply return to her own life and accept her perversity. Significantly, the final lines of the novella describe how Anjuta, oblivious to a farmer and his son nearby, tears off her scarf and bares her neck to the sun, as if in defiance of the covering up Erwin compelled in her.

Whereas Anjuta resents the limitations of traditional gender roles, Esther of "Ein Todesfall" accepts them unquestioningly, affirming woman's subordination to her husband both personally and theoretically. Her foster brother, whom she had once loved, dies young and, lamenting any role she might have played in his early death, she wonders if she should not have married him instead of the man she did marry. Drawing on the traditionally established gender roles of bourgeois marriage, her foster father reminds her why a marriage to the sensitive and artistic Eberhart could not have worked: "'Du bist geschaffen zum Sorgen und Pflegen, zur Frau und zur Mutter . . . jetzt gibt es Frauen, die ihre Männer stützen und leiten müssen, und es gibt Männer, denen das gefällt. Das ist der Selbstmord der Frau'" (303–4; "'You were created to care and tend, to be a wife and mother . . . now there are women who must support and guide their husbands, and there are men who like that. That is suicide for the woman,'" 168). Esther quickly acknowledges the truth of her foster father's statement, comes to terms with her grief, and returns happily to her authoritarian husband, the head of their household. As in Anjuta's case, Esther finds herself forced into an examination of her life's decisions because of a relationship with a man who sought intimacy with her and wanted something from her that did not conform to her own desires. Unlike Anjuta, Esther delights in traditional female roles, even seeing pregnancy as a kind of vacation because it corresponds for her to a loss of control, a time in which life does with her what it will. Both Anjuta and

Esther consider how a realignment of their desires and goals might allow for the relationships that are otherwise doomed to fail.

Comparing and contrasting the novellas reveals how the authority of the gaze exists regardless of a woman's decisions and even if those decisions appear to defiantly undercut the male gaze. In fact, the comparison makes it evident that it is precisely she who attempts to undercut the male gaze who suffers most from its authority. Esther's foster brother finds her beautiful when he sees her rushing about in the world, weighed down with packages: "'Bleibe doch nur, bitte, so schwer beladen stehen! Du bist schön wie ein Bild, wie du dastehst'" (284; "'Stop right there! Please just stand there so heavily laden! You're pretty as a picture the way you're standing there,'" 157). She, on the other hand, associates this activity with a man's lifestyle and is critical of him because he doesn't relieve her of her packages. Esther embraces her foster father's and husband's traditional definitions of femininity and is irritated by both her foster brother's admiration of her unusual traits as well as by his own delicacy and vulnerability. Anjuta struggles with the same visions of femininity imposed from outside that Esther covets. She questions herself and her decisions more than Erwin's assumptions about her, which he bases on her nationality and gender. Like Fenitschka and Adine, Anjuta may be forging ahead into new territories of feminine identity, but she must remain alone in order to do so.

Marfa of "Ein Wiedersehen" devotes herself, like Anjuta, to bringing enlightenment to backward corners of Russia. Influenced by Saitzew, who traveled Russia preaching that people, in particular Russian women, ought to spend their lives helping the poor and bringing culture and medicine to them, she becomes a doctor who does exactly what he called her to do. In Vienna ten years later Marfa finds him again and hopes that she can convince him to join her in Russia to share both her life and her work. They had loved each other when they first met, but Saitzew's wife was alive, preventing them from developing their relationship. Shaped by Saitzew's ideas, Marfa is dismayed to find that he has reneged on those same ideas. He now enjoys a luxurious and narcissistic life that he does not want to give up and even tries to convince her to follow in his footsteps, to stay in Vienna with him and marry him. She has internalized his earlier authority and injunctions to such a degree that even if the Saitzew who created her, as it were, no longer exists, the moral compass he offered her does. Although Marfa is disappointed in her experience of what Andreas-Salomé repeatedly depicts as a "God is dead" moment, she does not allow the beliefs he instilled in her to be shaken.[6] She ignores Saitzew's request that she come back to visit him the next day, and when he goes looking for her he discovers that she has already left Vienna and sent him a letter. Instead of returning home directly to read the letter, Saitzew stops to observe the railway from above and studies the men working on the tracks. His contemplation of how the iron bends under their hammers constitutes a perhaps less than subtle allegory for his earlier relationship to Marfa. The novella offers an interesting paradox of a young woman whose fierce independence and commitment to a cause beyond herself is predicated on her absolute obedience to the authority of a man.

In "Kein weibliches Schreiben? Fragen an Julia Kristeva," Kristeva, like Judith Butler later in *Gender Trouble*, argues for plurality in representations of femininity: "Ich bin für eine Konzeption des weiblichen, für die es so viele 'Weiblichkeiten' gibt wie Frauen" (I'm in favor of a concept of the feminine for which there are as many femininities as there are women).[7] Andreas-Salomé does not explicitly argue in her works for a heterogeneous femininity or for a redefinition of femininity, but she does suggest that a variety of constellations of adherence to and deviation from traditional feminine norms are a necessity for both reality and representation. *Menschenkinder* points to a contemporary understanding of femininity as a set of specific qualities such as motherhood, submission, and dependence, and demonstrates how women who find contentment in what is prescribed can lead relatively uncomplicated lives. It also acknowledges, however, that women do and will stray from what is prescribed and thereby push at the boundaries of the acceptable. Such women may then experience more distress and anxiety in their daily lives but are engaged, whether consciously or not, in the business of gradually shifting the terms of discourses on femininity and, inevitably, on masculinity too.

Andreas-Salomé's representation in fiction of complex theoretical concepts of identity as they related to changes ushered in by feminism makes these concepts accessible to, and concrete for, a wide readership. Each woman in the collection *Menschenkinder* has a complex relationship to her own sexuality, her social position, and her personal circumstances. The diverse depictions of women in *Menschenkinder*, together with the multitude of other female characters discussed in earlier chapters, emphasize the risks of reducing identity to a neatly prepackaged set of gendered qualities. Though we are perhaps more conscious of the problems of such reduction in the wake of postmodernist theories of identity formation, we still often instinctively ratify a kind of identity politics that we intellectually oppose. Andreas-Salomé argues in "Der Mensch als Weib" that woman is more of a type than man, but her depictions of women in fiction suggest otherwise. That her concept of woman lacks coherence and consistency across works and that her fictional representations of women complicate her theoretical representations constitutes a strength rather than a weakness.

Destabilizing the Gaze: Formal Considerations

In "The Situation of the Looker-on: Gender, Narration and Gaze in *Wuthering Heights*," Beth Newman confirms that the gaze functioned for a long time in Western culture as "the privilege of a male subject, a means of relegating women to the status of object (of representation, discourse, desire, etc.)."[8] And E. Ann Kaplan asks if the gaze is always, even if not literally, male "for reasons inherent in the structure of language, the unconscious, symbolic systems, and thus all social structures."[9] *Menschenkinder* contests as well as investigates ownership of the gaze in formal as well as thematic ways. All novellas in the collection begin with an external, omniscient point of view, making the central female character in each case the object of a gaze that she, at least initially, fails to challenge. Aligned with the knowledge and judgment of an external observer, the gaze represents the belief that an individual's identity can be determined from without, projected onto that individual by a knowing onlooker. This setup results then in the complicity of the reader in the gaze.

The first paragraph of the opening novella of the collection, "Vor dem Erwachen," will serve as a case in point. It reads as a series of stage directions for a play that would be impossible to stage. It therefore conjures up the directions from a screenplay:

> Die Waggonfenster sind von der Januarkälte so beschlagen, daß man das Hereindämmern des Morgens kaum gewahr wird. Die Eisfiguren auf den Scheiben färben sich bläulich, und auf dem schmalen Gange, der in den Waggon des Harmonikazuges an den Einzelcoupés entlang läuft, hört man von Zeit zu Zeit den kleinen Kellnerjungen mit klirrenden Tassen aus dem Küchenraume vorübereilen. (9)

> [The windows of the railroad car are so frosted over from the January cold that the passengers barely discern the dawn's light shining in. The ice figures on the windowpanes take on a bluish tint, and from the narrow gangway that runs the length of the passenger car of the composite train, the little serving boy can be heard as he hurries along from the dining car with his tray of clinking cups. (1)]

To introduce the novella's main characters the narration switches from this omniscient perspective to the perspective of an older woman. Traveling on a train with Edith and Klaus, this woman will provide her interpretation of the relationship between the two and then disappear entirely from the narrative by page three. She judges Edith and Klaus to be father and daughter, and they are described in enough detail to make the woman's assumptions about their relationship convincing. The narrator adopts the old woman's categorizations of these two people, lending even more credence to her interpretative vision. In the conflation of the omniscient narrator's and the woman's perspectives and in the inactivity of the young woman, the reader experiences a sense of control and security. By making the main object of the onlooker's and thereby the reader's interest the young girl, Andreas-Salomé emphasizes the idea that woman is always being looked at by women and men alike. Introducing conventional interpretations of gendered identity and sexuality via a third person observer, she shrewdly leads the reader to share the older woman's gaze and to accept her perspective as knowing.[10]

The power of the gaze is undermined, however, by a shift to yet another perspective, that of the young woman herself, who awakens and speaks to the onlooker. The new perspective reveals the gaze the reader has adopted to be a gaze that imposed meaning through recourse to a series of standard interpretations of gender and sexuality. In the moment in which the older woman enters into dialogue with the young woman, a moment that is coterminous with the young woman's first look back at the older woman, the reader discovers that Edith and Klaus are, in fact, husband and wife. Edith suddenly becomes, to use Mulvey's vocabulary, the maker rather than simply the bearer of meaning, moving from a peripheral to a central place in the narrative. The older woman's eyes register surprise and shock at this development: "Die Augen der alten Dame vergrößern sich unnatürlich und bleiben voll Staunen und Schreck an dem ungleichen Paar haften. Es ist gut, daß niemand Zeit hat, es zu beachten" (10; "The old lady's eyes widen unnaturally and rest on the dissimilar pair with a look of startled astonishment. Good that no one has the time to notice," 2). Because looks are communicative, the onlooker is relieved that she is not being observed at this moment. Her surprised look divulges something that she does not wish to vocalize, and a returned look in this instant would immediately expose the onlooker. Andreas-Salomé's narrative technique here demonstrates that while the gaze offers a sense of control, it also leaves the one who wields it vulnerable. Thus from the outset the gaze is shown to be a contestable arena, a place not simply where control originates but also where control might be resisted.

In these opening pages Andreas-Salomé has clearly sought to draw the reader's attention to the limitations of external vantage points. She encourages the complicity of the reader in the old woman's gaze, only to show it to be faulty. The old woman, like the reader, enjoys a voyeuristic position. The gaze of the voyeur is generally not returned, and this position therefore allows uninhibited reactions. The reader's privilege is further underscored by the fact that the woman, her curiosity piqued by the new configuration of this pair, would like to see more but cannot: "Die Augen schauen ihr aus dem Gesicht, als wollten sie noch um die Ecke sehen" (11; "Her eyes are staring out of her head as if she were trying to look around the corner," 2). While her voyeuristic pleasure is denied, the potential of the reader's pleasure is maintained, since the narrative records what happens after Edith and Klaus turn the corner the old woman can only wish to see around. Yet the privilege of even the reader's gaze has been compromised, because the narrator's trick alienates and makes uncertain. The external constituting power of identity, the gaze, and how it operates in conventional narratives, has been undermined, and the reader's voyeuristic desires have been laid bare. Unlike traditional omniscient narration, this narrative disrupts the scopophilic and voyeuristic pleasure of the reader.

Both the opening and closing of "Eine Nacht" ("One Night") similarly emphasize the gap between what is surmised by an outsider and what is unfolding internally in a particular character. Whereas the gaze might be associated then with power and the policing of social norms and rules, it is shown to be neither all-encompassing nor all-powerful. Again the novella begins with an omniscient narrator who describes for the reader how Elly, the main character, walks into the grounds of a hospital, only barely attracting the attention of the gatekeeper and the attendant. Elly does not arouse interest because she has been a patient in the hospital in the recent past. However, her visit to a young doctor on this particular evening is not for medical reasons. Although Elly feels conspicuous and therefore nervous, she is all but invisible to others. John Berger argues in *Ways of Seeing* that women internalize the male looker.[11] They become, he contends, both the looker and the looked-at, seeing themselves as they are seen by others. Elly bears this out in the opening paragraphs of "Eine Nacht." She is acutely aware of herself as someone being looked at, and her behavior is determined by her own awareness of a gendered social code.

During her visit to the young doctor, Berthold, he is called away to visit a dying man and asks Elly to wait for him until he returns. With some apprehension, she agrees to do so, but Berthold does not return until the early morning, leaving Elly in a compromised position. It is too late for her to leave alone and too late for him to be seen in the streets with her. Distraught from watching a man he knew die, Berthold pours his heart out to Elly, who comforts him, lulls him to sleep, and in the liminal space between darkness and dawn undergoes an existential crisis, a loss and regaining of her love for Berthold, and a rebirth as a confident and self-determining individual on the one hand and as an insignificant part of humanity as a whole on the other. In an interesting narrative conceit, Andreas-Salomé locates Elly in a small hospital apartment that she cannot leave for the duration of her journey inwards and her self-discovery. As if from a cocoon, Elly emerges from the hospital alone in the early morning hours completely forgetful of herself as a watched woman and in possession of a brand new consciousness. In an inversion of the opening, she is invisible to herself and visible to others:

> Ein Arzt, aus dem zweiten Hof des Krankenhauses kommend, durchquert die Baumanlagen. Wie er eine weibliche Gestalt auf den Hauptausgang zugehen sieht, hält er inne und schaut ihr aufmerksam nach. Irgendwo wird eine Thür geöffnet. Zwei Wärterinnen huschen in leisem, übrigens ganz vergnügtem Gespräch vorüber. Auch sie wenden die Köpfe und stutzen. Elly bemerkt es nicht. . . . In diesem

Augenblick sind für sie die Menschen nicht gefährliche Späher oder neugierige Verleumder. (137–38)

[A doctor coming from the inner courtyard of the hospital is walking through the trees. Seeing a woman walking toward the main exit, he stops and watches her attentively. Somewhere a door is opened. Two nurses sweep past in quiet but quite amiable conversation. They too turn their heads and stare. Elly does not notice. . . . In this moment she does not see people as dangerous spies and nosy gossips. (74–75)]

In the span of a few hours Elly has not only overcome her compulsion to watch herself as she imagines others watch her but has also repressed the knowledge that others watch her. Though perhaps shortlived, this is a triumphant moment of freedom in Andreas-Salomé's narrative: "Und glutrot geht hinter ihr, in dampfenden Frühnebeln, die Sonne groß und still auf und umspinnt die hineilende Gestalt mit feierlichem Licht" (138; "And glowing red in the early morning mist the sun rises behind her, large and silent, wrapping the hastening figure all round in a solemn light," 75).

Each novella introduces a new series of questions about the dynamics of looking and being looked at. "Vor dem Erwachen" foregrounds the undermined gaze; "Eine Nacht" examines the internalized gaze; and "Mädchenreigen" ("Maidens' Roundelay") illuminates what I call the confounded gaze. "Mädchenreigen" begins with a wallpaperer's interpretation of two hotel rooms, one inhabited by Alex, the main male character, and the other by Hans, the main female character. The wallpaperer examines the traces, the objects, and the use of space in the rooms to summon their inhabitants in his mind. He is a reader of space and decor. After seeing Hans's dressing-table, he concludes that it could not be a vain man who grooms himself here in the mornings and is utterly perplexed when he discovers that a young woman occupies this room (80). He is similarly perplexed when he sees Alex's room and realizes that a young man resides in it. Interpreting the discrepancy between biological sex and gendered space as a sign of a world losing its center, he ponders: "Wenn das so weiter ging, dann konnte man in dieser verkehrten Welt bald die Wohnungen der Frauenzimmer wie die der Mannsleute einrichten, und auch umgekehrt" (81; "If things kept on this way, then in this topsy-turvy world they would soon be doing the women's rooms like those of the men, and vice versa," 41). Expecting correspondence between the space and the subject who occupies that space and trusting long-tested reading strategies, the wallpaperer is confounded. In the wallpaperer's unconscious there is a link between space, identity, and ideology, but he can only articulate it in the form of a fear that the world is being turned on its head. By focusing on the wallpaperer's perspective at the opening of the novella, Andreas-Salomé exposes how spaces are shaped and decorated in accordance with typically gendered social relations that we overlook or take for granted. In his essay "Über Arbeitsnachweise" ("On Employment Agencies"), Siegfried Kracauer expounds on the relationship between spatial arrangements and the social unconscious, maintaining "[d]ie Raumbilder sind die Träume der Gesellschaft. Wo immer die Hieroglyphe irgendeines Raumbildes entziffert ist, dort bietet sich der Grund der sozialen Wirklichkeit dar" ("spatial images are the dreams of society. Wherever the hieroglyphics of these images can be deciphered, one finds the basis of social reality").[12] Andreas-Salomé's foray into similar issues in "Mädchenreigen" demonstrates that the "abnormal" can induce critical reading that exposes the social relations that generally go unnoticed and lays bare the assumptions of ideology and its tendency to naturalize certain behaviors.

The novella, "Abteilung: Innere Männer" ("Unit for 'Men, Internal'") mixes omniscient narrative and epistolary form in order to expose Otto Griepenkerl's long-held assumptions about femininity and appropriate female behavior as stifling both for women and for himself. It also serves to emphasize, once again, the discrepancy between the world's and one's own understanding of identity. Griepenkerl, in contrast to Max of *Fenitschka* and Benno of *Eine Ausschweifung,* does not engage in real dialogue with women about his understanding of femininity and thus, though he experiences melancholy, attains no meaningful enlightenment through self-reflection. The novella consists of two parts: his reminiscences, embedded in omniscient narration, about his relationship to Christiane von Brinken, followed by Christiane's version of their breakup, expressed in a posthumous letter to him. His decision to sever all ties to her constitutes the focus of the competing narratives. Her letter serves as a corrective and complement to his perspective on the events and shows him to be both the subject and the object of the gaze, despite the fact that he never perceives himself to be the latter. The events that transpired between Otto Griepenkerl and Christiane von Brinken recall what we have encountered elsewhere in Andreas-Salomé's prose: for women the link between sexuality and identity is paramount. That is, how a woman conducts herself sexually and whether or not her behavior is seen are vital elements in determining whether she is integrated into or marginalized from society.

The form of each character's thoughts points to fundamental differences in each character's relationship to the world. Christiane sends Otto a letter in which she explains the events that led to his spurning of her. In the letter she also confesses to a lapse of which he was unaware and reveals a process of self-reflection and increased self-knowledge. Whereas she begins the letter calling him a "Mitschuldigen" ("guilty accomplice"), she arrives at a conclusion that not only excuses but elevates Otto: "Ich nehme dieses Wort [Mitschuldigen] zurück und lege mein Erkenntnis als das der allein Schuldigen in Ihre Hände, als in die eines Menschen, der es offenbar besser verstanden hat als ich, sich rein und fest zu erhalten in den Wirrnissen und Versuchungen, die uns umgeben" (76; "I take back this word [guilty accomplice] and place my confession as the lone guilty one in your hands as if in the hands of a person who clearly knew better than I did how to keep himself pure and resolved amid the confusions and temptations that surround us," 39). Access to Otto's thoughts, on the other hand, is only possible through the conceit of an omniscient narrator. Whatever criticisms and self-criticisms he may have remain unarticulated, and the process evident in his thoughts represents a mirror image of Christiane's. Whereas he begins with a sense of melancholy and sadness in the immediate aftermath of Christiane's death, he goes through a process of self-justification:

> Aber ohne diesen Augenblick, diesen rettenden, Erkenntnis bringenden, wäre Schwester Christa heute seine Frau. Das ist keine gemütliche Vorstellung! Wenn sie ihm kommt, dann denkt er nicht, wie vorhin, in einer Regung unwillkürlichen Mitleids: "Christel hatte kein Heim!" sondern er denkt nur, nachträglich erschreckend: "An wie wenig hing es, und ich hätte sie in mein Heim aufgenommen." (55)

> [But were it not for this instant, this saving, insight-bringing instant, Sister Christa would be his wife today. That is not a pleasant thought! Whenever it occurs to him he does not think, as he did before, in a spontaneous feeling of sympathy: "Christel had no home!" but instead he just thinks with a feeling of belated fear: "If it hadn't been for that, I would have taken her into my home!" (28)]

Thus the title would seem to refer not only to the hospital ward in which Christiane's lapses occurred (*Abteilung: Innere Männer* — a ward for internal disorders) but also to Otto's own internal disorder: an inability to translate his feelings and thoughts into a language accessible to others.

Whereas Otto then is condemned to personal solitude despite the outer trappings of familial and professional success, Christiane is condemned to social solitude, forever frozen in the moment in which Otto saw her kiss a male patient and in which his gaze imposed a problematic identity upon her: "Ich sah mich selbst als Dirne, erkannt und gebrandmarkt von dem, den ich liebe" (69; "I saw myself as a whore, exposed and branded by the man I loved," 35). Appalled with herself as she sees herself seen by him, Christiane proves unable to move beyond this moment other than by embarking on a path of self-dissolution, a self-inflicted punishment: "Ich durfte, ich sollte mich im Dienst der anderen vergessen, mit allem was an Reue oder Sehnsucht, an Weh oder Glück in mir gelebt haben mag, und ich that das so getreulich, bis ich im Grunde kein rechtes eigenes Selbst mehr besaß" (75; "I was allowed — I was supposed — to forget myself in the service of others, with all that may have lived in me in the way of regret or longing, of sorrow or happiness, and I did that with such dedication that basically I no longer possessed a real self of my own," 39). While the theme of the story alone is interesting, then, its presentation in this form serves the further purpose of exposing the unchallenged gaze as a privilege of the male, to be sure, but also of warning against the unquestioned assumption of that privilege. Christiane's letter challenges Otto's gaze but simultaneously allows for the possibility that he continue to ignore that challenge. She not only explicitly excuses him in the end but also divulges a second lapse of which he was unaware, providing him further opportunity for self-assurance. The novella ends with the end of Chritiane's letter, refusing to privilege his gaze by allowing it to completely frame the narrative.

Christiane's letter reveals Otto's actions to have been dictated by ignorance, his refusal to communicate or listen, and a series of rigid gender expectations that in his mind elevated, and in Christiane's and others' minds unduly burdened, her. Griepenkerl's thoughts on his relationship to Christiane demonstrate a vexing self-confidence: "Doktor Griepenkerl hätte um die Welt sein Christel nicht kompromittiert. 'Ansehen, nicht Anfassen!' lautete sein Wahlspruch in dieser Beziehung" (51; "Doctor Griepenkerl would not have compromised his Christel for all the world. 'Look, don't touch!' was his motto at this point," 25). Otto's motto underscores his privileging of the gaze, of a mono-directional connection. Ironically it is precisely the fact that he wants only to look at Christiane that compromises her and leads to the end of their relationship. Despite advice from Hans Ebling, the suitor of Christiane's sister Lieselotte, who finds Otto's demands on Christel to be unreasonable, Otto refuses to reflect on his preconceptions about feminine identity. Ebling's advice reads as a summary of Silvia Bovenschen's argument in *Die imaginierte Weiblichkeit* and calls on Otto to consider the role his own shortcomings might play in his expectations of Christiane:[13] "Unsre eigenen Schwächen und Fehler spielen nicht zum wenigsten mit bei der Bildung unsrer sogenannten Ideale, mein Lieber. Besonders unsrer Frauenideale. Es wäre interessant, dies in Ihrem speziellen Fall ein wenig zu detaillieren, — Übrigens ist es ziemlich unangenehm für die Betreffenden, 'idealisiert zu werden,' wie ich es sehe" (54; "'Our own weaknesses and faults play no small role when we give shape to our ideals, my dear fellow. Especially our ideals about women. It would be interesting to detail this a bit in your special case. — In any case it's rather unpleasant for those concerned 'to be idolized,' as I see it," 27). Ebling introduces the topic of projection here, raising the possibility of a psychological flaw on the part of Otto and prodding his friend to reconsider his conviction that Christiane must undergo a "Probezeit" (53; "period of trial," 26). And, indeed, later references to Otto's extramarital affairs point to the legitimacy of Ebling's suggestions. Otto's

discussions with Hans Ebling during his courting of Christiane bring
to light his already unquestioning acceptance of the double standard of
morality for men and women. While he conscientiously refrains from
touching Christiane, he has surrogates: "Zum Anfassen sind ja andere
Frauen in die Welt gesetzt, mit denen man sich schlecht und recht
durchschlägt, bis man in die solide Futterkammer der Ehe gerät" (51;
"For touching there are other women in the world, with whom a fellow
can get by as well as he can until he makes it into the respectable feeding
grounds of marriage," 25). After he marries, he also justifies his affairs
to himself: "Niemand lebt, der ihn nicht als vortrefflichen Gatten, Vater,
Bürger und Berufsmenschen anerkennen müßte. . . . Das andere, — ob
man gelegentlich der kleinen Seitensprünge, ob man gelegentlicher Pri-
vaterholungen ein wenig abseits bedarf: das ist am Ende doch nur eine
Temperamentsfrage" (58; "There is not a living soul who would not
have to admit that he is a perfect husband, father, citizen, and professional man. . . . The other things — the fact that a fellow has occasional
need of a small fling, of an occasional bit of private rest and relaxation
on the side — that is ultimately really only a question of temperament,"
29). Unfaithful himself, Otto projects unfaithfulness onto Christiane
and makes her unacceptable.

The fact that Christiane von Brinken first represented for Otto the
possibility of social mobility also supports Ebling's hypothesis. A petty
bourgeois with significant ambition, Otto glorified the nobility, feeling
both inferior to and envious of people of such status. His association of
Christiane with representations of women in works by Goethe imply his
early reification of her and indicate his inability to experience women in
terms other than virgin or vamp.[14] The possibility of a much more complex feminine identity stares him in the face out of this mixture of images
of women from Goethe, as well as out of a photo he still has: "eine
kleine Photographie, etwas verblaßt, ein ganz junges Mädchen in der
Tracht der barmherzigen Schwestern vom Sankt-Michaelshause. . . . ein
sehr liebes Gesicht, aus dem nußbraune Schelmenaugen keck herauss-
chauen" (47; "a small photograph, somewhat faded, of a very young girl
in the uniform of the merciful sisters of the House of St. Michael. . . . a
very dear face, from which roguish brown eyes gaze out," 22). Otto's
contemplation of the photo emphasizes conflicting images of Christel. On the one hand, she represents a de-eroticized and unthreaten-
ing femininity; she is dressed in white and is a young, innocent girl in
reference to whom he uses the word "sister."[15] On the other hand, her
eyes respond impishly and sassily, but he seeks to erase all traces of this
latter femininity. Thus Christiane's relatively innocent kiss of a dying
man banishes her definitively to the category of vamp for Otto. In her
letter, Christiane addresses Otto's reification of her in her reference to
this very same photograph:

Vielleicht besitzen Sie noch das kleine Bild, das Sie sich gleich nach meiner Einkleidung von mir erbaten: "Um des reizenden Kontrastes willen," sagten Sie, "den dieses Kleid zu diesem Antlitz bildet." Es schmeichelte mir damals, ich begriff noch nicht das Mittleidlose und Kaltherzige darin, daß Sie mich gerade so ausstaffiert vor sich sehen wollten. (65)

[Perhaps you still have the little picture that you asked for right after my convocation: "All for the charming contrast," you said, "in which this uniform stands to your countenance." I was flattered then; I did not yet grasp the lack of sympathy and cold-heartedness in the way you wanted to see me dressed up just that way. 33)]

Otto's desire for this particular photograph of Christiane testifies to his problematic psychology, his exacting concept of feminine identity, and his fragile relationship to Christiane from the beginning. Her words confirm Ebling's accusations against Otto and further underscore Otto's desire for something immobile and fixed in accordance with his enormously limiting, simplistic, and selfish projections. Only in retrospect does Christiane realize that his relationship to her was never about her but about his own desire to climb socially and to be aided in this by a suitably respectable, dutiful, and submissive woman. Her letter shows a life-long dilemma of attempting to reconcile how she experiences and sees herself with how she knows herself to be experienced and seen from without. Whereas Christiane comes to a realization of the conflicting pulls on her and the unavoidable negotiation among them, Otto resists such self-knowledge and suppresses self-criticism. Ultimately, however, he suffers the same dilemma.

Although the second half of this novella is a letter and thus something that suggests dialogue, it provides for no interaction, since it is posthumous. Additionally, Andreas-Salomé does not return us to the frame at the end of this novella and therefore offers no insight into Otto's reaction to Christiane's confession. The letter functions then as a returned gaze similar to the gaze its female author suffered many years earlier at Otto's hands. Just as Otto ended their relationship without dialogue, without offering Christiane any chance to explain herself and to adjust his perception of her, she offers him no possibility of rebuttal or response. Although in the closing paragraph of the letter she retracts her accusation that he too is guilty, the letter leaves open the possibility that Otto Griepenkerl will perceive himself differently once presented with a narrative snapshot of himself produced and sent by Christiane.

Narrative structure plays an important role in this collection of novellas and is repeatedly linked to the gaze which is, in turn, repeatedly linked to concepts of identity. The open ending of "Abteilung: Innere Männer," as of all but a couple of the novellas in *Menschenkinder*, compensates for the narrowing narrative gaze. Just as a photograph is a moment in time that, in the same moment that it offers insight into identity, exposes its own limits in capturing identity, so too a narrative both informs and constrains. Andreas-Salomé's open endings and writerly texts point beyond narrative and closure, however, and, given the tight links between narration and identity, indicate that there can be no closure. As Whitinger argues in relation to *Fenitschka,* Andreas-Salomé works against traditional notions of development as presented in the Bildungsroman, which traces an individual's path toward an inevitable integration into society. Her choice of what initially seem to be relatively traditional narrative forms in *Menschenkinder* actually involves an interesting experimentation that inaugurates a female subject who is always first an object, observed, judged, and defined by others.

As a genre, in fact, the novella seems particularly suitable for what I see as Andreas-Salomé's repeated insistence on the fact that there is no final attainment of, in Alice Kuzniar's words from a different context, "a transparent, sincere relationship between self and society."[16] If the novella focuses on a single, life-changing moment, then it suggests the fragmentary nature — in the German romantic sense of the word — of narrative and of the identity that can be represented in narrative. Andreas-Salomé depicts female subjectivity as something that slowly emerges through a series of necessary conflicts that force repeated self-evaluations and the subsequent development of a new skin. Underscoring a process through which one constantly reinvents oneself, she challenges any notion of a stable or fixed feminine self and cultivates the idea of a fluid self. Buttressing her thematic choices, Andreas-Salomé's formal choices in *Menschenkinder* contest the promise of a coherent identity. In this sense, I argue that she engages in a Butlerian project throughout her writings, undermining and questioning identity categories rather than reifying them and using them to unite women around, as she depicts it, equally faulty and inflexible feminist notions of femininity and masculinity. Refigurations of traditional narrative allow for a refiguration of female identity and self-definition. Formal elements of the stories provide commentary on the emergence of new ways of conceiving of identity and demonstrate both the author's engagement with modernist literary practices and her interest in and incorporation of new modes of seeing into her texts.

Gender and Gaze

Given that cinema could only come into existence because someone imagined it as a medium for carrying narratives, it is not that surprising that what is nowadays common screenplay style would be already present in narratives written down before cinema became a widespread and very accessible phenomenon. What is surprising, perhaps, is that

Andreas-Salomé already seems to identify problems with visual narratives and undercut them in ways that feminist filmmakers and authors will also invoke later. This has rarely been recognized or analyzed in her work, however. Among her fictional works, *Menschenkinder* in particular foregrounds a narrative perspective that is very much, as I have discussed in preceding pages, tied to the visual and that refers repeatedly to acts of seeing and to the exercise of the gaze.

Cross-dressing in "Mädchenreigen" integrates both subversive and conventional approaches to theories of gender and the gaze. In her recent book entitled *The Representation of Masochism and Queer Desire in Film and Literature,* Barbara Mennel argues that "womanliness as masquerade becomes visible precisely at the historical juncture when gender definitions shift and women redefine the radius of their actions" (134).[17] Andreas-Salomé writes at, and sets these novellas in, a time in which femininity was being radically redefined, and "Mädchenreigen" deals with a particularly compelling set of redefinitions of gender and of prescribed gendered behaviors. In an interesting twist, Andreas-Salomé turns the male character into the object of the gaze in what is generally the most masculine of moments, the moment in which a woman submits entirely to a man and promises to follow and obey him forever.

Alex, the central male figure, is a looker from the beginning. He likes to look, sketch, and record what he sees. One of the first things he sketches is the head and face of a young girl whom he finds attractive and who will from this moment on be referred to in the narrative as the *Madonnenkopf* or *Madonnenköpfchen* ("Madonna face" or "little Madonna face"). This naming and Alex's sketch of her head both fragment and reduce the girl, functioning similarly to close-ups of specific female body parts in Hollywood cinema. It allays, as Laura Mulvey argues, the fear of castration or loss of power for the man who looks. In order to draw the girl's head, Alex must look at her carefully for extended periods of time with his "dunklen Augen, die ausgezeichnet fein und scharf zu sehen verstanden" (86; "dark eyes that could see so exceptionally finely and sharply," 44). While he is happy to stare at the young girl and happy to have his friend Ferdinand stare at her, he reacts vehemently to the young girl's return of Ferdinand's gaze: "Während Ferdinand sich langsam mit seinem etwas hinkenden Schritt entfernte, sahen die drei am anderen Tisch unwillkürlich hinter ihn her. Die beiden alten Herren gleichgültig, der kleine Madonnenkopf mit einer leichten Neugier, die Alex plötzlich abstieß" (87; "While Ferdinand left with his somewhat limping gait, the three people at the other table involuntarily watched him go. The two gentlemen indifferently, the little Madonna face with a mild curiosity that suddenly put Alex off," 45). This young woman's active observation of Ferdinand feminizes him, thus weakening him in a way that Alex would prefer not to witness. Alex's own interactions with Ferdinand validate this feminization. In contrast to

Alex, Ferdinand has weak eyes: "Ferdinand strengte seine kurzsichtigen Augen an" (86; "Ferdinand [strained] his myopic eyes," 44); he cannot own and activate the gaze as Alex does; he is in poor health and wears the signs of it on his body; and he obeys Alex, who sends him to bed earlier than the others out of concern for his health. The forcefulness of the verb "abstoßen" (put off / repel) to express Alex's distaste is remarkable and indicates that he sees the gaze very much as the privilege of the male, a privilege that his emasculated friend cannot assert. Beth Newman argues that "when a woman looks back she asserts her 'existence' as a subject, her place outside the position of object to which the male gaze relegates her and by which it defines her as 'woman.'"[18] And indeed, this seems to be what is at stake when the *Madonnenkopf* stares at Ferdinand. Asserting the privilege of a male subject, she relegates Ferdinand to the status of object. Her look confirms what Alex already knows, that Ferdinand is "abnormal" or other.

Whereas Alex has difficulty accepting a woman's gaze at a man, he is attracted to Hans, a twenty-one-year-old woman who dresses as a man, observes other young women, and engages in flirtations with them. When Alex first meets Hans, she is described as sizing him up with "ein paar wundervolle braune Augen [die] ihm voll Spannung ins Gesicht sahen. . . . Augen wie ein Untersuchungsrichter" (88; "a pair of wonderful brown eyes, full of expectation, gazed into his face. . . . eyes like an examining magistrate," 46). Alex remains unperturbed by the curiosity in Hans's gaze despite the fact that he was repulsed by the *Madonnenkopf*'s curiosity about Ferdinand. Again Mennel's discussion of cross-dressing and masquerade provides a useful foundation for understanding why Hans's ostensibly subversive behavior proves less disconcerting for Alex than the *Madonnenkopf*'s gaze: "It is precisely in her attempt to pass as what she is not that woman reveals herself as what she cannot be."[19] Hans does not represent the same kind of threat as the *Madonnenkopf* because she challenges only her own position as object and, in her cross-dressing, even acknowledges and affirms the gaze as the privilege of the male.

Assuming the privilege of the male gaze, Hans also seems utterly oblivious to the gaze that would seek to make her its feminine object. When Alex reacts in surprise to her plans to take the *Abitur* (School Leaving Examination), Hans responds to what she thinks surprised him rather than to what actually surprised him. Alex wonders why a young woman would have any interest in sitting for examinations such as the *Abitur,* but Hans responds as if his surprise had to do with the timing of the exam: "'Ja, mein Gott, es ist spät dazu,' bemerkte sie schnell, seinen erstaunten Blick nicht verstehend" (93; "'Yes, my God, it's late to be doing that,' she commented quickly, not understanding this astonished gaze," 47–48). Her own perception of herself as someone who would self-evidently take the *Abitur* counters Alex's perception of her as first and foremost a young woman. Hans's cross-dressing creates a space in which she can operate outside the constraints of the gaze that would fix her in a series of feminine roles and pursuits without really threatening that gaze in general terms. In fact, Hans even explains her flirtations with other young women as an attempt to offer them gentle introductions to adolescent sexual awakening. Pretending to be a young man, she attracts them in traditional terms but provides a safe context in which they can role-play before they are overly hastily assimilated into traditional feminine and heterosexual roles. That this ought to be the eventual outcome for these girls is never questioned in and of itself, however.

Hans's adoption of the gaze in more or less traditional terms becomes evident too in her collection of photographs. She displays them on the wall in her room, explaining to Alex that they are "fremde Mädchen und Frauen, deren Photographien ich mir ihrer Schönheit halber zu verschaffen gewußt habe. Manchmal zu meiner großen Freude auch ihren Umgang" (94; "Girls and women I don't know, but whose photographs, owing to their beauty, I was able to acquire. And sometimes, to my great pleasure, their company," 49). Just as Hans has usurped the masculine role, she has usurped the gaze, which in her control operates both similarly to and yet differently from Alex's gaze. While Hans, like Alex, keeps images of the women she has found attractive, her images are photographs, and it is improbable that she is the photographer, the producer of the images, given that she speaks of procuring (verschaffen) these photographs rather than of taking them. Alex, on the other hand, sketches young women. He is the author, that is, of the images he collects. Whereas Hans's gaze might be seen to allow for reciprocation in that she takes pleasure in meeting the women in her photographs and appreciates life-like images of them, Alex's gaze runs one way. He sees, creates, and collects. Although, or perhaps because, many writers and artists contested the idea of the photograph as a natural image in the late nineteenth and early twentieth century, it is clear that discourses on photography as an authentic, artless form of representation dominated its early history.[20] Thus the differences between Alex's artistic and Hans's photographic gaze point to Hans's gaze as one that fixes and shapes the women in less directly subjective fashion than Alex's. In the early parts of this novella, then, masculinity corresponds to control of the gaze. Alex is in control of the gaze, Hans, masquerading as a man, is in control of it, and Ferdinand, a handicapped man, is in control while seated but also becomes its object and is thus feminized when he stands up and reveals his handicap, his otherness.

In *Three Essays on Sexuality*, Freud discusses a model of development for girls whereby they have to repress their juvenile masculinity to become adult women. "Mädchenreigen" might be read as a literary realization of this theory of the establishment of femininity, because Hans literally enacts juvenile masculinity but surrenders her masquerade and all of its benefits in order to be integrated into a socially sanctioned, heterosexual relationship. She falls in love with Alex, becomes quieter, talks about letting her hair grow, and envisions a life of submission and service to Alex: "mir scheint jetzt, als ob ich immer — immer auf dich allein gewartet hätte. Um dir allein zu folgen, um zu dir allein aufzusehen" (105; "But now it seems to me as if I had always — always been waiting for you. To follow you alone, to look up to you alone," 56). I want to focus here on the choice of the verb "aufsehen" which surely cannot be incidental. While its idiomatic usage points simply to a declaration of respect and admiration, its literal meaning of "to look up" cannot be ignored in a novella so explicitly focused on looking. When Hans relinquishes her masquerade, her gaze becomes more subversive. Alex finds himself placed on the kind of pedestal that Bovenschen identifies in eighteenth-century texts. Recognizing his objectification and idealization, he rejects such positioning and leaves Hans:

> Hans würde immer einen idealen, unerhörten Maßstab an ihn legen, dem er entsprechen mußte, wenn ihr Rausch von heute abend je mehr werden sollte als nur ein verfliegender Rausch — wenn sie ihn lieben sollte. Sie wußte genau, was sie wollte, und erwartete alles von ihm. In ihrer Demut lag etwas verborgen, wovor ihm graute. (108)

> [Hans would always measure him against an ideal, incredible standard, which he would have to meet if her euphoria of this evening were ever to become more than only a fleeting enthusiasm — if she was to love him. She knew exactly what she wanted, and expected everything of him. In her humility there was something hidden that he dreaded. (57)]

Perhaps because Hans has so expertly wielded the gaze from the masculine vantage point for so long, she has a very clear idea about what role she should play as a woman, as the epitome of femininity. She has not really relinquished the gaze at all, it turns out, but seeks to control it by becoming its ultimate object. If she is to truly fill the role she perceives as feminine, she needs Alex to fill the other role, to be the epitome of masculinity, to wield the gaze, and thus create the appropriate pole against which Hans can define herself. The ideal of femininity to which she has fallen prey demands a counter ideal of masculinity, and when Alex asks Hans if she might still love him if she were to find out that he were not that ideal of masculinity that she expects, she shakes her head. If the gaze operates then as a kind of guardian of femininity, Andreas-Salomé seems to say, it must also operate as a guardian of what femininity is not, namely of masculinity. Femininity can only be safeguarded if its binary opposite is equally safeguarded. Hans's understanding of femininity and masculinity are shown to be extremely limited and entirely dependent on one another and on who owns the gaze and how he activates it. Ironically, in the very moment that Hans desires traditional gendered relations, confers mastery on Alex, and offers herself up as the object of his gaze, she destabilizes the gaze, not only because her explicit requirements of the person to whom she assigns the gaze limits him, but also because her actions reveal an active decision to take on a new role rather than a natural slippage into such a role. If one decides to be rather than simply is a gendered being, then gendered identity must be artificial and flexible.

Similar alignments of the gaze with masculinity are to be found in "Abteilung: Innere Männer." Otto Griepenkerl's look, be it his look of desire or his look of disgust, is a powerful one that exercises real power over the life of Christiane von Brinken. He rarely speaks to her, moves in very limiting and limited circles with her, and eventually discards her without any exchange of dialogue, because he brands her in accordance with what he sees and his interpretation of what he sees. Griepenkerl represents Hans's male counterpart. He allows no outside interference with his notions of femininity and masculinity, purity and impurity, having defined them well in advance and in such a way that they complement each other entirely. Demanding perfection from Christiane, his ideal of femininity, Griepenkerl forces a "Probezeit" ("period of trial") upon her for which there could be no outcome other than failure (53). Proving a negative is always easier than proving a positive, so regardless of how long Christiane remained pure before marriage, she could never show that she would always remain so. Any minor slipup, however, undercuts her perfection. Even his acquaintance Hans Ebling warns Griepenkerl about the pitfalls of his idealizations and expectations: "Wer die Frauen weniger hoch taxiert, ist barmherziger gegen sie" (54; "Those who tax women less highly are more sympathetic toward them," 27). Having a more flexible concept of femininity, Hans Ebling sees women as *Menschenkinder* with the same potential frailties and shortcomings or strengths as men. Griepenkerl's judgmental gaze, a look that allows for no response from Christiane, paralyzes her, decides the outcome of her life, and, in the end, fails to acknowledge her as a human being, as a *Menschenkind* (member of the human family), someone whose identity cannot be captured in the reductive terms masculine and feminine. That both Hans of "Mädchenreigen" and Otto of "Abteilung: Innere Männer" drive their loves away with similarly extravagant gender expectations emphasizes, even if it does not condemn, the complicity on the part of both men and women in regulating gender and in maintaining problematic gender distinctions that undermine a more compassionate humanity. Andreas-Salomé's novellas as a whole highlight women's essential humanity, however, and the title of the collection draws our attention to the similarities across gender rather than to the differences that a concentration on gender inaugurates and exaggerates.

Decadence as Resistance to the Gaze

The final story in *Menschenkinder*, "Zurück ans All" ("At One, Again, with Nature") presents a very interesting triangle of women: Ella, a traditional young woman who wants to marry, settle down, and raise a family, Frau Dr. Fuhrberg, a scholar and active feminist, and Irene, a young, unmarried misanthrope. Ella accepts her role as object of the gaze; Frau Dr. Fuhrberg rejects such objectification and fights for women's equality with men; and Irene seeks an existence beyond social power structures entirely. Irene is misanthropic to the point of comedy, providing a sardonic commentary on her wholesome cousin, Ella, who embraces traditional femininity. The triangular constellation reads as an attempt to differentiate the decadent woman from both traditional and feminist woman, to suggest, that is, that associating feminists with decadence is erroneous, and to suggest that there is a means of existing otherwise for women, a decadence, that implicitly resists rather than simply seeks to invert the gaze.[21]

In her late teens the protagonist, Irene, turned down her sixty-year-old uncle's marriage proposal but accompanied him nonetheless to his isolated farm in the country where she has, in the meantime — she is now in her late twenties — restructured the entire farm to make it a better and kinder environment for all of its animals and plants. The animals and plants thrive in her care because she is interested in them in their own right and wants an environment that is pleasant for them rather than one that is a productive food source for humans. An early environmentalist, Irene shuns people and avoids situations in which they congregate if at all possible, explaining: "Alle Nähe macht mir Übelkeit" (338; "Anything close disgusts me," 187). The novella begins, however, with a brief visit to the town of Königsberg that emphasizes Irene's distaste for normal, everyday human life and underscores people's sense of her as an anomaly: "Fast ein jeder, der ihr begegnete, wandte den Kopf nach ihr um, doch hätte keiner zu sagen gewußt, was an ihr auffiel" (315; "Almost all who encountered her turned their heads; yet no one could have said what was so striking about her," 174). Irene, on the other hand, is indifferent to them and to their gaze, going about her business with an expression of "tiefster Gleichgültigkeit für das Getriebe der Menschen und Wagen um sie" (315; "profoundest indifference to the bustle of the people and carriages around her," 174). But if she is oblivious to the gaze, if she strides around the city in a manner that makes people notice a difference that they are unable to articulate, she does so not as a feminist rejection of traditional women's roles but as a rejection of human life patterns as a whole. When Frau Dr. Fuhrberg tries to win her over to the feminist cause precisely because she appears to reject traditional feminine roles, Irene explains: "Weil ich gegen die Männer bin, bin ich noch lange nicht für die Frauen" (319; "The fact that I am against men does not by any stretch mean that I am for women," 176).

Irene demonstrates an excessive and misanthropic individualism, a physical and mental androgyny, and a desire to escape from a mechanized, collective way of life as represented by the city and the family. When she returns to her hotel in Köngisberg, she is dismayed to hear from the porter that two women await her outside her room: "Der helle Ausdruck schwand aus ihren Augen, sie stieg müde die kurze Treppe hinauf und betrat ihre Stube mit einer Miene so starrer Gleichgültigkeit, daß es wie ein kühler Lufthauch von ihr auf die beiden anwesenden Damen auszugehen schien" (318; "The bright expression vanished from her eyes; wearily she climbed the few stairs and entered her room with a look of such fixed indifference that it seemed to hit the two ladies there like a cold draft," 176). Irene's indifference is repeatedly highlighted in conjunction with seeing and being seen and reads as an extreme, whether conscious or unconscious, resistance to the gaze in the form of self-isolation. By implicitly contrasting Irene with feminist women, the text criticizes a feminist ideology that remains caught up in the logic of the gaze and of patriarchal society. It also, however, demonstrates that feminism and feminists contribute a great deal to society, guided, as they are, by a concept of justice and focused on future generations. Whereas Frau Dr. Fuhrberg may deviate from traditional feminine roles, she is productive and participates in other arenas. Irene, on the other hand, represents a greater "perversion" than women who are feminists and choose less traditionally feminine paths in life. When Frau Dr. Fuhrberg tells her that her way of thinking and her lifestyle connect her to feminism whether she likes it or not, because her choices indicate that she must want the same rights as men, the right to do anything they can do, Irene responds: "Mich reizt nicht, was Männer besitzen. Mannesrecht ist ja, alles mitzumachen, — und ich mag nichts mitmachen" (320; "I find no appeal in what men possess. Man's right is to take part in everything — and I don't care to be part of anything," 177).

Irene is, in her own words, a "ganz unproduktiver Mensch" (336; "quite an unproductive person," 186). She plays the piano beautifully but doesn't consider this a productive endeavor because she has never composed anything and simply copies what others have done before her. She refuses to play for others, only playing alone in a room after lunch. An orphaned aristocrat, she does not want contact to her equally marginalized brother and, though she lives with her uncle, she does not interact with him, preferring the company of the animals and plants she so carefully tends. She underscores the absoluteness of her isolation when she tells her cousin Ella "Ich glaube nicht daran, daß die Liebe uns aus unserer Vereinzelung erlöst" (329; "I don't believe that love saves us from our isolation," 182). Irene also displays all of the standard outward signs of the decadent. She has "blasse Züge," "eine marmorbleiche Stirn," and "kühle Finger" (321; "pale features," "marble-pale brow," and "cool fingers," 177). Unlike her healthy cousin, Ella, who is eager to marry and reproduce, Irene has no appetite and is referred to by some in the area in which she lives as "ein zartes, gebrechliches fin de siècle-Wesen" (325; "a delicate, frail, fin-de-siècle creature," 180). She and her brother, a "ziemlich verlebte[r] Weltmann [sind] die letzten eines alten Geschlechts" (326; "rather dissipated man of the world constituted the last of an old family," 180).

Ella, by contrast, is repeatedly described as "lebhaft" ("lively") and is outraged when Irene tells her that she cannot stand the thought of human reproduction. Irene does not mean that she personally does not want to have children but rather that she rejects reproduction in principle: "Ein Mörder, der da tötet, ist mir lieber, als dies —, dies verfluchte schmutzige Leben machen" (341; "A murderer who kills I prefer to this — this making of damned, filthy life," 189). Ella accuses Irene of indulging in "unmenschliche Gedanken" (342; "inhuman thoughts," 190) and commands her to clear the way for those human beings to whom the future really belongs. Here, as in *Fenitschka* and *Eine Ausschweifung*, Andreas-Salomé links decadence for women to a refusal or failure to reproduce and links this refusal to reproduce and participate in society to a resistance to preestablished identity categories and thus to the gaze that polices those identity categories. It may be interpreted as decadent to be promiscuous, to participate in the commodification of sex by offering it at a price, but it is more decadent, Andreas-Salomé suggests, to refuse sex and to render oneself useless within a patriarchal economy. The refusal to reproduce marginalizes woman beyond compare, rendering her worthless and unproductive in conventional, and even in tolerated unconventional, terms. Irene's lack of productivity, her refusal to be seen in utilitarian terms as a link between past and future generations, represents an aestheticization and perversion of the feminine and a valorization of an "artificial" relationship to the world. Irene's decadence in "Zurück ans All" amounts to a resistance to the gaze. Her argument to Ella that "all forms of closeness disgust her" results in Ella questioning if Irene is "überhaupt ein Mensch" (338; "human at all," 187). Her extreme form of resistance makes Irene's interpellation into a comprehensible feminine, or even human, subject position exceedingly difficult, if not impossible. By denying her relationship to others as well as their attempts to identify her, Irene rejects identity, denies her own existence, and, at the end of this novella, literally ceases to exist.

After having devoted herself for years to the animals and plants she loves on the farm, Irene obeys Ella's command to get out of the way of those such as Ella to whom the future belongs. She walks out into nature, away from the farm that Ella will now inherit, and simply dissolves into the environment: "Und dann unterschied sie [Irene] sich kaum von den

Bäumen . . . und Äste und Zweige und alle Linien ringsum schienen sich hinter dem Rücken der Sonne zu neuen bizarren Formen zu verbinden, in denen Irenens erhobener Arm und feine Rückenlinie nur ein paar dunkle Linien mehr bildeten" (363; "And then she could hardly be distinguished from the trees . . . and branches and twigs and all lines all around seemed behind the sun's back to be joining into fantastic new forms, in which Irene's outstretched arm and fine line of her back merely formed a few more dark lines," 202). Irene wholeheartedly accepts her own demise and the end of herself and her line. The last image recalls a literal decadence in the sense of decay, that which rots and returns to the earth. Irene does not merely accept a kind of organic decay but strides willingly into it, concluding about herself: "Nie wird ein zartes Wiesenhälmchen zu einem Fruchtbaum" (360; "Never will a delicate blade of meadow grass turn into a fruit tree," 200). Her decadence becomes the ability to become invisible, to self-efface and dissolve into thin air. Decadence, taken to its logical limits as an embrace of the end and the opposite of regeneration, would mean a kind of voluntary human extinction and a vision of human beings as merely part of a continuum of existence rather than as its pinnacle. It would not be narcissistic but altruistic.

The gaze emerges here then as not merely an instrument of power wielded by men but also as a tool of narcissism on the part of the object of the gaze who allows her emotional and ego sustenance to be based on the reactions of others and on their approval. In a refreshingly prickly turn, Andreas-Salomé's depiction of Ella suggests that reproduction and gender normalcy, rather than decadence and abnormality, might qualify as the ultimate narcissism. At the end of "Zurück ans All," Ella, the woman who sticks wholeheartedly to social conventions and embraces and celebrates her role as the object of the gaze emerges as utterly narcissistic, so much so, that within seconds of Irene's departure, she begins to lose any sense of gratitude that she might have felt for everything Irene has given her. She has assumed unquestioningly that her desire to marry and have children is superior to Irene's desire to create a more humane life for animals, and, before Irene has dissolved into nature, Ella has decided to forget about her and focus on her new opportunity.

The abundance of references to easily identifiable decadent traits in Irene points to Andreas-Salomé's conscious investigation of the construction of decadence. Her depiction of Irene draws on a set of well-established conventions. Thus it is hard not to see her revision of the decadent woman as a direct intervention in contemporary cultural understandings of decadence and its relationship to looking and being looked at. By examining decadence in women in connection with the gaze and feminism, Andreas-Salomé complicates a number of contemporary discourses, literary and other, encouraging the engaged reader to see beyond the ubiquitous binaries that often constitute the limits of those discourses:

feminist/traditional, decadent/wholesome, narcissistic/selfless, and subject/object. In her contrast of Ella to the other women in the text, for example, she implies that it would be possible to interpret everything beyond primal instinctive urges as decadent, and that civilization, modernity, culture, sublimation, and concepts of progress all contain decadent undercurrents. She questions a clear distinction between decadence and the sort of normative social behavior that constitutes civilization.

The overt invocation of decadence in this final novella of the cycle significantly influences rereadings of the other novellas in the cycle. In retrospect, for example, "Unterwegs" ("On Their Way") seems to offer a tongue-in-cheek look at extreme civilization. A young city couple, Martin and Lisa, make an excursion into the mountains with the goal of committing suicide, because they realize they probably cannot afford a life in which he is a poet and she his muse. When Martin wavers and argues that there are other things in life and that they at least have each other and their love, Lisa chastises him:

> "Werde nicht wankelmütig! Wozu kann denn das führen? Willst du etwa ein Leben wie Gevatter Schuster und Schneider? Nein, laß uns groß und uns selbst treu bleiben, —: wenn du nicht, unbeschwert von niedrigen Sorgen, streben darfst, einst unsterbliche Werke zu schaffen, und wenn ich an deiner Seite nicht deine Muse werden darf —" Sie vollendete nicht. (149)

> ["Don't start equivocating," . . . "what can that lead to, then? Do you want to live like some good little cobbler or tailor? No, let us remain great and true to ourselves — if you are not allowed to strive, free from common cares, to create works that might one day be immortal, and if I am not to be allowed to be the muse at your side —" She did not finish. (81)].

Humorous in its absurdity, this justification for suicide implies that there is an inherent alienation in civilization, something that deviates from the so-called natural order. The novella presents the latter in the form of the peasants and farmers of whom Martin says somewhat condescendingly: "Glücklich sind diese einfachen Menschen mit ihren Illusionen" (160; "These simple people are happy with their illusions," 87). Mali and Aloys live hand-to-mouth, work the land in a very rural area, and are concerned primarily with survival. Unlike Martin and Lisa, whom Mali perceives as riding a carousel, they are so caught up in the basics of surviving that they do not have time to think about the luxuries that Martin and Lisa deem necessities. City life and civilization emerge here as artificial, decadent structures, and the novella poses the question of how civilization, always already artificial, is any different from decadence except in its ideological function.

In most cases the novellas in this collection are stories of thwarted love that end with the decision on the part of the majority of their protagonists to opt for a life beyond marriage, family, and traditional gender roles. Andreas-Salomé's female characters who "exist otherwise" are women who devote their lives to some greater cause: Christiane of "Abteilung; Innere Männer" nurses the sick devotedly and Marfa of "Ein Wiedersehen" goes back to Russia to practice medicine in an area where she will be poor and overworked but where they desperately need qualified doctors. Both have to forego a comfortable bourgeois lifestyle with a man who loves them because of the man's refusal to accept any level of compromise on the expected roles within a heterosexual relationship. In the case of Irene in "Zurück ans All," it is her cousin who rejects her unique lifestyle and forces her out of existence. All transfer whatever maternal or wifely instincts they might have had to people and services beyond their families; they do not reproduce and they are not integrated. But their acceptance of their own extinction functions as a kind of manure. They are the dung, the decaying waste products that contribute to the regeneration of the Other and to the gradual transformation of femininity.

The narrative perspective employed throughout *Menschenkinder* seems designed to help the reader understand this dialectic of social expectation and the changing formation of feminine identity. It introduces the reader first to the cultural panorama, to the landscape in which the women who populate Andreas-Salomé's fiction exist, before cutting to the internal space being constructed — cut and edited — by these women, who are all intimately aware of the script that has been written for them. The first person perspective follows on from and amends the introductory perspective, undermining and complicating it in a variety of ways. While *Menschenkinder* offers us ten very different women in ten very different situations, each story employs the same textual movement to elucidate the complexities of women's negotiations of both social and personal spaces at the turn of the twentieth century. Andreas-Salomé's technique and her repeated examinations of people looking and being looked at suggest a keen awareness of how looking and being looked at, being the subject or the object of the gaze, is and was an important constitutive aspect of gendered identity. She demonstrates a clear interest in how the gaze functions as an instrument of ideology and offers a sophisticated analysis of it, suggesting that it is at once powerful and masculine and yet vulnerable, unstable, and appropriable.

Notes

[1] Lou Andreas-Salomé, *Menschenkinder: Novellencyklus* (Stuttgart: Cotta, 1899).

[2] Laura Mulvey, "Visual Pleasure and Narrative Cinema," *Screen 16.3 (1975): 6–18.*

[3] I am thinking here of works such as De Lauretis's *Alice Doesn't: Feminism Semiotics Cinema* (Bloomington: Indiana UP, 1984); Mary Ann Doane's "Film and the Masquerade: Theorising the Female Spectator," *Screen* 23.3–4 (1982): 74–87; and parts of Luce Irigray's *Speculum of the Other Woman*, trans. Gilliam C. Gill (Ithaca, NY: Cornell UP, 1985), especially the chapter "Another 'Cause' — Castration" (46–54).

[4] All translations for the stories in *Menschenkinder* are taken from Raleigh Whitinger's excellent translation of the collection. Lou Andreas-Salomé, *The Human Family: Stories*, trans. and with an introduction by Raleigh Whitinger (Lincoln and London: U of Nebraska P, 2005).

[5] Brigid Haines, "'Ja, so würde ich es auch heute noch sagen': Reading Lou Andreas-Salomé in the 1990s," *Publications of the English Goethe Society* 62 (1992): 77–95.

[6] In "Die Stunde ohne Gott" (The Hour without God) Andreas-Salomé narrates the story of her first realization that God had disappeared from the world. She repeats this tale at the beginning of her autobiography, *Lebensrückblick* (Looking Back). The loss of God in Andreas-Salomé's narratives functions as an allegory for the loss of a clear authority and morality represented generally by an altruistic man who reveals his tragic flaw. See Lou Andreas-Salomé, *Die Stunde ohne Gott und andere Kindergeschichten* (Jena, Germany: E. Dietrichs Verlag, 1922). See also *Lebensrückblick: Grundriß einiger Lebenserinnerungen*, ed. Ernst Pfeiffer (1951; repr., Frankfurt am Main: Insel, 1998).

[7] Julia Kristeva, "Kein weibliches Schreiben? Fragen an *Julia Kristeva*," *Freibeuter* 2 (1979): 79–84. Many parallels have been drawn between Kristeva and Andreas-Salomé. They both tend to essentialize femininity in their theoretical tracts and link it to motherhood; they both dislike political feminisms; they both argue that seeking equality with men will eliminate femininity. Compare, for example, Andreas-Salomé's "Der Mensch als Weib," *Neue Deutsche Rundschau* 10 (1899): 225–43, repr. in Lou Andreas-Salomé, *Die Erotik: Vier Aufsätze*, ed. Ernst Pfeiffer (Frankfurt am Main: Ullstein, 1985), 7–44; and Kristeva's "Women's Time," in *Feminisms: An Anthology of Literary Theory and Criticism*, ed. Robyn R. Warhol and Diana Price Herndl (New Brunswick, NJ: Rutgers UP, 1997). See also Karla Schultz, "In Defense of Narcissus: Lou Andreas-Salomé and Julia Kristeva," *The German Quarterly* 67.2 (1994): 185–96.

[8] Beth Newman, "The Situation of the Looker-On: Gender, Narration, and Gaze in *Wuthering Heights*," in Warhol and Herndl, *Feminisms: An Anthology of Literary Theory and Criticism*, 451.

[9] E. Ann Kaplan, *Women and Film: Both Sides of the Camera* (New York: Routledge, 1990), 24.

[10] That the external observer is a woman further complicates things and points to the possibility of the gaze as potentially owned and activated by either sex, an issue discussed in detail by Kaplan in *Women and Film*.

[11] John Berger, *Ways of Seeing* (London: BBC & Penguin, 1992).

[12] Siegfried Kracauer, "Über Arbeitsnachweise," *Frankfurter Zeitung* (June 17, 1930). Translation from "On Employment Agencies," in *Rethinking Architecture,* ed. Neil Leach (London: Routledge, 1997), 60.

[13] Bovenschen argues that women placed on a pedestal were bound to fail, because expectations were too high and too limiting. See the introduction to this volume, note 19.

[14] He thinks of the poem about "Christiane" that Goethe wrote because the names match but cannot imagine that his Christiane has anything in common with Goethe's Christiane, whom he sees as a loose woman of a lower class. He then also associates his Christiane with Lottchen from *Die Leiden des jungen Werthers* (The Sorrows of Young Werther). The image he recalls is one of Lottchen cutting bread for her siblings, Lottchen as a pure, innocent sister taking care of her family. While Christiane von Brinken's class origins are significantly different, she too takes care of others.

[15] Although "sister" refers to Christiane's profession here, there is something familial and familiar about the title "sister" as given to all nurses. It names those who take care of men in nonsexual terms, raising the specter of the incest taboo to perhaps prevent sexual attraction.

[16] Alice Kuzniar, *The Queer German Cinema* (Stanford, CA: Stanford UP, 2000), 200.

[17] Barbara Mennel, *The Representation of Masochism and Queer Desire in Film and Literature* (New York: Palgrave Macmillan, 2007).

[18] Beth Newman, "The Situation of the Looker-On, 453.

[19] Mennel, *The Representation of Masochism and Queer Desire,* 137.

[20] See John Hannavy, ed., "Historiography of 19th Century Photography," *Encyclopedia of 19th Century Photography* (New York: Routledge, 2007), 664–68.

[21] See chapter 1 for a fuller discussion of decadence.

6: Articulating Identity: Narrative as Mastery and Self-Mastery in *Fenitschka*

> *Coherence and closure are deep human desires that are presently unfashionable. But they are always both frightening and enchantingly desirable.*
>
> — A. S. Byatt

FENITSCHKA, published in 1898 together with *Eine Ausschweifung*, has undoubtedly received the most critical attention of any of Lou Andreas-Salomé's fictional works, perhaps because it offers such an interesting window into the debates of the turn-of-the-century women's movement. That the environment in which Fenitschka lives presents her with an unsolvable dilemma — she wants love and passion but not marriage, and she wants a career as a teacher — has been analyzed lucidly and thoroughly in a number of publications that focus exclusively on the novella, from Brigid Haines's "Fenitschka: A Feminist Reading" (1990) to Raleigh Whitinger's "Lou Andreas-Salomé's *Fenitschka* and the Tradition of the Bildungsroman" (1999).[1] From a variety of compelling perspectives, the essays focus on how Andreas-Salomé treats aspects of the turn-of-the-century emancipation debate and undermines the antifeminist position by demonstrating, in the figure of Max Werner, how limiting and imbalanced it is.[2] In addition, Whitinger tackles the character of Max in detail, arguing that he represents the confinement that traditional, male-authored narratives and artworks exercise on women. He highlights how Max continuously seeks to steer Fenitschka toward more conventional women's choices and how he nevertheless achieves some level of insight and growth over the course of his relationship with Fenitschka that bodes well for the future of feminism. Whitinger's study is replete with fascinating details that emphasize Andreas-Salomé's clear contribution to formal as well as thematic innovations.

Shifting the emphasis away from Fenitschka's dilemma, as Whitinger does, and onto Max's, I argue here that Max is a more central character in this text than is generally appreciated. Throughout the novella we have access not only to what Max says aloud to Fenitschka but also quite frequently to what he thinks before, during, and after he says what he says. His particular perspective is enhanced, in other words, but readers are denied the same access to Fenitschka's private thoughts, to her internal reactions to Max's behaviors and statements. We find ourselves in Max's shoes, in an identificatory position with him, forced to guess what Fenitschka might actually be thinking when she falls silent and when she thanks her lover profusely at the end.[3] Focusing on his centrality reveals aspects of the novella formerly overlooked: first, Lou Andreas-Salomé's interest in man's negotiation of identity in the same volatile context in which she examines woman's and second, her clever textual mirroring of feminist discourse's marginalized cultural status at the time. By aligning the reader with Max and making Fenitschka the Other, she pushes feminist discourse and those who support it to the sidelines.

Max is not merely the embodiment of everything Fenitschka must fight against and overcome in her pursuit of freedom in this particular time and place, and the problematic discourse that he represents is shown to be not so much a male discourse on women (compare Doll Allen and Whitinger) as it is the socially sanctioned discourse on women.[4] Andreas-Salomé emphasizes Fenitschka's deviation from other women's concepts of normal life narratives throughout this novella. In the café in Paris she reacts very differently from her female colleagues to the unpleasant scene unfolding in front of her. In her uncle's home, she seems unperturbed by rumors that he believes will damage her reputation. Her cousin, by contrast, admits to having been worried to the point of a migraine by these rumors that don't directly involve her (32). Max also reflects that his fiancée would have been very out of sorts were she to hear any such rumors about herself (33). Fenitschka is clearly operating in accordance with a deviant narrative, one outside the consciousness of her family, one with which she struggles, and one to which she nonetheless attempts to adhere. Hence Fenitschka constitutes a truly tragic character in the Nietzschean sense: she sees what others cannot see and cannot be integrated.

Max's Dilemma: Fenitschka as Moving Target

Although we seem to be dealing in *Fenitschka* with a third person, omniscient narrator, the narrative actually predominantly represents Max's perspective.[5] That Max and the narrator are in fact one is supported by the narrator's expression of regret for Max's having been young and foolish at the time of his first acquaintance with Fenitschka: "Ach, er war noch sehr jung damals!" (16; "How young and naïve he had been then," 10).[6] "Ach," an exclamation of regret or resignation, demonstrates an emotional investment in, and a visceral response to, the events at hand. It suggests a narrator who at the very least is sympathetic to Max's plight and hence someone closely associated with, if not in fact identical with, Max himself. Furthermore, as Julie Doll Allen points out, we get no detailed external description of Max. We do not know what he looks like, what he wears, or what color his eyes are, but we do get several details about Fenitschka's attire and appearance.[7] Max's hat is mentioned briefly as Fenitschka flees his room in Paris but is not described in any physical detail and has significance only in that its absence reflects Max's psychic state at this moment, as he struggles with a loss of sovereignty or dominance.[8] These references to Max's hat reveal an intimate knowledge of his psychic life.

Doll Allen argues that we are dealing in fact with an unreliable narrator, a narrator set up as omniscient but who knows only one side of the story well. What we may have, in fact, is Max masquerading as an omniscient or objective narrator. The fact that this kind of tactic — Max's elevation of himself to one who knows, who can lecture and inform from a knowing and external perspective — would fit in general with his tendencies in speech within the novella further supports the notion that the seemingly third-person narrator is Max. When he speaks to Fenitschka, he attempts to take on a universalist or objective position. He has a tendency to lecture her and responds best when she asks him questions. Their first conversation is composed of her short questions to him, almost rhetorical questions, to which he nonetheless responds at length, as if already in his role as professor at the lectern. When he speaks of the world and how the people in it exist, he does so from what he projects as an authoritative and all-knowing perspective. He knows what the French are like, what Russian women are like, what women are like. Though she does not generally question Max's adoption of such an authoritative position, toward the end of the novella when the issues under discussion have become more personal for Fenitschka, she does interrupt him to ask if what he has just related to her about love has any basis in his own personal experience. He can only respond that he has no personal experience of what he has just lectured her about but that he has heard it elsewhere and believes it. He adds that it would not, in any case, apply to him as a man. Max's retrospective narrative, whether he himself a reflector or mirror narrator tells it to us, a narrative including moments of regret, representing him at times in questionable light but ultimately redeeming him, indicates that his time with Fenitschka, though brief, was significant. After all, it warrants telling. And in the telling lie other important and interesting revelations about Max and processes of telling in general.

Although he repeatedly represents the traditionalist standpoint to Fenitschka, Max is one of the more positive characters in the story. He is at once the most and least ambitious proponent of the male-authored discourse on women, in that he represents it to Fenitschka but also acquiesces to discussing the possibility of something different. Thanks to these discussions, he achieves a few moments of rational understanding of Fenitschka's perspective and an awareness that his own concerted attempts to pigeonhole her might be questionable. In their creation and exchange of narratives, each attempts to "master," to come to terms with, both the Other and the self. The text pits a conservative, antifeminist Max against the feminist Fenitschka in an ideologically charged confrontation and emphasizes, as Allen argues, dialogue, conversation, and communication between these two divergent ideologies.[9] This emphasis on exchange and dialog suggests that legitimized, authoritative discourses can only be undermined and replaced with something new through patient and persistent conflict and argument, which might someday lead to consensus.[10] Like Fenitschka, Max is part of the narrative structure he wants to impose and thus likewise confined or empowered by it. He is not simply trying to make sense of Fenitschka's life by casting it in terms of a narrative with which he is familiar. He is equally trying to make sense of his own life both in terms of his relationship to her and to his fiancée, Irmgard. Max's personal identity crisis is, in other words, as acute as Fenitschka's.

Fenitschka underscores how the changes that feminist ideology ushered in at the turn of the twentieth century affected men as well as women. Max's development shows how ideological shifts, such as feminism, affect the narratives through which men, as well as women, account for themselves and their relationships to others and hones in on the relationship between reason and reflex, between the logical and the habitual, between new ideologies that need time to be absorbed and old ideologies that are second-nature and have been granted the status of "natural." The role narrative conventions play in both accounting for the past and scripting present and future possibilities is intimately linked to questions of ideological change and self-representation and similarly plays a large role in determining how the relationship between Max and Fenitschka unfolds. Certain narratives are not only part of our cultural and ideological heritage, Andreas-Salomé suggests in this novella, but they are quite literally part of us, written on the body, whether we like it or not.

Max's first encounter with Fenitschka in Paris sets up the terms of his personal dilemma. I want to trace here the progress of what is termed his relationship to Fenitschka, emphasizing his greater investment in it from the beginning. Unable to account for Fenitschka, Max proves unable to account for his own behavior toward her. She has a visceral effect on him: "Eine Art von stiller Wut kam über ihn. Seine Unklarheit über dieses Mädchen quälte ihn" (16; "He became incensed; his confusion about this young woman plagued him," 10).[11] The only way his reaction to Fenitschka (his failed attempt at seduction followed by the threat implied in his locking of the door and removal of the key) can be accounted for is by underscoring his own inability to assess it. Three times in a very brief textual segment his behavior is described as devoid of intention: "Er hatte sie *ohne irgendeine klare Absicht* hier eingeführt . . . *ohne noch selbst recht zu wissen*, was er eigentlich damit bezweckte, stürzte er an ihr vorbei zur Tür. . . . Seine Hand fuhr, *ohne daß er es ihr im geringsten anbefohlen hätte*, in seine Tasche" (17–18; "He had brought her here *without a clear notion* of what he wanted . . . and *without knowing what he was really trying to do,* he reached for the door before she could get to it. . . . His hand slid into his pocket *quite involuntarily, and without notice of its owner,"* 11, emphasis added). As readers, we might assume then that Max has never behaved in this manner before. Frustrated by the challenge Fenitschka poses, he becomes erratic in, and out of control of, his behavior. If Max is to be able to integrate these events into his self-representation, the relationship to Fenitschka cannot end here, as he himself realizes. He wants to find her again in Paris to make amends, but by the time he picks up the courage to do so, she is gone. Then the chance to make amends and achieve closure presents itself unexpectedly over a year later, when his sister marries a relative of Fenitschka's in Russia. With the exception of the first chapter, the novella delineates the terms of their more positive relationship and reads as Max's effort to reconcile himself to the past. Most analyses of *Fenitschka* have gone along with the narrator's perspective, which interprets what Max did to Fenitschka in Paris as a minor glitsch, an infelicitous approach. However, it consisted of a gesture and an intention that are far more problematic than youthful fervor. His actions, predicated on the idea that a woman who behaves independently must be sexually active and therefore sexually active with anyone who wants her, betray a deep-seated misogyny. The remainder of his narrative becomes his attempt to compensate for his Parisian transgression and thus manage to integrate it into a coherent and positive self-narrative.

From the outset of his time in Russia, Max throws himself into his relationship with Fenitschka, wanting it to become very familiar very quickly. He is annoyed, for example, when the whole wedding party drinks to brotherhood but then fails to follow up on what drinking to brotherhood in this manner would imply, namely the use of "du," the informal second person pronoun (21). He tries using it with Fenia, but when she fails to react, he reverts to "Sie" (22–23). He is also the first to share intimate details of his private life, revealing during a sleigh ride his secret affair with Irmgard. The dynamics of this and other conversations demonstrate that it is Max who is most invested in seeing intimacy develop between them. He drives the narrative, and his expectations of closure and conciliation become those of the readers. While Max is shown to be willing to betray Irmgard, revealing a secret that is more threatening to her than to himself, the narrator underscores Fenitschka's tendency to remain tight-lipped: "Fenia schwieg einige Minuten. Irgendein Gedanke schien sie zu beschäftigen" (24; "Fenia remained silent for a while; something seemed to occupy her mind," 16). In their discussion about relationships she reveals little or nothing about herself, and when she does speak, she asks a question that is so clearly formulated from her own very specific perspective that it perplexes Max: "Und trotzdem, — trotz all diesen schwierigen Umständen, — will sie [Irmgard] Sie [Max] noch nicht heiraten?" (24; "And for all that — in spite of this difficult state of affairs, she does not want to marry you yet?" 16). He cannot conceive of a case in which a woman would not want to marry, and his response silences Fenia once again: "Fenia verfiel in Nachdenken. Sie saß mit gesenktem Gesicht, als horche sie aufmerksam auf das Schellenklingel der Schlittenpferde" (24; "Fenia lost herself in her thoughts. With bowed head she listened to the jingling sleigh bells," 16). When they later revisit their discussion of love after seeing illustrations of Lermontov's demon in a window, Max has to draw Fenitschka out on her opinion of love, asking her how she would respond to an examination question about its nature. Throughout parts two and three of the novella, she falls silent or breaks off in mid-sentence, indicating her engagement with thoughts that she is reluctant to share. When Max finds her outside a convent in a somewhat questionable area of St. Petersburg, for example, she interrupts a sentence that could compromise her because it reveals that she expected to be able to preserve her anonymity in this area: ". . . Man kann fast sicher sein, daß man —" (26; "One can almost be certain not to —," 17). Shortly thereafter, when he asks her how she feels about her impending return to work, she again holds back: "Darauf schwieg sie wieder mit nachdenklichem Gesicht, als beschäftige sie etwas Unausgesprochenes" (27; "Then she became quiet again and lost herself in thought. Something seemed to occupy her mind that she had not been able to express," 18). She does not automatically make Max her confidant as he wishes she would, and she is far slower to reveal details about her private life than he is.

So what motivates Max's unusually strong interest in achieving some level of intimacy with Fenitschka? Why does he repeatedly seek her out and try to engage her in conversation? Why is he more invested in a relationship with her than she is in one with him? While our narrator presents his interest as a kind of intellectual curiosity in a mystery that Max would like to solve, it seems more likely that Max is motivated by what Fenitschka means to his understanding of himself, to his self-image and self-representation. Max's excitement when he does finally achieve a more substantial level of intimacy with Fenitschka underscores his curiously exaggerated interest in doing so. As he comes home one evening, she passes him by, heavily veiled, on the stairs of his boarding house. He pretends not to recognize her in deference to social codes that make her presence there shameful. Unable to tolerate what his pretense implies, Fenitschka reveals herself to him and accuses him of treating her like a criminal or breakable doll. Max's reactions in the conversation that follows warrant closer examination. Although the exchange suggests a turning point in their relationship, namely a shift to a more reciprocal friendship, Max seems preoccupied with himself during the interaction and unable to subordinate his own desires for intimacy to Fenitschka's need for support. At first Fenitschka's responses to him seem less eager or warm than he might desire. When he tries to comfort her after her initial outburst, she pushes his hand away, and when she finally speaks again, she seems to have missed or chosen to ignore what is a fairly major declaration of affection and concern on his part; he refers to them as "feste, gute Freunde" ("good, trusted friends") and tells her he would go through fire for her (42; 30). Fenitschka is still upset by the misfortune of having seen him here at all and indulges in a series of self-accusations "Wie sollte ich wissen, daß Sie hier wohnen. . . . Sonst wäre ich — hätte ich — " (43; "How could I have know that you were staying here. . . . I should have, would have — ," 30). When, in a fit of rage, she tells him that she is involved in a secret affair, he finds her all the more alluring: "Er fand sie herrlich, wie sie mit fliegendem Atem das sagte" (43; "He was full of admiration for her as she blurted this out breathlessly," 30). He thanks her profusely for telling him this: "Er faßte ihre Hände und küßte sie. 'Danke, Fenia!' sagte er ernst, 'ich danke Ihnen!'" (43; "He took her hand and kissed it. 'Thank you, Fenia,' he said, 'I thank you,'" 30).

Max is overjoyed to have the opportunity to be Fenitschka's confidant, as his desperate attempts to prolong the interaction indicates. He tries to get her to stay when he fears she might flee and feels particularly successful when he gets her to talk: "Damit hatte er das richtige Wort getroffen. Sie setzte sich wieder und blickte ihn erstaunt und erwartungsvoll an" (44; "He had found the right word. She sat down again and looked at him surprised and expectant," 31). Whereas Fenitschka experiences great distress and vacillates between feeling relieved to have told someone and wanting to flee from the spotlight, Max celebrates the moment of "Brüderschaft" ("brotherhood") and the "du" (informal "you") that her predicament triggers (47–48). Doll Allen emphasizes the condescending, patriarchal tone he adopts with Fenitschka in these interactions, arguing convincingly that he takes on an authoritative, doctor-like demeanor that implies hysteria in Fenitschka (487). His giddy excitement might also be read as relief in finding himself in a situation in which he knows exactly how to behave. Max, at last, is in a role he knows and likes because it institutes him as the protector and places him in a position of power. He seeks to comfort her with his words. All the while, however, he is thinking only of the prospect he now has of getting closer to her and of how enticing, interesting, and attractive he finds her in this condition. Romanticizing Fenitschka's dilemma, he sees a fiery passionate woman, someone risking everything for love, instead of seeing a woman at risk. He seizes the opportunity to wrap her around his finger in a manner that he is unable to do when she is not under severe personal duress. The gap the narrative reveals between what Max says and what he thinks in this interaction detracts attention from the mere content of their dialogue and calls attention instead to Max's underlying motives and his contradictory and primarily self-interested relationship to Fenitschka: he wants to be her friend and confidant because this will compensate for his past transgression, but becoming her friend involves the reestablishment of a conventional gendered narrative in which he becomes a knight in shining armor, her guardian or protector. Thus the very role that, in its familiarity, offers him some relief makes her uneasy and returns them to square one.

This uncomfortable seesaw relationship and the past's tendency to repeat itself explain Max's repeated annoyance at the clash of their perspectives on practically every subject. Because she does not behave as women should, she thrusts him out of his comfort zone, confusing and angering him. In Paris, when he first meets Fenitschka, she is dressed in black. In Russia, when he meets her again, she is wearing white (21). On each occasion he settles on an interpretation of her appearance very quickly. He sees women in very simplistic terms, the text suggests, namely in black and white. When he first arrives in Russia, Fenitschka, dressed in white, is welcoming to him, and he therefore sees her as softer and more feminine than earlier. He expects that she has become what he understands a woman to be and relaxes. Whereas he literally locked Fenitschka into a room in Paris, literally confined her, in Russia he does so metaphorically. For him, there are clear-cut distinctions between two different kinds of women, with no grey areas in between, and Fenitschka challenges his self-assurance in that she resists such categorization. In his developing relationship to Fenitschka, Max must learn to function in a relationship with which he has no experience. During their conversation on women's education in Paris, for example, he explains that women should receive whatever intellectual stimulation and knowledge they need from men, and from his tendency to lecture Fenitschka on the French and on women's education, it is evident that he has been socialized in accordance with such a belief (15). He automatically takes on authority in discussions with her, interpreting reality from his very tidy, prepackaged perspective and then delivering that interpretation to her as a corrective to her own understanding of the world. For Max, repeatedly telling Fenitschka how women really feel or really are does not give rise to any degree of self-consciousness. Andreas-Salomé makes it abundantly clear that Max simply recites age-old notions of what women should be, influenced, she suggests, by his scholarly training in psychology, one of the disciplines so taken with the woman question at the turn of the century.

Max genuinely seems to want to solidify a relationship to Fenitschka and, over time, even comes to genuinely care for her, but behavioral reflexes based on gender repeatedly undo any gained intimacy. He is an example of a man not unwilling to listen to the voice of feminism, perhaps not even unwilling to slowly accept some of its doctrines, but for every moment of self-reflection he gains from the relationship to Fenitschka, he experiences a moment of knee-jerk reaction to anything she says or does that might suggest a vision of the sexes on a a more equal footing. Depicted as undergoing a learning process in which he makes an effort to absorb Fenitschka's rational explanations of the desires and behaviors that differentiate her from what he understands women to be, Max struggles to quell his instinctive rejections of those explanations. Slowly, though, Fenitschka does manage to temper his masculine postures and encourage him to transcend the limits of his narrow perspective. As the narrative progresses, he becomes less able to speak about the topics on which he earlier claimed authority without finding her voice and perspective first.

Despite all Max's faults, Andreas-Salomé does not depict him as a despicable or unlikable figure. Rather she seems at pains to emphasize that he makes progress with the new ideology with which he is confronted. At dinner at Fenitschka's uncle's house, Max reflects on how Fenitschka must feel about people who make problematic assumptions about the freedom she simply assumes for herself: "Wie oft mochte sie in ihrem freien Studienleben im Auslande Verachtung empfunden haben für die Menschen, deren billige Klugheit ihre Freiheit mißverstand und deren weises Urteil auf den ersten besten Schein hereinfiel" (32; "How often she must have felt scorn for people whose lack of education did not let them comprehend her unrestrained manner and whose wise judgment rested on quick and superficial impressions," 22). Oblivious nonetheless to how this thought might apply to his own treatment of Fenitschka, in the next moment he jumps to her defense in a knightly gesture that implies his continued adherence to the petrified and traditional gender roles he appears to have understood.[12] Early on in part 3 the narrator suggests Max's awareness of his problematic tendency to categorize women in accordance with simple formulas: "Warum nur? Warum hatte er in beiden Fällen ihr Wesen so typisch genommen, so grob fixiert? . . . Es war ganz merkwürdig, wie schwer es fiel, die Frauen in ihrer rein menschlichen Mannigfaltigkeit aufzufassen und nicht immer nur von der Geschlechtsnatur aus, nicht immer nur halb schematisch" (36; "Why? Just why had he regarded her, in both cases, as personification of a particular type? . . . It was strange that he found it so difficult to comprehend women in the manifold ways of their humanity and not just in some schematic way as representations of their gender," 25). Yet he continues to assess Fenitschka rather than meet her on her own terms in the next couple of chapters. This back and forth on Max's part is significant in that it makes him much more than simply a representative of limiting male discourse on women. Just as Andreas-Salomé demonstrates in *Das Haus* that the rationally argued advantages of feminism could not rearrange overnight a feminine desire that had been masochistically organized for hundreds of years, she demonstrates here too that men are equally the recipients of ingrained behaviors, of socializations that can also not be changed overnight.

The relentless return of the dominant trait Fenitschka possesses in Max's eyes, namely her femininity, the relentless return, that is, of the pre-scripted narrative to which Fenitschka fails to adhere, thwarts Max's efforts to understand her stance on a variety of topics. When they discuss the question of intimate relationships and secrecy from, as usual, very different perspectives, Max knows that this topic is more than simply theoretical for her and, for one of the first times, listens intently to what she says with a new result: "Die ein wenig frivole Spannung, in der Max Werner heute zu ihr gekommen war, verlor sich mehr und mehr; je länger er ihr zuhörte, desto *menschlicher* kam er ihr nah" (38; "Max Werner had been in a slightly frivolous state of tension this morning. But that began to disappear gradually now. The longer he listened to her, the closer he felt to her as *a human being*," 26, emphasis added). Because Fenitschka challenges everything he says, however, his masculine ego slowly gets the better of him. He launches into a condescending tirade on how "kampflustig" and "entsetzlich positiv und aggressiv" women have become (39; "belligerent" and "so terribly positive and aggressive," 27). This occurs only three pages after he appears somewhat self-critical for persistently attempting to classify Fenitschka in accordance with female stereotypes. What had been a relatively pleasant disagreement about intimacy and secrecy becomes an all-out attack by Max. No sooner has he calmed himself again than her response to his bottom line on love causes renewed consternation. He informs Fenitschka that the main thing for two lovers is "wie sie zueinander, nicht wie sie zur Welt stehen. — Wie lange das Glück währen mag, — wie gefestigt es ist, — oder ob man sich bei der ersten Not wieder verläßt, — das quält viel mehr" (40; "their relationship to one another, not to the world at large. How long will the happiness last? Are we secure with one another? Or are we going to part at the first sign of a problem? These are agonizing questions," 28). Max speaks here in general terms, using the pronoun "man" as if what he says were applicable to all human beings. When Fenitschka interprets it in this way, taking "man" (one) to mean any human being, male or female, and insists that she would never leave someone in their time of need, he flounders. What he in fact meant by "man" (one) was "Mann" (man), it appears, given that he cannot conceive of the idea of a "verlassenen Mann" (40; "deserted man," 28). Whereas he speaks to Fenitschka here as he would to a man and thus shows signs of being able to briefly forget her ubiquitous femininity, when she responds by assuming the same rights as a man, that is the right to be the one who leaves rather than the one who is left, Max is taken aback. Fenia's understanding of herself as someone with the same freedoms guaranteed to men strikes Max as bizarre and objectionable on a visceral if not on a conscious level, and he therefore reacts in very macho fashion. Similarly when Fenitschka later bemoans the marriage proposal she has received, Max sees her behavior as masculine and thus perplexing:

Er war offen gestanden, bezüglich des Mannes, der da soeben
Fenia einen Heiratsantrag gemacht hatte, nicht ganz ohne
Schadenfreude, — aber da hinein mischte sich ein ganz sonder-
bares Gefühl, — fast ein verblüfftes, beleidigtes, — fast als sei
er es, den sie abgewiesen habe. — Das war die Verblüffung über
die Worte, — Worte einer Frau, die ganz so sprach, als sei sie ein
Mann. (56)

[Quite honestly, as far as the man was concerned who had just proposed marriage to Fenia, he could not repress a malicious glee; but it
was mixed with a very peculiar sensation. He was almost nonplussed,
offended — almost as if he himself had been rejected. That was what
was so perplexing in her words, words of a woman who spoke as if
she were a man. (40)]

By drawing attention to Max's assumptions in this manner, Andreas-
Salomé subtly undermines the claims to universality that he makes for
his discourse, a discourse that represents general social attitudes toward
gender. She emphasizes that even when he speaks in general terms, using
"man" (one) as if to include all, we have little more than a rhetorical turn
used to suggest the universality of the male-authored position which, if
then truly interpreted and acted on as universal, becomes problematic.

Emphasizing that Max has come to Fenitschka's space in part 3,
Whitinger argues that Max demonstrates an increasing willingness to
meet Fenitschka on her own terms. He sees Max's "toying . . . with the
bundles of thread and wool on her sewing table" as indicative of "a lat-
ter-day Hercules, submitting to Queen Omphale, shedding, if only in
symbolic and unconscious gesture, his usual armor and weaponry for
women's work" (9). Focusing on what can be termed Max's feminization here, Whitinger reads his fidgeting positively, as the sign of a conces-
sion on Max's part, a sign of his understanding for Fenitschka's position.
Max's grasping at her balls of yarn at precisely this moment, his feminization, however, seems accompanied by strong feelings of a loss of authority and dominance. He is not simply "playing" with the balls of yarn but
clenches them nervously: "Etwas nervös griff er in Fenias Garnröllchen"
(40; "He became nervous and started to play with the spools of thread,"
28). Only seconds before this description Fenia introduces what for Max
is the problematic notion of a woman leaving a man and thus provokes
discomfort and mistrust on Max's part: "Fuhrte sie ihn vielleicht doch
hinters Licht?" (40; "Was she still deceiving him?" 28). In its implied
empowerment of women, Fenia's comment feminizes men and offers an
understanding of women's freedom that Max had never imagined possible. Discovering himself in a position in which the male privilege, masculinity, and its alignment with freedom, choice, and control has been
threatened by Fenitschka's words, Max responds passive-aggressively,

announcing that he saw her *Doppelgänger* the previous evening and thus dealing her a knock-out blow: "Sie sah blaß und in sich verkehrt aus" (41; "She looked pale and withdrawn," 28). In this state, refeminized as it were, Fenitschka becomes endearing to Max again: "Sehr lieb sah sie aus" (41; "She looked very sweet," 28). Within half a page he has gone from feeling a kind of passionate annoyance at Fenitschka ("Er wurde sogar plötzlich ganz irre . . ." and "Wäre sie nun doch wieder in Wirklichkeit die unschuldige Fenia, so wäre das ja einfach, um aus der Haut zu fahren" 40; "But now he became thoroughly confused . . ." and "If in reality she was, after all, the innocent Fenia — it would be enough to drive him out of his mind," 28) to finding her "very sweet." The change in Fenitschka that corresponds to the change in his feelings toward her is one from a sense of security with him and herself to a sense of vulnerability, exposure, and defenselessness brought on by his underhanded comment revealing that he had seen her in a compromising situation. Interestingly then, however, he immediately feels guilty for his nastiness: "[Er] schämte sich seiner unritterlichen Aufwallung" (40–41; "[He] felt ashamed of having blurted this out so unchivalrously," 28). The close attention paid to Max's psychic permutations here, his back and forth between defensive aggression and affection, is surely designed to hammer home that ingrained behavioral tendencies cause visceral responses. Something makes Max want to belittle Fenitschka and put her back in her place when he feels his own masculinity and masculinity in general threatened. That he is capable of reflecting rationally on his behavior and seeing that he behaved spitefully rather than rationally underscores again the gap between a rational understanding of an argument or position and an instinctive socialization that can be equated with a set of reflexes. If Andreas-Salomé indicates here, as Whitinger argues she does, that the patriarchal narratives with which Max is familiar are inadequate for the complex truths of reality, so too she indicates that the feminist narrative is inadequate for the complex truth of reality. It may reveal aspects of women's lives hitherto ignored and suppressed, but it too fails to account for the complexity of men and women as socialized beings. Undercutting master narratives as a whole then, Andreas-Salomé indicates that while they may be necessary and inescapable, they are always reductive and inadequate.

Max proves incapable of controlling his reflexes one final time in the fourth part of the novella, when he argues that if a woman doesn't want to marry a lover, then it can only be because what she feels for him is not love but sensual desire. He interprets the latter to be unwholesome and inappropriate for a woman of Fenitschka's standing. Initially taking this to heart, Fenitschka withdraws completely for a couple of days, and the next two times she sees Max, she does so only because he seeks her out or it cannot be avoided. On the second to last occasion, she asks him to leave, and on the last occasion she is not at all pleased to see him:

"Das ist ein großes Unglück . . . ein wahres Unglück, daß du gekommen bist" (64; "How unfortunate! . . . It is singularly unfortunate that you came just now," 45). She receives him because if she does not, she will also be unable to receive her lover, who is due to arrive at any moment. Fenitschka later revises and softens her initial displeasure at seeing him, asking if he is her true friend and, if so, if he can stay. But this request is related to self-interest and a tactic that she hopes will help her leave her lover. Thereafter, Fenia never wants to see Max again: "Zwei Tage später reiste er aus Rußland fort, ohne Fenitschka wiedergesehen zu haben. Sie wollte es so" (67; "Two days later he left Russia without seeing Fenia again. She had wished it this way," 47). While her refusal to see him could be attributed to her grief over the loss she had just endured, given the one-sided interest Max has had in her and her own increasing disinterest in Max in the denouement, it seems more likely that she has simply not found in him the confidant he had hoped she would.

In the end, it appears that Max may just be another example of the men Fenitschka spent time with in Zürich, men who sought out her friendship but were then unable to differentiate it from romance and love, feelings that never developed in her from such a relationship. She explains these relationships in detail to Max when he asks if she never loved any of the men she spent so much time with:

> Nein. Nie. Um manchen, der um deswillen fortging, trauerte ich. Aber was konnte das ändern? Ich wartete darauf, daß die Freundschaft in mir bis zur Liebe stiege — — . Sie stieg auch zuweilen, — immer höher und höher, — — aber nicht in die Liebe hinein, — sie wurde dann zugleich immer dünner und spitzer, — — und eines Tages brach stets die Spitze ab. (45)

> [No, never; Sometimes I mourned the loss of one who left for no reason. But what could I have done? I waited for the friendship I felt to grow into love. It grew sometimes, more and more — but never developed into love. It always became frailer and more fragile and invariably one day the point broke off from it." (32)]

Although Fenitschka has managed to escape the confining aspects of one potential narrative then, she seems powerless to effect a change in a new and unsatisfactory narrative. The trajectory she describes above is the trajectory of her relationship to Max, too.

There is no evidence of a love relationship developing from Fenia's perspective, but Max is obsessed with her during his time in St. Petersburg, dreams of her, and comments a number of times that he finds her attractive, endearing, even that he feels a little in love with her one morning. The retrospective narrative from his perspective, ostensibly about her, similarly suggests his greater investment in the relationship. Fenitschka, on the other hand, gives no signal that the relationship to Max is something new or special. In the end Max proves relatively satisfied with what he achieves, but in general the relationship involves a one-sided intimacy. He tells her all about his secret affair, though there is no reason to do so, whereas she tells him of hers only when he sees her in compromising situations; he wants her to take comfort in his presence, wants to help her, defend her, whereas she wants none of this and wants to be left to fend for herself. Max then finds a new narrative trajectory and a relationship to a woman that he has not experienced before: "Welch eine seltsame Rolle spielte er doch da in Fenias Leben" (65; "What a strange role he had assumed in Fenia's life!" 46). Until the narrative trajectories defined by or enacted in Max's and Fenitschka's relationship and in Fenitschka's relationship to her lover — narrative trajectories whose presence in discourse is becoming possible only because of a burgeoning feminist movement and its accompanying feminist ideology — move from the realm of conception to the realm of more general experience, Fenitschka is doomed to "fail," that is to remain incapable of finding a personal narrative that can be integrated into the master narratives of gender and experience. In this novella therefore, Andreas-Salomé examines the links between narrative and life, between conception and experience, ideology and practice and suggests that experience is governed by dominant and authoritative narratives that can only gradually be challenged and eventually altered through repeated conflict and consensus.

That the time spent with Fenitschka has begun to affect the narratives Max lives by and expects women to live by is evidenced by an encounter late in the novella in which he seeks to make up for having hurt her with one of his reflex reactions. Having incited enormous self-doubt in Fenitschka with his comments about the relationship between love, sensuality, and marriage, Max reflects on how his ideas may not apply in her case:

> Und doch, fragte sich Max Werner, können dafür denn nicht dieselben Gründe maßgebend sein, die den Mann so leicht dazu verführen, seiner Liebe nur einen Teil seines Innern zu öffnen, ihr Grenzen zu ziehen, sie *neben,* und nicht *über* seine sonstigen Lebensinteressen zu setzen? Die Frau, die ihr Leben ganz so einrichtet und in die Hand nimmt wie der Mann, wird natürlich auch in ganz ähnliche Lagen, Konflikte und Versuchungen kommen wie er, und nur, infolge ihrer langen andersgearteten Frauenvergangenheit, viel schwerer daran leiden. (59)

> [And yet, Max Werner asked himself, were the reasons not the same here as for a man who opens up only part of his inner self to his love? He sets limits for it; he puts his love next to the other interests in his life and not above them. A woman who takes her own life in hand and arranges it just as a man would, of course, find herself in

similar situations, conflicts, temptations, as he would; but because of women's long and different tradition, she would suffer from them more. (42)]

What he recognizes here is that the narrative that accommodates a man's life may have relevance beyond men in certain cases. This moment of reflection seems to be the only one that allows him to behave somewhat differently toward Fenitschka, the only one that is not almost immediately followed by behavior that would emphasize the split between *ratio* and reflex. When he visits Fenitschka shortly thereafter, hearing that she is sick, he tries to convince her that the dream in which she saw herself as a *grisette* is not to be taken to heart. He is more sympathetic of her plight than in the past and more focused on her than on either his desire to correct her or his desire to get closer to her. He is thus determined to say something to make her feel better rather than something that emphasizes the aberration that she and her approach to life represent. Fenitschka's voice has finally succeeded in disrupting the conventional narrative to which he adheres. Max's attitude in the end reflects a communal perspective, one that combines aspects of prefeminist and feminist ideologies.

Over the course of his dealings with Fenitschka, Max learns to listen and begins to open up to the possibility of other narrative trajectories. The form of the narrative we finally read reveals that Max has listened and has heard something: it is retrospective, suggesting that something has remained with him that is worthy of passing on, and it allows for repeated undermining of the illusion of the omniscient narrator in its use of direct speech from Fenitschka, thus mimicking a disruption in authoritative and dominant narrative perspectives. Fenitschka's voice always ruptures the conventional and easy narrative Max proffers, offering alternative interpretations and examples of a woman's life. The narrative structure points to the fact that her developing narrative of resistance leads to a loss of confidence on Max's part in the time-honored gendered narratives that he has repeatedly drawn on to speak authoritatively about women and their life choices.

Once we accept Max's more central role in *Fenitshcka,* it becomes evident that he functions as an example of the challenges men face in this changing ideological world and not merely as an example of what Fenitschka fights on a daily basis. Through him, Andreas-Salomé underscores that with the advent of feminism men too face new ways of seeing and new ways of being in the world. She shows that, when men resist ideological change, they, like women, do so not necessarily out of some conspiratorial undermining of the feminist movement and the rights of women. It is perhaps the case, this depiction of Max suggests, that they do it because of ingrained, rehearsed and well-established patterns of behavior. Whereas Fenitschka has arrived at an understanding of herself and her relationship to men that she knows is at odds with the dominant social roles allotted to women at the time, Max is only beginning his journey toward such knowledge. Whereas Fenitschka has clearly relinquished the possibility of complete social integration, Max is still very much in search of it. Through his relationship to Fenitschka he gains awareness at least that the commonly accepted ideology on women and on relationships between men and women that would ease such integration is a problematic and limiting one. Yet he finds himself repeatedly defending that ideology to Fenitschka and suppressing its problems to himself. Fenitschka has arrived at a point at which the majority of her battles are with externals, but Max is still battling something within.

Narrative Aporias

The relationships being examined in this text are therefore twofold: in terms of content, we are dealing with a potential friendship between a man and a woman; in terms of form, we are dealing with a variety of different levels of narrative, narrative as straightforward storytelling, narrative as self-representation, narrative as ideology, and narrative as an epistemological tool. Andreas-Salomé's narrative in *Fenitschka* is, in other words, self-reflexive. It is a narrative about narrative and how narrative functions as a master trope in our worlds and lives, how it functions as a means of making excuses for oneself, a means of justifying the "truths" we live by, a means of shoring up ideology. Yet because it operates as one of our primary epistemological tools, it is also the only means of undermining that same ideology, the same truths, and the same excuses that it maintains. Andreas-Salomé exposes the master trope that is narrative and how narrative is tied to ideology, whether it be prefeminist, antifeminist, or feminist. A question posed by Julia Kristeva in "Women's Time" captures this dilemma *in nuce:* "No longer wishing to be excluded or no longer content with the function which has always been demanded of us (to maintain, arrange and perpetuate this socio-symbolic contract as mothers, wives, nurses, doctors, teachers . . .), how can we reveal our place, first as it is bequeathed to us by tradition, and then as we want to transform it?"[13] In order to orchestrate change, one is dependent both on the traditional narrative and on the potential for rescripting that narrative, but in either case one is dependent on creating a narrative that has resonance. If the traditional narrative represents the perceived, the new narrative represents the conceived, and in the interaction between the two, experience might be altered. It is impossible to debunk preceding narratives without calling into question the role of narrative, but if the power of narrative is undermined, what tool remains to facilitate the articulation of the transformation at which one aims?

For Fenitschka, a traditional, conventional, male-authored narrative (a narrative that claims to describe what is) has been replaced by a feminist narrative (a narrative that seeks to relate what could be). For Max, the latter has not replaced the former. Therefore in their meeting in this novella Andreas-Salomé pits narrative against narrative. Because the narrator figure in *Fenitschka* slowly loses authority, the gap between what his narrative is trying to support (Max's traditional views on women and their place in the world) and the reality (Fenitschka and her decisions, behavior, thoughts) becomes increasingly visible. Thus it seems that how narrative functions can be best exposed by showing how it fails in its attempt to function. Max and the reader have little or no recourse to narratives that accommodate mere friendship between the sexes. The ability of the narrator — and this includes Max, whether we see him as the actual narrator or merely as someone who passed the events along to the narrator — to render the story of Max's relationship to Fenia is hampered by the narratives available to him, narratives of heterosexual relationships that end in love and marriage. The narrator is similarly hampered by his desire or need to justify Max's past behaviors and incorporate them into an acceptable self-narrative or self-image. Such constraints influence Max in his actual interactions with Fenitschka and in his personal metanarrative, that is in his attempt to make sense of his personal experience.

Whitinger draws the reader's attention to the text's allusions to famous artworks and to Max's co-option by the male-authored narratives that such artworks sustain. Summoning the aesthetic tradition that depicts women in very limited fashion, either as weak and vulnerable or as sensuous, Whitinger argues that this tradition determines how Max sees Fenitschka and is a factor in his constant desire to impose a pre-scripted narrative on her. An analysis of Max's personal attraction to Fenitschka and the manner in which it is anchored in moments of her vulnerability, a vulnerability he sometimes induces, adds further to Whitinger's compelling argument. As I argued earlier, Max finds Fenitschka most alluring in the moments in which she is weakened both physically and mentally. The first time he sees her in positive terms in Paris — apart from the kissibility of her mouth — is when she becomes insecure and seems weakened in her resolve. After responding spontaneously to the *grisette's* predicament in the café, she becomes aware of her reaction and is described as follows from Max's perspective: "Im selben Augenblick ward sie sich ihrer spontanen Bewegung bewußt, hielt sich zurück und errötete stark, wodurch sie plötzlich ganz lieb und kindlich und ein wenig hilflos aussah" (9; "Immediately, though, she became aware of her spontaneous gesture, and she began to blush. All of a sudden she appeared quite childlike and appealing and as if she were in need of help," 4). When she stands at the window in her uncle's house at the end of chapter 2, Max imagines her similarly as weakened and feels the return of the "Zauber" (magic) that she initially held for him.[14] Later again, when Fenitschka realizes that she has been proposed to and grows pale and nervous and seems dazed and confused (54), Max finds that she looks "unendlich lieb" (56; "infinitely sweet").[15] And finally, in part 5, when he visits her in her room the day before she leaves her lover and has declared herself "sick" so she doesn't have to go out or receive anyone, he is again drawn to her: "Ihre Stimme fiel ihm auf. So sanft und lieb klang sie, daß sie Rührung in ihm weckte. Aber ein so matter Ton klang darin mit, — und weckte Sorge, wie man sie etwa am Krankenbett von lebhaften Kindern fühlt, wenn sie plötzlich gar zu artig und gut werden" (61; "He noticed her voice — so soft and full of affection that he was quite touched. But it had a weak sound, too, and he started to worry, the way one feels about a vivacious child who is ill and becomes too good and obedient," 43). Completely deprived of her usual independence and her strength, in both appearance and voice, and described as the unwell woman, stretched out on the couch, hands above her head, Fenitschka has been refeminized: "Sie selbst lag, in einem Schlafrock von feinem weichem Stoff, auf ihrer Ottomane ausgestreckt, das Haar in zwei hängenden Flechten und die Hände hoch über dem Kopf verschränkt" (60; "She herself lay on her day bed in a robe of soft, elegant material. She was stretched out with her arms folded under her head and her hair hanging down in two braids," 42). All these images of Fenitschka and Max's tendency to find her most beautiful at these moments are in keeping with the concept of feminine beauty examined by Bram Dykstra in *Idols of Perversity* and with the late nineteenth-, early twentieth-century upper-middle-class obsession with sickliness and weakness in women as signs of status, as reaffirmations of their femininity and of the masculinity of those attracted to or married to them.[16]

Andreas-Salomé does not simply examine how narratives conceived influence lives lived in this text but also implies that the desire to protect narrative and narrative conventions is an innate drive and that people have developed wide-ranging strategies to this end. She focuses the reader's attention on one of Max's strategies for protecting the narratives with which he lives and which empower him when, in the opening pages of the novella, she depicts his attempts to account for his inconsistent response to Fenitschka. Although he subscribes to a personal narrative in which he finds frigid, intellectual women unattractive, he is drawn to Fenitschka. Rather than therefore revise his self-narrative, the story with which he accounts for himself to himself and others, he adjusts his image of Fenitschka so that his attraction can fit into the familiar narrative of self he wants to protect. Thus he decides that Fenitschka must in fact be simply hiding a sensuous, sexually active self under the austere exterior he sees. Whitinger's analysis of Max's imposition of a narrative on Fenitschka, particularly in the scene where she leans into the curtains and the window at her uncle's home, underscores Max's tendency to protect the narratives with which he is familiar and with which he can best function.[17]

By creating this slippery narrator, who may or may not be Max, Andreas-Salomé demonstrates how difficult it is to write the story of a male/female relationship without awakening notions of an erotic attraction between the main characters on the part of the reader as well. The predominant narrative trajectory available for mixed gender relationships at this time, namely the love story, constantly threatens to absorb the unscripted narrative of female-male friendship. At the same time, the unscripted narrative of female-male friendship constantly threatens to disrupt the traditional narrative and in the end, despite its own lack of success in arriving at closure, does disrupt it. What the narrator tries to tell is the story of how an unusual relationship developed, but the beginning of the story points readers down a familiar path. Fenitschka and Max meet and establish a conflictual relationship. A little more than a year later, they meet again, smooth over the past and begin to spend a lot of time with each other. The initial dislike or conflict that leads to a love affair is a narrative with which readers are generally familiar, from *The Taming of the Shrew* to *When Harry Met Sally*. Max and Fenitschka even jokingly refer to the Paris event as their "Liebesroman" (romance) calling attention to narrative conventions and expectations that failed to be fulfilled in their first encounter (21). Andreas-Salomé sets the reader up, in other words, such that the reader's expectations mirror Max's difficulty in adapting to the new role that a real friendship with Fenitschka would demand.

Fenitschka demonstrates how narrative conventions affect the narratives of our lives and/or how narrative conventions can not only prove inadequate to the stories of our lives, particularly in times of radical ideological change, but also how they shape those lives in negative ways, because we tend, it suggests, not only to interpret the past in terms of narratives told and rhetoric familiar to us, but also to script the future based on familiar and available narratives. The novella presents narrative as something that structures self-representations, interactions with others, concepts of the future, and perceptions of others. The failed or repeatedly ruptured narrative form implies that the narratives that mirror lived experience also limit it. Max's investment in patriarchal ideology and his loyalty to the narrative structures that shore up that ideology lead to a failure in real terms for his relationship to Fenitschka, and Fenitschka's resistance to that ideology leads to a failure in narratological terms for this text in that closure is not achieved. Max fails to truly listen to and grasp Fenitschka's perspective until it is too late, because he focused for too long on himself and the potential for saving the narrative he knew by forcing some kind of intimacy between them. The corresponding romance narrative then similarly fails because it veers off the beaten path. In the end, the failed narrative represents a kind of success in that the old structure is ruptured so that something new can emerge. One of the real tragedies of the novella *Fenitschka* then is not the failure of Fenitschka's love relationship that corresponds to the failure of the romance narrative. The actual failure in this story is overshadowed by our narrative expectations of love and marriage, and that failure is the failure of friendship, Max's inability to adapt enough early enough to make a successful, even-footed friendship between himself and Fenitschka possible.

The breakdown of communication that occurs because of the characters' reliance on divergent narrative trajectories can perhaps be best illustrated by the recurrence of the word "erniedrigend" (denigrating). In one instance Fenitschka invokes it and in one instance Max does so. In each case it is very differently couched. When Max and Fenitschka are first talking about secret affairs, she expresses annoyance at the fact that women not only have to hide such affairs but then also have to be thankful to men for not exposing them:

> Ja, wissen Sie, das ist doch wirklich etwas Abscheuliches! Ich meine, daß den Frauen in manchen Beziehungen die Heimlichkeit einfach aufgezwungen wird! Daß sie auch noch froh sein müssen, wenn sie gelingt, — und vom Mann wie etwas Selbstverständliches erwarten, daß er sie durch seine Diskretion, seine Schonung, seine Vorsicht schütze und beschirme. — Ja, es mag notwendig sein, so wie die Welt nun einmal ist, aber es ist das *Erniedrigendste,* was ich noch je gehört habe. Etwas verleugnen und verstecken müssen, was man aus tiefstem Herzen tut! Sich schämen, wo man jubeln sollte. (37–38, emphasis added)

> [Yes, you know it is really disgusting! I mean the fact that women are simply forced into secrecy on many occasions and have to be happy yet when that succeeds. It is taken for granted that a man protects and shields them against the whole world through his precaution and his discretion. Well, it may be necessary, taking the world as it is. But it is *the most denigrating* thing I have ever known. Why should you have to deny and hide something that you do from the bottom of your heart; why be ashamed when you want to be jubilant! (26, emphasis added)]

Fenitschka underscores again the constraints of the public and dominantly accepted narrative on women and their sexuality that is the romance narrative, a narrative that allows for woman's two natures — sexual and pure — to be reconciled because her sexuality can be contained within a monogamous, life-long relationship. Her self-critical dream emphasizes the deeply negative impact on her of the duplicity that society forces upon women who deviate from the norm.[18] Fenitschka's decisions deny the possibility of the reconciliation and closure that the romance-narrative promises and that Max pursues on her behalf.

Fenitschka is remarkably calm during the discussion of her dream, but Max grows angry about her self-comparison to a *grisette,* terming it "Selbsterniedrigung" (62; self-denigration).[19] He now finds himself in the position of defending her relationship to her Russian lover as something more than what he called it only a day before. But it is this defense and his constant insistence that there must be more to the relationship than there is that is "erniedrigend" (denigrating) in the sense that Fenitschka addressed earlier. Max's notion of what is "erniedrigend" for Fenitschka then makes him behave toward her in a way that she actually finds "erniedrigend." Whereas for her "erniedrigend" has to do with the collusion of an entire society in the denial of an acceptable female sexuality outside marriage, for him "erniedrigend" has to do with active female sexuality in the absence of a love that leads to marriage. For her to imagine herself as a *grisette,* a sexually active but unmarried woman, is "erniedrigend" in his eyes, and yet this is what Fenitschka acknowledges herself to be. For her, to have to deny that she is a sexually active but unmarried woman is the "Erniedrigung."

Birgit Wernz argues that too much attention has been paid to Fenitschka and how she revises her understanding of herself over the course of her encounters with Max. Fenitschka knows who she is from the beginning, Wernz contends, represents a decisive position, and forces Max to revise his understanding of women. This particular set of interactions, however, reveals that Fenitschka is still involved in a process of weighing, reflecting, and changing. Max's pursuit of the traditional narrative affects Fenitschka seriously and throws her back into the conventional narrative, where she begins to see herself again in its terms and thus as a woman who can't possibly love her lover if she doesn't want to marry him. But one last interaction with her lover reminds her again of the existence of possibilities other than the one Max continually promotes. In the final intimate moment with her lover, the lover asks Fenitschka if she could ever forget what they mean to each other. Her response reflects deep gratitude: "'Niemals! Niemals! . . . niemals kann ich es vergessen, daß ich dein bin. Und mit einem Ausdruck, der Max durch alle Nerven ging, fügte sie hinzu: 'Ich danke dir! ich danke dir!'" (66; "'Never! Never! . . . Never will I forget that I am yours.' And in a tone that went through his every nerve, she added, 'Thank you! I thank you!'" 47). Given the recent self-doubt, her exuberant thanks to her lover can be read as thanks for the renewed conviction that the relationship she had to him was not "erniedrigend," even if it did end in this separation. In the same way that Fenitschka's narrative pushes against and affects Max's throughout the story, Max's is shown here to still be present for Fenitschka and to cause at least occasional relapses. This mutuality plays an important part in Andreas-Salomé's creation of a model of effective, if laborious, exchange, of dialogue between opposing positions, and of the rocky and meandering path on which we move toward new understandings of ourselves and others. *Fenitschka* illuminates how narrative, in the form of gender ideology, among other things, stands alongside and influences logic and knowledge in our attempts to organize our experience and construct reality.

Notes

The epigraph at the start of this chapter is from A. S. Byatt, *Possession: A Romance* (New York: Random House, 1990), 456.

[1] The complete list follows: Julie Doll Allen, "Male and Female Dialogue in Lou Andreas-Salomé's *Fenitschka*," in *Frauen: Mitsprechen, Mitschreiben; Beiträge zu Literatur- und sprachwissenschaftlichen Frauenforschung*, ed. Marianne Henn and Britta Hufeisen (Stuttgart: Akademischer Verlag Hans-Dieter Heinz, 1997), 479–89; Brigid Haines, "Lou Andreas-Salomé's *Fenitschka*: A Feminist Reading," *German Life and Letters* 44 (1991): 416–25; Raleigh Whitinger,"Lou Andreas-Salomé's *Fenitschka* and the Tradition of the Bildungsroman," *Monatshefte* 91 (1999): 464–81. There are also two chapters in books, chapter 6 in Biddy Martin, *Woman and Modernity: The (Life)Styles of Lou Andreas-Salomé* (Ithaca, NY: Cornell UP, 1991); and chapter 10 in Uta Treder, *Von der Hexe zur Hysterikerin: Zur Verfestigungsgeschichte des "Ewig Weiblichen"* (Bonn: Bouvier, 1984). Gahlinger, Schütz, and Wernz also all devote considerable time to interpretations of *Fenitschka*.

[2] Haines, for example, discusses the novella's narrative viewpoint as one that "exposes how norms of gendered behaviour govern social intercourse between men and women" ("Lou Andreas-Salomé's *Fenitschka*: A Feminist Reading," 421) and points to its examination of a subjectivity that is always in process. Whitinger, in his "Lou Andreas-Salomé's *Fenitschka* and the Tradition of the Bildungsroman," examines how the text manipulates and parodies the Bildungsroman tradition; and Doll Allen, in "Male and Female Dialogue in Lou Andreas-Salomé's *Fenitschka*," analyzes not just the said of the dialogues between Max and Fenitschka but the acts of saying. Treder takes up the concept of love developed in the novella, concluding that it is a love that is an erotic drive, free of all social conventions and something fundamentally narcissistic (*Von der Hexe zur Hysterikerin*, chapter 10). Finally, Martin analyzes how the man's perspective in the novella contributes to "exploring and even diagnosing masculine projections of femininity" (*Woman and Modernity*, 177).

[3] There is one exception to the statement that we do not have access to Fenitschka's private thoughts, one that can be accounted for perhaps by the fact that most people could probably guess what might be going through her head during their first encounter in his room when he locks the door. Fenia's eyes flit around looking for an escape and come to rest on the bell: "Aber konnte sie den Garçon herbeiläuten und sich von ihm zu dieser Stunde in dieser Stube mit dem Fremden finden lassen? — Und in den Hof hinunterspringen konnte sie ja doch auch nicht" (18; "But could she ring for the garçon, to let herself be found in this room with a stranger at this hour? A jump into the yard was equally impossible," 11). While it is entirely possible that Max could deduce her perspective at this moment and

write it into the retrospective narrative, it is an unusual instance of emphasis on Fenitschka's perspective not rendered in what she specifically utters.

4 Although the socially sanctioned discourse may be predominantly male-authored, it is important to underscore that, with the exception of Fenitschka, everyone in this novella supports the same discourse, women as much as men.

5 Compare Haines, "Lou Andreas-Salomé's *Fenitschka:* A Feminist Reading," 419.

6 Except where otherwise noted, all translations for *Fenitschka* are from Lou Andreas-Salomé, *Fenitschka and Deviations: Two Novellas,* trans. Dorothee Einstein Krahn (Lanham, NY, and London: UP of America, 1990).

7 Julie Doll Allen, "Male and Female Dialogue in Lou Andreas-Salomé's *Fenitschka,*" 483.

8 See Whitinger, "Lou Andreas-Salomé's *Fenitschka* and the Tradition of the Bildungsroman," 469–70 for an excellent discussion of the choreography of this scene and how it emphasizes Max's loss of authority.

9 Allen, "Male and Female Dialogue in Lou Andreas-Salomé's *Fenitschka.*"

10 Haines's discussion of a feminist poststructuralist subjectivity in "Lou Andreas-Salomé's Fenitschka: A Feminist Reading" supports this argument (417).

11 There are a number of other references to how Fenitschka gives rise to anger and discomfort in Max in this opening chapter. When they discuss women's education, for example, he is described as answering "fast gereizt" (14; "with some irritation," 8), and what he interprets as her "einfache Bereitwilligkeit" ("obligingness") as he leads her away from rather than toward her hotel irritates him (16/10).

12 See Doll Allen for a discussion of Max's knightly behaviors throughout.

13 Julia Kristeva, "Women's Time," in *The Kristeva Reader,* ed. Toril Moi (New York: Columbia UP, 1986), 187–213, here 199.

14 See Whitinger, "Lou Andreas-Salomé's *Fenitschka* and the Tradition of the Bildungsroman," for an extended discussion of this scene (471) as well as an interesting position on the role of windows and doors, figuratively and literally, in the novella (468).

15 Krahn leaves out the following part of the sentence in her translation: ". . . unendlich lieb schaute sie dabei aus, mit ihren halbgeöffneten Kußlippen" (56). The following is a rough translation: ". . . she looked infinitely sweet as she listened, with her half-opened lips, made for kissing" (40). It is unclear to me why Krahn might have left this part out. It is important in that it is yet another instance of Max's attraction to what he perceives as Fenia's vulnerability.

16 Bram Dykstra, *Idols of Perversity: Fantasies of Feminine Evil in Fin-de-Siècle Culture* (New York and Oxford: Oxford UP, 1986).

17 Whitinger also underscores the gap between Fenitschka's desire here to get out of the confining space, both literal and figurative, in which she finds herself, and Max's fantasy that she has suddenly become passive and physically weakened and is crying: "Es war wie eine Zwangvorstellung, aber nicht durch seelische Eindrücke oder Mutmaßungen hervorgerufen, sondern wie ein malerischer Zwang, der in

den Linien lag, die durchaus in dieser Weise zusammenfließen wollten, — hartnäckig alle Wirklichkeit fälschend" (34; "Lou Andreas-Salomé's *Fenitschka* and the Tradition of the Bildungsroman," "It was a compulsive notion — not caused by emotional impressions or assumptions, but simply by the artful sweep of the lines which evoked that apparition through the way they seemed to flow together, obstinately denying all reality," 24). Images of artworks that depict woman in a particular way force Max, as it were, into certain patterns of behavior with Fenitschka, into perceiving and conceiving of her in a certain way, as, to invoke Whitinger once again, "'a' woman" rather than "as 'the' individual he knows — trying to capture an image of her as the weeping and suffering fallen woman in need of his heroic help" (471). The fantasy that Max's image of Fenitschka, influenced by aesthetic traditions, encapsulates is no different from the fantasies that narrative (as both fiction and ideology) impart and articulate. Accounting for Max's relationship to Fenitschka throughout the novella involves a constant back and forth between his expectations of a romance narrative bolstered by the artistic images of women with which he is familiar and Fenitschka's resistance to the same.

[18] Andreas-Salomé invites us to apply Freud's theory of dream interpretation — Fenitschka asks Max if he understands "Traumdeutung" (61; the interpretation of dreams) — to her dream. If all dreams are seen as an expression of wish fulfillment linked to something both in the distant and and in the recent past, then we can relate Fenitschka's dream of herself as a *grisette* to the most recent past, that is to Max's comment distinguishing love from sensual passion, and thus understand the impact of his comments on her. It is also undoubtedly linked to her recent change in situation: back in Russia, surrounded by family members, dependent on a respectable teaching job, she cannot nonchalantly enjoy the relationship to her lover, be it sensual or otherwise. Sigmund Freud, *Die Traumdeutung*, vol 2 of *Gesammelte Werke*(Frankfurt am Main: Fischer, 1968–78).

[19] Krahn translates "Selbsterniedrigung" as "self-abasement" which is obviously a fine translation. I choose "self-denigration" here in order to underscore the return of the word Fenitschka had used earlier.

Conclusion: Women Who Move Too Much

IN THIS BOOK I have focused on Andreas-Salomé's depictions of independent, intellectual, and creative women muddling through a time and society in which their place was uncertain and their concept of self threatening to both themselves and others. Following in the footsteps of critics such as Gisela Brinker-Gabler, Brigid Haines, Raleigh Whitinger, and Biddy Martin, I have tried to elucidate this author's various attempts to complicate the contemporary definition and regulation of sexual difference and gender in her fiction. Her informed interest in literary, medical, scientific, feminist, philosophical, psychological, and political discourses allows her to recontextualize them in her fiction in ways that expose how the binaries that tend to form the basis of any particular discourse constitute simplifications of immensely complex and irreducible psychological processes. Though one might well call her a disciple of such intellectuals as Nietzsche, Rilke, and Freud, Andreas-Salomé clearly had her own intellectual agenda, and it manifests itself throughout her body of work. For her there was no contradiction in listening to and absorbing the theories of renowned male intellectuals and concomitantly developing her own theories, which often read as refinements of and correctives to theirs. Andreas-Salomé was interested in any discourse that could help her in what I interpret to have been her primary quest, namely to figure out what identity meant in the contemporary moment. Her novels, novellas, and essays ask how issues such as class, gender, ethnicity, religion, nationalism, culture, and location inform both concepts of identity and identity formation itself. Her wavering characters offer compelling insights into the fate of the modern self, caught up in past practices and customs, current circumstances, and future possibilities among which this modern self perpetually negotiated. Exploratory rather than conclusive, her depictions of both women and men leave the reader with questions, puzzles, and uncertainties, encouraging ongoing and infinite deliberations about gender and identity.

By way of conclusion, I would like to revisit a selection of the works already discussed as well as briefly introduce a much later novel, *Ródinka,* in order to show that Andreas-Salomé's female characters are essentially women who, like herself, moved too much and refused to be pinned (or penned) down.[1] Although the female figures in Lou Andreas-Salomé's fictional works have often been read as models of conservatism and although her theory of gender as expressed in essays such as "Der Mensch als Weib" and "Ketzereien gegen die moderne Frau" points to a mirroring of Freud's castration complex onto women in art — gender identity becomes constituted around the presence or absence of artistic ability — her own life has interested biographers because of her free movement through a variety of classes and artistic, theoretical, and intellectual communities. Reading backward, then, from life to works, employing the same kind of movement that she seemed to find productive, it is hard to not to see her depictions of women and her understanding of identity formation as more complex and subversive than they initially appear or than they have often been described.

At the end of the nineteenth century the majority of Lou Andreas-Salomé's female characters exist between two worlds (old-world Russia and new-world Germany) and two spaces (the domestic sphere and the realm of the public and professional). They move back and forth between the two, just as they negotiate traditional and enlightened concepts of female identity and female roles, constantly crossing borders and thresholds and donning, as it were, new skins. Rarely, however, do these women arrive at a final destination or a stopping point. Andreas-Salomé's endings are almost always open, and her female characters are generally most content when literally in motion: on a train, walking through the streets, moving toward, rather than arriving at, a place and an understanding of themselves.

Fenitschka, as we have seen, leaves Russia as a young woman to study in Zürich, vacations in Paris briefly at the end of her studies, and finally returns to St. Petersburg to prepare herself for a job as a teacher. The novella focuses on an evening she spends in Paris and on a couple of weeks she spends in St. Petersburg.[2] Her border crossings are as metaphorical as they are literal, allowing, and in some cases compelling, her to redefine herself as a woman. Bridging place and time are the protagonist's love of walking the city streets without a particular aim, her flaneurism, and her acquaintance with an Austrian man, Max Werner. Fenitschka's flaneurism offers her freedom from a variety of constraints, because of the anonymity it allows. It represents the space of the in-between, which, as Jean-Xavier Ridon argues in his article "Between Here and There: A Displacement in Memory," "can be seen as the moment of a negation, the confrontation with a space which no longer has an identity to offer" (720).[3] Ridon's formulation (he writes primarily about francophone literature and the postcolonial) suggests a somewhat negative interpretation of the in-between — a space with no identity to *offer* — but a slight reformulation of this position — a space in which no identity is *imposed* — would seem to correspond to Andreas-Salomé's positive understanding of the in-between.

Fenitschka's walks are a space and time in which, however briefly, she is not interpellated. To be sure, she cannot escape a general identification as a woman in these public spaces, but she chooses clothes in both Paris and St. Petersburg that deflect attention away from her. In Paris she wears her "schwarz[es] nonnenhaft[es] Kleidchen" (black dress as a nun would wear) that, although "fast drollig unpariserisch" (almost drolly unparisian) conceals her shape so that she at first makes "keinerlei besonderen Eindruck" (no particular impression) on Max Werner, the man from whose perspective the story is told (7).[4] In St. Petersburg she wears traditional women's winter clothing that, again from Max Werner's perspective, makes her indistinguishable from any other woman on the street (32–33). Werner, who insists on accompanying her on walks, represents that dominant gender ideology that would locate her neatly in the social, organizational structure. Repeatedly disrupting her "in-between," he spends the entirety of their acquaintance trying to figure her out for once and for all. His tactics involve engaging her in discussions about woman's "natural" tendencies in love and marriage and reading her responses and behavior in general through the lens of traditional gender ideology. In Paris he thinks that her outfit suggests a chaste, reserved, and boring woman, but when she stands up in a café and reaches her hand toward a *grisette* who is under attack from her male companions, he decides that her sympathy for this woman must point toward a promiscuity obscured by her nun-like attire. He therefore waylays her, takes her to his hotel room and tries to force himself upon her. When Fenitschka rejects him and tells him that he is the first indecent man she has encountered, he returns to his original reading of her as chaste (19). In St. Petersburg he sees her at a wedding, dressed in white, and interprets this as a confirmation of his most recent reading of Fenitschka, only to later find out that she is in fact involved in a secret, illicit affair with a man she does not want to marry.

Fenitschka confounds Max Werner utterly because he cannot adequately categorize her. She contests both his professional judgment (he is a psychologist) and his male authority, pushes back, and confronts him with "unanticipated agency."[5] She moves too much, literally and figuratively, and her movement moves him, literally and figuratively. Fenitschka causes gender trouble. The woman Werner sees her perform is not the woman she "is" because there is no "is," no essence, and no location or definite coordinates. Fenitschka offers only performances and movement among and in those performances. She, in Judith Butler's terms, "destabilizes the very distinctions between the natural and the artificial, depth and surface, inner and outer through which discourse about genders almost always operates."[6]

In "Eine Ausschweifung" Adine's relocations serve as allegories of identity change. She never completely leaves any place or time behind, however, and negotiates constantly between a masochistic desire to remain in a traditional and confining relationship that makes her seriously ill and a desire to be different, free, and able to express herself artistically. The negotiation of traditional and more modern gender identities is reflected in her travel between Brieg and Paris, between her "home" with her mother and cousin/fiancé — a constellation that emphasizes the notion of origins/family — and her atelier in a foreign and hedonistic city. Adine's first change of location occurs after her father's death and represents a loss of freedom and agency. The apartment to which she moves is directly across from the city's penitentiary and the insane asylum where Benno, her fiancé, works. She describes both buildings as "Gefängnisse leidender Menschen," and her new home becomes just such an institution for her (76; "prisons for humanity's suffering outcasts," 54). Although she consciously affirms the gendered identity that is thrust upon her, her unconscious rejection of it wins out. She spends her days staring out the window at the prisoners and patients, stops painting and eating, and thus slowly makes herself sick. Adine immobilizes and paralyzes herself and waits for Benno and her mother to set her in motion again by sending her away and deciding to end the engagement. She reluctantly and sadly changes country but, in time, rediscovers her art and a more fluid notion of her own identity, one that allows her to regain agency and to restore psychological balance. Her recovery depends on an ability to play different roles, to move back and forth between the submission that a love relationship sometimes requires and the self-assertion and narcissism that a commitment to art/work requires.

Adine describes her trip back to this isolated eastern town of Brieg years later in a manner that draws on the vocabulary of motion and stasis in interesting ways and leaves the reader wondering whether her trip to Brieg results in a relapse or whether the onset of a relapse results in her trip to Brieg. She embarks on the trip in a nostalgic mood, hoping that she will find the town exactly as she left it: small, confined, and a little bit backward. She finds it "förmlich *eingesargt* im tiefen weißen Winterschnee" (83; "almost *buried* in deep white winter snow," 60, emphasis added) and this initial impression of stasis pleases her. But modernization has begun — "Auch Brieg *ging* also vorwärts!" (83; "So Brieg was *moving* forward also," 60, emphasis added) — and this disappoints her. Adine's rendering of her first Benno sighting suggests an immediate loss of agency. Walking toward her house, she sees him standing in the lamplight, feels a compulsion to stop in her tracks, but finds herself blown toward him by the force of nature: "Mich ergriff eine kindische Freude, so groß, wie ich sie nie für möglich gehalten hätte, zugleich mit dem Verlangen *stehnzubleiben* [*sic*]. Aber das erlaubte der Sturm nicht; er *blies* mich von hinten an, als *wehe* er mich ihm einfach entgegen" (83; "I was seized by a childlike joy, greater than I would have thought possible; and at the same time, I felt a desire *to stand quite still*. The wind did not allow that. It *gripped* me from the back and literally *blew* me toward him," 60, emphasis added). In fact, within a few days the old symptoms begin to manifest themselves, and she has to leave much earlier than she intended. Adine comes back in search of origins, a point from which she departed that promised a sense of feminine authenticity, but the point from which she departed is no longer what it was. She never truly arrives where she was going. Lou Andreas-Salomé's depiction of Adine's quest implies that the search for an origin, a point of departure, a true and authentic femininity, which Adine associates with her mother, marriage, and Brieg, is bound to fail. When Adine tries to locate a lost femininity that can serve as the basis of her identity by returning to something in her own or other women's pasts, she becomes unstable and ill.

Her experience during the return visit to Brieg prompts the letter that becomes the narrative we read. She writes the letter when she is back in her atelier in Paris, and it begins as an explanation of a breakup to the person with whom she has broken up. Her opening paragraphs seem very definite, concluding "mich hat eine lange Ausschweifung zu ernster und voller Liebe unfähig gemacht" (71; "a long, passionate affair . . . left me impervious to a serious and all-embracing love," 51). But in the process of writing, in the expression, that movement of what is inside to the outside, she restates this position, changes the position, returns to the position, departs from it again, and finally breaks off the letter very suddenly, without any real conclusion, implying that this letter is never sent. Paradoxically, this sudden paralysis, the inability to continue with the letter, her reduction to silence, is encouraging. Because she stops asserting her identity, this letter, like she herself, remains a work in progress. Just as Max Werner failed to figure out Fenitschka, Adine has failed to figure out herself. Lou Andreas-Salomé demonstrates again and again that identity cannot be fixed and that the ability to move between performances and negotiate among multiple possibilities is essential. She also suggests, however, that such movement and negotiation can be psychologically exhausting and that feminism is neither a panacea for the difficulties of identity negotiation nor a practice that can change the collective unconscious overnight.

Motion matters in *Das Haus* too. Gitta demonstrates an incurable giddiness and a delight about change and new things that make her parents eager to confine her and slow her down. Because she is attracted to three different men in a relatively short period of time, they see her as endangered and believe that the answer lies in taming her through marriage. Rather than risk the downfall they see as inevitable if Gitta is free to move about as she wishes, they concede to a marriage with which they are not entirely satisfied. It is precisely their ideology of stasis, however, that then threatens that marriage. Interpreting marriage as a set of physical, emotional, and spiritual limitations, as her parents have taught her to do, Gitta attempts to settle, denying herself the freedoms she had previously enjoyed. Her self-denial eventually causes her to run away, to respond to the domestic carceral by resolutely breaking free from it. The answer to Gitta's marital problems is presented to her by her new husband, who incorporates concepts of freedom and motion into his understanding of marriage. Unlike her parents, he does not want to confine her. He encourages her solitary walks, wants her to have a room of her own, and underscores the inevitability of a chronic vacillation between distance and closeness in marriage. For Markus, Gitta's restlessness does not constitute a threat, and she rewards his acceptance of that restless physical and psychical motion by including him now and then in her walks.

The female characters in *Ma: Ein Porträt, Menschenkinder,* and *Jutta* find themselves similarly in motion, confronted by a variety of new possibilities for self-determination and, at the same time, by conservative guidelines, conventional gendered expectations, and familial duties. Cita and Sophie want freedom from their home and their homeland and see Western Europe as a place full of the kinds of professional and personal freedoms denied them not only in their motherland but also, at least partially, by their mother. Changing spaces will allow them new opportunities for self-definition. In their journey toward self-sufficiency they need to engage in the same back and forth in their relationship to their mother that Markus and Gitta engage in to save their marriage. Even Ma, though nostalgic for a traditional woman's role as wife and mother, is in constant motion and takes solace in her walks, her work, and the manner in which her departure each day heightens the intensity of her time with her daughters in the evenings. Ma too is caught up in, and even takes some pleasure in, the restless motion that appears to characterize the modern condition and, in the end, rather than settle into a marriage in which she would be taken care of and secure, she chooses solitude. Our last image of her is a familiar one: Ma moving through Moscow and, like Anneliese at the end of *Das Haus,* seen and at the same time not seen by a male observer.

The novel *Ródinka,* published later (1923) than the other works discussed in this book, tells of a somewhat different movement, a movement back to Russia, back in time, and I focus on it in closing in order to underscore Andreas-Salomé's back and forth among apparently contradictory positions and her occasional complete reversal of a series of conventional associations. Of interest here is the ironic twist by which a fundamentally conservative, agrarian move becomes liberating for Margot, the protagonist. The daughter of German immigrants, Margot grew up in St. Petersburg, moved back to Germany with her father in her early teens, married a German, and now, as a kind of therapy for the recent loss of a child, travels back to a family of old friends who live on an estate called Ródinka in rural Russia. The chapter relating Margot's travel to Ródinka is titled "Einfahrt" (83; journey inward), and the details of her journey into the almost exotic interior of Russia, her journey inward, emphasize that this is "the road less traveled." No train goes where Margot is headed, and she has to ride on a horse-drawn cart, seated in the hay, over poorly paved and unpaved paths, driven by an old farmer who is in no hurry to get where he is going. Margot's choices here are unusual for the time, Andreas-Salomé indicates, but the possibility of these choices is as important as the possibility of Fenitschka's or Adine's choices. It is not so much the forth that matters, Andreas-Salomé demonstrates, but the back and forth, not so much the there, but the here and there.

Margot's narrative has a lot in common with what Rita Felski discusses as the literary tradition of "imagining non-Western cultures as exotic zones of spiritual plenitude and erotic transfiguration" (137).[7] Felski goes on to explain that "instead of affirming the hegemony of modern civilization over less developed territories, this latter motif privileges those very territories as a redemptive refuge from an overbearing modernity" (137). Ródinka becomes such a refuge for the protagonist Margot. At the end of *Ródinka,* in fact, on the night before she is to travel back to Germany she cannot sleep and wants to empty her suitcase again. Though she does not explicitly state her intention to remain at Ródinka, the ending implies that she might well do so. She hears a *troika* pass by outside: "Dort, weit fort, jagt eine Troika übers Land. Weit fort — weit, weit an uns vorbei. . . . Eilig, eilig, Zukünften entgegen, die uns nicht angehen" (262–63; There, off in the distance, a *Troika* chased through the countryside. Off in the distance — far, far away, passing us by. . . . In a hurry, a great hurry toward futures that didn't concern us).[8] The "us" here refers to a group of women who have been left behind on Ródinka after the Faustian, modern, individualistic men have left. Two brothers have abandoned rural Russia, their wives, their mother, their children, the widow of a friend killed by a train, and Margot in their search for something better. Progress, the text implies, is robbing Russia of its traditions, tearing apart its families, and leaving its children and women yearning for their fathers and husbands. While the women represent ties to a community, selflessness, primitiveness, and love, the men who have left them represent hyper-individualism, selfishness, progress, and rationality. Rural Russia is feminized in *Ródinka,* and that feminization constitutes a privileging of traditional women's roles in order to question the masculinist, progressive, mono-directional drive representative of the West and of feminism, among other things. What seems like a conservative move on Andreas-Salomé's part, then, is merely an underscoring of the idea that what matters most is the movement, the negotiation, and the proliferation of possibilities that these concepts imply. The questioning of tradition is productive, but so too is the questioning of the new, of modernization and feminism, and their foundation on the assumption of the primacy of the individual and his/her needs and desires. In this novel, what seems atavistic or reactionary at first represents, in fact, an important moment of resistance.

The endings of *Eine Ausschweifung, Jutta, Ma,* and *Das Haus* similarly resist resolution. Adine's letter simply breaks off before she has been able to come to terms with her masochistic dilemma. Jutta's narrative ends abruptly too, with a return to the divided self that she had sought to master through writing. There is no "happily ever after" in *Das Haus,* nor in *Ma.* Andreas-Salomé's narratives do not prescribe what is necessary for a fulfilled life as a woman but show instead that achieving fulfillment amounts to an endless negotiation of positions, ideals, and convictions. In one of the few stories where there is some sense of resolution, "Das Paradies" ("Paradise") in the collection *Menschenkinder,* that resolution corresponds to a failure to take flight and is ultimately quite tragic:

> Hildegard kam es dunkel in den Sinn, als ob sie jetzt gleich zwei große, lichtgraue Flügel aufschlagen müßte und sich mit ihnen erheben, — hoch, hoch wie im Traum. Aber sie fühlte auch dunkel, wie es manchmal im Fiebertraum ist: als ob etwas in ihr hilflos, machtlos mit den Flügeln schlüge, — und man plötzlich nicht mehr weiß, ob man fliegt, — oder fällt — (238)

> [Hildegard sensed darkly that she would now at once have to spread two light gray wings and let them lift her up — high, high, as in her dream. But she also sensed darkly how it is in feverish dreams; as though something in her were helplessly, powerlessly beating its wings — and suddenly she didn't know whether she was flying — or falling —[9]]

Having escaped one unwanted marriage, it appears that Hildegard is about to consent to a second one. "Das Paradies" opens with a description of Hildegard in imaginary flight, of her landing to chat affably with a friend of her deceased father and suitor as "junge Mädchen thun sollen" ("young girls are supposed to do") and as her mother has advised her to do, and then taking off anew, uninterested in her mother's matchmaking (195; 106). Hildegard reflects that she has nothing against the man in question but merely finds it cumbersome to have to engage in boring and polite conversation when she could be flying. Hildegard's imaginary flights reveal her desire for personal freedom, a fantasy world in which she is not weighed down by social convention, and in which she can focus on herself.[10] They also emphasize her very real tethering to house and hearth. In this case, unlike in most of Andreas-Salomé's stories, the ending is dispiriting precisely because it apparently offers closure. There is a sad finality to the moment in which Hildegard, in a domestic setting in which he finds her particularly alluring, gives Dietrich her hand, "Über ein Paradies hinweg" (238; "Reaching out over a paradise," 132). This closing phrase, together with her sense that her flight has turned into a fall, emphasizes sacrifice and loss. Although the traditional comedic ending, the coming together of a heterosexual couple, is achieved, Andreas-Salomé refuses to depict it as triumphant. The joining of their hands, Hildegard's consent to marriage occurs at the expense of her movement, both psychic and physical, at the expense of a potential experience of paradise.

Aware of the weight of a social tradition that had contributed to and continued to contribute to the training of women to be wives and mothers, and that could lead a young woman like Hildegard to settle for security and stability instead of freedom and perpetual motion, Andreas-Salomé did not believe that the articulation of a new identity for women could change women's lives, desires, needs, and self-images in and of itself. She acknowledged that feminism and the women's movement had ushered in a period of discord, confusion, conflict, and anger for women and men and underscored the fact that feminism could not simply and quickly create new identities and bring freedom and a sense of fulfillment. Problems of identity, freedom, and fulfillment would remain an everyday part of life, and the new conditions of women's lives would bring new dissatisfactions and new difficulties for both themselves and men.

Through a mapping of the figurative motion of negotiation onto the literal motion of travel, Andreas-Salomé proposes that the big advantage of feminism might not be simply that it points forward, toward something new and away from something old. Anticipating Judith Butler's positive construction of identity performance in *Gender Trouble*, she suggests that the real gain is to be found in the coexistence of the traditional and the modern, the possibility of a back-and-forth movement between the two, and the flexibility that a variety of roles provides people, women in particular, as they seek to define and redefine themselves. Migration and the exploration and negotiation of identity that it often promotes, motion or movement, appear, in the end, to be key in all of her depictions of women. A fixed gender identity in her depictions is part of a political and ideological process that, in Althusserian terms, takes the raw material that is the human being and transforms it into a product that can be easily integrated in a pre-defined web of power relations. Fenitschka, Adine, Margot, Anjuta, Gitta, Marfa, and Irene, among others, battle with this process of interpellation and thus do not come to rest. Andreas-Salomé's women are women in motion.

Notes

[1] Lou Andreas-Salomé, *Ródinka: Russische Erinnerung* (1923; repr., Frankfurt am Main: Ullstein, 1985).

[2] Laura Deiulio couples a discussion of the gaze with a discussion of urban space and its effects on identity and growth in "A Tale of Two Cities: The Metropolis in Lou Andreas-Salomé's *Fenitschka*," *Women in German Yearbook* 23 (2007): 76–101. Interestingly, Deiulio argues that St. Petersburg, a traditionally less

"modern" city in the consciousness of the time, offers Fenitschka more room for growth than Paris does.

[3] Ridon, Jean-Xavier, "Between Here and There: A Displacement in Memory," trans. Alistair Rolls, *World Literature Today: A Literary Quarterly of the University of Oklahoma,* 71.4 (1997): 717–22.

[4] To allow a better fit with the sentence structure, these phrases are my own translations.

[5] Judith Butler, *Gender Trouble: Feminism and the Subversion of Identity* (New York: Routledge, 1990), vii.

[6] Butler, *Gender Trouble,* viii.

[7] Rita Felski, *The Gender of Modernity* (Cambridge, MA: Harvard UP, 1995).

[8] Translations from *Ródinka* are my own.

[9] Translation taken from Lou Andreas-Salomé, *The Human Family: Stories,* trans. Raleigh Whitinger (Lincoln and London: U of Nebraska P, 2005), 132.

[10] See Birgit Wernz's very interesting discussion of the story "Das Paradies" in *Sub-Versionen: Weiblichkeitsentwürfe in den Erzähltexten Lou Andreas-Salomés* (Pfaffenweiler, Germany: Centaurus-Verlagsgesellschaft, 1997), 91–121. She examines this phenomenon of "fliegen" (flying) in greater detail and in connection with dreams and Freud's *Traumdeutung.* She also reads Hildegard's embroidery as equivalent to her imaginary flight: it offers her a refuge from daily life and conversation, a time during which can engage in a "Sich-selbst-Ausdenken" (thinking through of herself): "Der Text suggeriert, daß sich Hildegard Formen und Farben nicht bewußt ausdenkt, sie ihre Stickarbeit vielmehr als 'interessante Lektüre,' als eine Form des Gesprächs auffaßt" (115; The text suggests that Hildegard does not consciously plan out forms and colors but rather interprets her needle work as 'interesting reading,' a kind of conversation; my translation).

Works Cited

I. Andreas-Salomé's Writings

Andreas-Salomé. *Amor, Jutta, Die Tarnkappe: Drei Dichtungen*. Edited by Ernst Pfeiffer. Frankfurt am Main: Insel Verlag, 1981.

———. *Die Erotik: Vier Aufsätze*. Edited by Ernst Pfeiffer. Frankfurt am Main: Ullstein, 1985.

———. *Fenitschka, Eine Ausschweifung: Zwei Erzählungen*. 1898. Reprint, Frankfurt am Main: Ullstein, 1983.

———. *Fenitschka and Deviations: Two Novellas*. Translated by Dorothee Einstein Krahn. Lanham, NY, and London: UP of America, 1990.

———. *Das Haus: Familiengeschichte vom Ende vorigen Jahrhunderts*. 1921. Reprint, Frankfurt am Main: Ullstein, 1987.

———. *The Human Family: Stories*. Translated by Raleigh Whitinger. Lincoln and London: U of Nebraska P, 2005.

———. "Ketzereien gegen die moderne Frau." *Die Zukunft* 7.26 (1898–99). Reprinted in *Literarische Manifeste der Jahrhundertwende: 1890–1910*, edited by Ruprecht and Bänsch, 566–69. Stuttgart: Metzler, 1981.

———. *Lebensrückblick: Grundriß einiger Lebenserinnerungen*. Edited by Ernst Pfeiffer. 1951. 5th ed., Frankfurt am Main: Insel, 1968.

———. *Ma: Ein Porträt*. 1904. Reprint, Frankfurt am Main: Ullstein, 1996.

———. *Menschenkinder: Novellencyklus*. Stuttgart: Cotta, 1899.

———. *Ródinka: Russische Erinnerung*. 1923. Reprint, Frankfurt am Main: Ullstein, 1985.

———. *Ruth*. Stuttgart: Cotta, 1895.

———. *Die Stunde ohne Gott und andere Kindergeschichten*. Jena, Germany: E. Dietrichs Verlag, 1922.

II. Secondary Literature

Bassin, Donna, Margaret Honey, and Meryle Mahrer Kaplan. *Representations of Motherhood*. New Haven, CT: Yale UP, 1994.

Bauer, Dale M., and Susan Jaret Mckinstry. "Introduction." In *Feminism, Bakhtin and the Dialogic*, edited by Bauer and McKinstry, 1–6. Albany: SUNY Press, 1991.

Bäumer, Gertrud. *Die Frau und das geistige Leben*. Leipzig: C. F. Amelangs, 1911.

Benjamin, Jessica. *The Bonds of Love: Psychoanalysis, Feminism, and the Problem of Domination*. London: Virago, 1988.

Berger, John. *Ways of Seeing*. London: BBC & Penguin, 1972.

Binion, Rudolph. *Frau Lou: Nietzsche's Wayward Disciple*. Princeton, NJ: Princeton UP, 1968.

Boetcher Joeres, Ruth-Ellen. *Respectability and Deviance: Nineteenth-Century German Women Writers and the Ambiguity of Representation*. Chicago and London: U of Chicago P, 1998.

Bovenschen, Silvia. *Die imaginierte Weiblichkeit: Exemplarische Untersuchungen zu kulturgeschichtlichen und literarischen Präsentationsformen des Weiblichen*. Frankfurt am Main: Suhrkamp, 1979.

Brinker-Gabler, Gisela. "Feminismus und Moderne: Brennpunkt 1900." *Kontroversen, alte und neue; Akten des VII. Internationalen Germanisten-Kongresses 1985* 8 (1986): 228–34.

———. "Perspektiven des Übergangs: Weibliches Bewußtsein und frühe Moderne." In *Deutsche Literatur von Frauen*, edited by Gisela Brinker-Gabler, 2:169–205. Munich: C. H. Beck, 1988.

———. "Renaming the Human: Andreas-Salomé's 'Becoming Human.'" *Seminar* 36:1 (Feb. 2000): 22–41.

Bülow, Frieda Freiin von. "Männerurtheil über Frauendichtung." *Die Zukunft* 7.26 (1898–99). Reprinted in *Literarische Manifeste der Jahrhundertwende: 1890–1910*, edited by Erich Ruprecht and Dieter Bänsch, 562–65. Stuttgart: Metzler, 1981.

Butler, Judith. *Gender Trouble: Feminism and the Subversion of Identity*. New York: Routledge, 1990.

Byatt, A. S. *Possession: A Romance*. New York: Random House, 1990.

Calinescu, Matei. *Five Faces of Modernity*. Durham, NC: Duke UP, 1987.

Cormican, Muriel. "Authority and Resistance: Women in Lou Andreas-Salomé's *The House*." *Women in German Yearbook* 14 (1998): 127–42.

———. "Female Sexuality and the Dilemma of Self Representation." *Seminar: A Journal of Germanic Studies* 36.1 (Feb. 2000): 130–40.

Daly, Brenda O., and Maureen T. Reddy. "Introduction." In *Narrating Mothers: Theorizing Maternal Subjectivities*, edited by Daly and Reddy, 76–93. Knoxville: U of Tennessee P, 1991.

De Lauretis, Teresa. *Alice Doesn't: Feminism Semiotics Cinema*. Bloomington: Indiana UP, 1984.

Deiulio, Laura. "A Tale of Two Cities: The Metropolis in Lou Andreas-Salomé's *Fenitschka*." *Women in German Yearbook* 23 (2007): 76–101.

Deleuze, Gilles. "Coldness and Cruelty." In *Masochism*, translated by Jean McNeil. New York: Zone Books, 1991.

Dietze, Gabriele, ed. *Die Überwindung der Sprachlosigkeit: Texte aus der Frauenbewegung*. Frankfurt am Main: Luchterhand, 1979.

Doane, Mary Ann. "Film and the Masquerade: Theorising the Female Spectator." *Screen* 23.3–4 (1982): 74–87.

Dohm, Hedwig. *Die Mütter: Beitrag zur Erziehungsfrage*. Berlin: S. Fischer Verlag, 1903.

———. "Reaktion in der Frauenbewegung." *Die Zukunft* 29 (1899): 279–91.

Doll Allen, Julie. "Male and Female Dialogue in Lou Andreas-Salomé's *Fenitschka.*" In *Frauen: Mitsprechen, Mitschreiben; Beiträge zu Literatur- und sprachwissenschaftlichen Frauenforschung,* edited by Marianne Henn and Britta Hufeisen, 479–89. Stuttgart: Akademischer Verlag Hans-Dieter Heinz, 1997.

Dykstra, Bram. *Idols of Perversity: Fantasies of Feminine Evil in Fin-de-Siècle Culture.* New York and Oxford: Oxford UP, 1986.

Eloesser, Arthur. "Neue Bücher." *Neue Deutsche Rundschau* (1901): 652–62.

Felski, Rita. *The Gender of Modernity.* Cambridge and London: Harvard UP, 1995.

Flax, Jane. "Multiples: On the Contemporary Politics of Subjectivity." In *Disputed Essays on Psychoanalysis, Subjects Politics and Philosophy.* New York: Routledge, 1993.

———. "Political Philosophy and the Patriarchal Unconscious: A Psychoanalytic Perspective on Epistemology and Metaphysics." In Harding and Hintikka, *Discovering Reality: Feminist Perspectives on Epistemology, Metaphysics, Methodology, and Philosophy of Science,* 245–81.

Foucault, Michel. *The History of Sexuality.* Vol. 1, *An Introduction.* Translated by Robert Hurley. New York: Vintage, 1990. Originally published as *Histoire de la sexualité 1: La volonté de savoir.* Paris: Gallimard, 1978.

Freud, Sigmund. *Beyond the Pleasure Principle.* Translated by James Strachey. New York: W. W. Norton, 1961.

———. *Dora: An Analysis of a Case of Hysteria.* Edited by Philip Rieff. New York: McMillan, 1963.

———. "The Economic Problem of Masochism." In *Essential Papers on Masochism,* edited by Margaret Ann Fitzpatrick Hanly, 274–85. New York: NYU Press, 1995.

———. *Die Traumdeutung.* Vol. 2 of *Gesammelte Werke.* Frankfurt am Main: Fischer, 1968–78.

Frevert, Ute. *Women in German History: From Bourgeois Emancipation to Sexual Liberation.* Translated by Stuart McKinnon-Evans. Oxford: Berg, 1989.

Gahlinger, Chantal. *Der Weg zur weiblichen Autonomie: Zur Psychologie der Selbstwerdung im literarischen Werk von Lou Andreas-Salomé.* Bern: Peter Lang, 2001.

Garner, Shirley Nelson. "Constructing the Mother: Contemporary Psychoanalytic Theorists and Women Autobiographers." In Daly and Reddy, *Narrating Mothers: Theorizing Maternal Subjectivities,* 76–93.

Gautier, Théophile. Charles Baudelaire: His Life. London: Greening & Co., 1915.

Gay, Peter. *The Education of the Senses.* New York: Oxford UP, 1984. Vol. 1 of *The Bourgeois Experience: Victoria to Freud.* 3 vols. 1984–93.

Gerhard, Ute. *Unerhört: Die Geschichte der deutschen Frauenbewegung.* Reinbeck bei Hamburg: Rowohlt Taschenbuch Verlag, 1990.

Gidion, Heidi. "Nachwort." In *Ma: Ein Porträt,* by Lou Andreas-Salomé. Frankfurt am Main: Ullstein, 1996.

Gilman, Sander L. *Difference and Pathology: Stereotypes of Sexuality, Race, and Madness.* Ithaca, NY: Cornell UP, 1985.

Gropp, Rose-Maria. "Das 'Weib' existiert nicht." *Blätter der Rilke Gesellschaft* 11–12 (1984–85): 46–69.

Haines, Brigid. "'Ja, so würde ich es auch heute noch sagen': Reading Lou Andreas-Salomé in the 1990s." *Publications of the English Goethe Society* 62 (1992): 77–95.

———. "Lou Andreas-Salomé's *Fenitschka:* A Feminist Reading." *German Life and Letters* 44 (1991): 416–25.

———. "Masochism and Femininity in Lou Andreas-Salomé's *Eine Ausschweifung.*" *Women in German Yearbook* 8 (1993): 97–115.

Hannavy, John, ed. "Historiography of 19th Century Photography." In *Encyclopedia of 19th Century Photography,* 664–68. New York: Routledge, 2007.

Harding, Sandra, and Merril B. Hintikka, eds. *Discovering Reality: Feminist Perspectives on Epistemology, Metaphysics, Methodology, and Philosophy of Science.* Dordrecht, Netherlands: D. Reidel, 1983.

Irigaray, Luce. *Speculum of the Other Woman.* Translated by Gilliam C. Gill. Ithaca, NY: Cornell UP, 1985.

———. *This Sex Which Is Not One.* Translated by Catherine Porter with Carolyn Burke. Ithaca, NY: Cornell UP, 1985.

Janssen-Jurreit, Marielouise. "Nationalbiologie, Sexualreform und Geburtenrückgang: Über die Zusammenhänge von Bevölkerungspolitik und Frauenbewegung um die Jahrhundertwende." In Dietze, *Die Überwindung der Sprachlosigkeit: Texte aus der Frauenbewegung,* 139–75.

Kaplan, Ann E. *Women and Film: Both Sides of the Camera.* New York: Routledge, 1990.

Kaufmann, Walter. "Foreword." In *Frau Lou: Nietzsche's Wayward Disciple,* by Rudolph Binion, v. Princeton, NJ: Princeton UP, 1968.

Keller, Evelyn Fox. "Feminism and Science." In *Feminism and Science,* edited by Evelyn Keller Fox and Helen E. Longino, 28–40. New York: Oxford UP, 1996. Originally published in *Signs: Journal of Women in Culture and Society* 17:3 (1982): 28–40.

———. "Gender and Science." In Harding and Hintikka, *Discovering Reality: Feminist Perspectives on Epistemology, Metaphysics, Methodology, and Philosophy of Science,* 187–205.

King, Lynda J. *Best-Sellers by Design: Vicki Baum and the House of Ullstein.* Detroit, MI: Wayne UP, 1988.

Koepcke, Cordula. *Lou Andreas-Salomé: Ein eigenwilliger Lebensweg; Ihre Begegnungen mit Nietzsche, Rilke und Freud.* Freiburg im Breisgau: Herder, 1982.

———. *Lou Andreas-Salomé: Leben, Persönlichkeit, Werk; Eine Biographie.* Frankfurt am Main: Insel, 1986.

Kracauer, Siegfried. "Über Arbeitsnachweise." *Frankfurter Zeitung* (June 17, 1930).

———. "On Employment Agencies." In *Rethinking Architecture,* edited by Neil Leach, 59–64. London and New York: Routledge, 1997.

Krafft-Ebing, Richard von. *Psychopathia Sexualis.* Translated by Franklin S. Klaf. New York: Bell, 1965.

Kreide, Caroline. *Lou Andreas-Salomé: Feministin oder Antifeministin? Eine Standortbestimmung zur wilhelminischen Frauenbewegung.* New York: Peter Lang, 1996.

Kristeva, Julia. "Kein weibliches Schreiben? Fragen an *Julia Kristeva.*" *Freibeuter* 2 (1979): 79–84.

———. *Revolution in Poetic Language.* Translated by Margaret Waller. New York: Columbia UP, 1984.

———. "Stabat Mater." In *The Kristeva Reader,* edited by Toril Moi, 160–86. New York: Columbia UP, 1986.

———. "Women's Time." In Warhol and Herndl, *Feminisms: An Anthology of Literary Theory and Criticism,* 860–79.

Kuzniar, Alice. *The Queer German Cinema.* Stanford, CA: Stanford UP, 2000.

Lange, Helene. *Kampfzeiten.* Berlin: F. A. Herbig, 1921.

Livingstone, Angela. *Lou Andreas-Salomé: Her Life and Work.* New York: Moyer Bell, 1984. Reprint. of *Lou Andreas-Salomé,* 1984.

Markotic, Lorraine. "Andreas-Salomé and the Contemporary Essentialism Debate." *Seminar* 36:1 (Feb. 2000): 59–78.

Martin, Biddy. *Woman and Modernity: The (Life)Styles of Lou Andreas-Salomé.* Ithaca, NY: Cornell UP, 1991.

Matysik, Tracie. "The Interests of Ethics: Andreas-Salomé's Psychoanalytic Critique." *Seminar* 36:1 (Feb. 2000): 5–21.

McGlashan, Ann. *Creating Women: The Female Artist in Fin-de-Siècle Germany and Austria.* PhD diss., Indiana University, 1996.

Mennel, Barbara. *The Representation of Masochism and Queer Desire in Film and Literature.* New York: Palgrave Macmillan, 2007.

Modleski, Tania. "Time and Desire in the Woman's Film." In *Film Theory and Criticism,* edited by Gerald Mast, Marshall Cohen, and Leo Braudy, 536–48. 4th ed. New York: Oxford UP, 1992.

Morrison, Paul. "Enclosed in Openness: *Northanger Abbey* and the Domestic Carceral." *Texas Studies in Literature and Language* 23:1 (Spring 1991): 1–23.

Müller-Loreck, Leonie. *Die erzählende Dichtung Lou Andreas-Salomés: Ihr Zusammenhang mit der Literatur um 1900.* Stuttgart: Akademischer Verlag Hans-Dieter Heinz, 1976.

Mulvey, Laura. "Visual Pleasure and Narrative Cinema." *Screen* 16.3 (1975): 6–18.

Newman, Beth. "The Situation of the Looker-On: Gender, Narration, and Gaze in *Wuthering Heights.*" In Warhol and Herndl, *Feminisms: An Anthology of Literary Theory and Criticism,* 449–66.

Peters, H. F. *My Sister, My Spouse: A Biography of Lou Andreas-Salomé.* London: V. Gollancz, 1963.

Petro, Patrice. *Joyless Streets: Women and Melodramatic Representation in Weimar Germany.* Princeton, NJ: Princeton UP, 1989.

Platzhoff, Eduard. "Ma." *Das literarische Echo* 4 (1901): 1573–74.

Prokop, Ulrike. "Die Sehnsucht nach Volkseinheit: Zum Konservatismus der bürgerlichen Frauenbewegung." In Dietze, *Die Überwindung der Sprachlosigkeit: Texte aus der Frauenbewegung,* 176–202.

Reik, Theodor. *Masochism and Modern Man.* New York: Farrar & Rinehart, 1941.

Ridon, Jean-Xavier. "Between Here and There: A Displacement in Memory." Translated by Alistair Rolls. *World Literature Today: A Literary Quarterly of the University of Oklahoma* 71.4 (1997): 717–22.

Salber, Linde. *Lou Andreas-Salomé.* Reinbek bei Hamburg: Rowohlt, 1990.

Schultz, Karla. "In Defense of Narcissus: Lou Andreas-Salomé and Julia Kristeva." *The German Quarterly* 67.2 (1994): 185–96.

Schütz, Karin. *Geschlechterentwürfe im literarischen Werk von Lou Andreas-Salomé unter Berücksichtigung ihrer Geschlechtertheorie.* Würzburg, Germany: Königshausen & Neumann, 2008.

Schwartz, Agata. "Lou Andreas-Salomé and Rosa Mayreder: Femininity and Masculinity." *Seminar* 36:1 (Feb. 2000): 42–58;

Sedgwick, Eve Kosofsky. *Between Men: English Literature and Male Homosocial Desire.* New York: Columbia UP, 1985.

Stöcker, Helene. *Die Liebe und die Frauen.* Minden, Germany: Bruns, 1908.

Streiter, Sabine. "Nachwort." In Andreas-Salomé, *Das Haus: Eine Familiengeschichte vom Ende vorigen Jahrhunderts,* 239–52.

Treder, Uta. *Von der Hexe zur Hysterikerin: Zur Verfestigungsgeschichte des "Ewig Weiblichen."* Bonn: Bouvier, 1984.

Van Santum, Lisa A. Rainwater. "Hiding Behind Literary Analysis: Heinrich Heine's *Shakespeares Mädchen* and Lou Andreas-Salomé's *Henrik Ibsens Frauengestalten.*" *Monatshefte* 89 (1997): 307–23.

Warhol, Robyn R., and Diana Price Herndl, eds. *Feminisms: An Anthology of Literary Theory and Criticism.* 2nd ed. New Brunswick, NJ: Rutgers UP, 1997.

Weininger, Otto. *Geschlecht und Charakter: Eine prinzipielle Untersuchung.* 1903. Reprint, Berlin: Kiepenheuer, 1932.

Weir, David. *Decadence and the Making of Modernism.* Amherst: UP of Massachusetts, 1995.

Welsch, Ursula, and Michaela Wiesner. *Lou Andreas-Salomé: Vom "Lebensurgrund" zur Psychoanalyse.* Munich: Verlag Internationale Psychoanalyse, 1988.

Wernz, Birgit. *Sub-Versionen: Weiblichkeitsentwürfe in den Erzähltexten Lou Andreas-Salomés.* Pfaffenweiler, Germany: Centaurus-Verlagsgesellschaft, 1997.

Whitinger, Raleigh. "Echoes of Lou Andreas-Salomé in Thomas Mann's *Tonio Kröger: Eine Ausschweifung* and Its Relationship to the Bildungsroman Tradition." *The Germanic Review* 75:1 (Winter 2000): 21–36.

———. "Lou Andreas-Salomé's *Fenitschka* and the Tradition of the Bildungsroman." *Monatshefte* 91:4 (Winter 1999): 464–81.

———, ed. *Seminar: A Journal of Germanic Studies; Special Issue on Lou Andreas-Salomé*, 36:1 (Feb. 2000).

Index